Astro Boy
Come to t

Astro Boy and Anime Come to the Americas

An Insider's View of the Birth of a Pop Culture Phenomenon

FRED LADD

with HARVEY DENEROFF

McFarland & Company, Inc., Publishers

Jefferson, North Carolina, and London

LIBRARY OF CONGRESS CATALOGUING-IN-PUBLICATION DATA

Ladd, Fred.
    Astro Boy and anime come to the Americas : an insider's view of the birth of a pop culture phenomenon / Fred Ladd with Harvey Deneroff.
        p.   cm.
    Includes index.

    ISBN 978-0-7864-3866-2
    softcover : 50# alkaline paper ∞

    1. Astroboy (Television program)   2. Animated television programs — United States — History and criticism.   I. Deneroff, Harvey.   II. Title.
    PN1992.77.A87L33   2009
    791.45'72 — dc22   2008044740

British Library cataloguing data are available

Cover art: Japanese artist Osamu Tezuka's 1951 creation *Tetsuan Atom* (Mighty Atom), known in America as *Astro Boy*; background ©2008 Shutterstock

Manufactured in the United States of America

McFarland & Company, Inc., Publishers
  Box 611, Jefferson, North Carolina 28640
    www.mcfarlandpub.com

To Eileen Laderman, whose computer skills and good sense made the production of this book possible; to Fred Patten and Frederik L. Schodt, whose scholarly research and passion for history-as-it-actually-happened were inspirational; to Harvey Deneroff, without whose persistent, indefatigable urging, this book would not have been written; to Kim Manning and Terry Kalajian, who have helped keep the history-making adventures of Astro Boy and Gigantor shining on Cartoon Network; to Takayuki Matsutani, president of Tezuka Productions, and to Tomoko Kanai, who provided rare images of Osamu Tezuka, Japan's "God of Comics," at work; and to the late Osamu Tezuka himself, the brilliant artist whose character *Tetsuan Atom,* our cherished *Astro Boy,* created the wave of anime that initiated today's multibillion dollar industry in the Americas, thus changing our pop culture forever, this author gives heartfelt thanks and appreciation. Without their efforts, this accounting of events that led to today's explosive growth of anime, told for the first time from an inside participant's point of view, would not have happened.

Table of Contents

Preface by Harvey Deneroff

I had first met Fred Ladd in 1996, when I interviewed him for a special anime issue of *Animation World Magazine* I was editing. At the time, anime had not yet achieved the widespread popularity in the United States it currently enjoys. However, interest in it was growing, anime clubs were popping up on college campuses, and the Society for Animation Studies was even planning a conference that focused on "Japanese Animation and Global Media." So, the special issue, to be published in August 1996, seemed a natural for the newly launched online animation magazine.

As I felt my knowledge of Japanese animation was rather modest, I was open to suggestions as to possible contributors and topics. One of the first people I contacted was anime historian and critic Fred Patten; he not only agreed to write for the issue, but also suggested we do an interview with Fred Ladd.

Ladd, he told me, had produced the English-language versions of such TV series as Osamu Tezuka's *Tetsuan Atom* (*Astro Boy*). Although I was aware of *Astro Boy,* at the time, I was more likely to associate Tezuka with his hilarious personal films, such as *Jumping,* than with his pioneering TV work. But it seemed like a good idea and I undertook to do the interview myself.

While I was pleased with the resulting story, I didn't realize how strongly it would resonate in the anime community. In fact, over the next few years, I probably received more responses from that story than from almost anything else I had written for the magazine. Though most of these were queries asking how people could get in touch with Ladd, I began to get some sense of his place in the world of anime fandom.

Actually, by 1996, I had written a number of pieces about the Japanese animation industry. Most of those articles, for the likes of *The Hollywood Reporter, Animation Magazine,* and *Animation World Magazine,* as well as my own industry newsletter, *The Animation Report,* were related to the international animation industry; like a number of other animation journalists, I was not above using Japan's example to browbeat Hollywood for its limited view of what one could do with animation. If I did need to know something about Japanese animation, I turned to people like Jerry Beck (who cofounded Streamline Pictures, pioneers of the distribution of such movies as *Akira* in the United States) or Fred Patten (whose voluminous writings on the subject have been compiled in *Watching Anime, Reading Manga*).

I recall being fascinated with stories Patten told me in the late 1980s about his role in starting the Cartoon/Fantasy Organization (C/FO), the first anime fan club in the United States. It was there that he and others got together to screen and discuss videotapes imported from Japan or taped from broadcasts aimed at Japanese Americans in Hawaii and Los Angeles.

I remember, several years later, observing animation historian Jerry Beck's enthusiasm about his plans to distribute Japanese animated movies on the cheap; his plans, with the help of Carl Macek, came to fruition under the banner of Streamline Pictures (in which Patten also became involved), and they were used to feed the growing appetite for anime created by C/FO and the hordes of other anime clubs that bloomed in its wake, especially on college campuses.

I especially recall Beck's hilarious stories of what happened when he screened *Akira* for Hollywood executives; he reported they would first get very excited about the film, but then realize they couldn't release such a violent film because it was a cartoon! It was only when *Pokémon* became a runaway hit on American TV a few years later that anime, almost overnight, became part of the mainstream American entertainment industry.

After the interview, Ladd and I kept in touch. In 2003, he asked me to moderate a panel discussion celebrating the opening of the Postwar Japanese Anime/Manga exhibit at the Japanese American Cultural and Community Center in the Little Tokyo area of Los Angeles on April 6, 2003. In preparing for it, Fred called several times to make sure I would cover all the bases in my introduction and questions for the panel. At the same time, he would regale me with stories and anecdotes about his career and anime.

It was then that I came to realize that Fred should be writing this down. I then casually suggested he write his autobiography and offered to help him do it.

My view of his importance was confirmed in witnessing Fred's commanding performance during the exhibit's opening ceremonies and the panel discussion itself. After all, Fred Ladd is America's direct link to the beginnings of the worldwide phenomenon that is anime. His successful English-language version of such TV series as *Astro Boy* played a key role in jump-starting today's Japanese animation industry, which has proved to be the only effective counter to Hollywood's traditional hegemony. In the process, anime has become a major influence not only on American and European animation, but also on many other aspects of international art and culture.

As happens with this sort of project, the process of writing the book took a lot longer than expected, especially since I moved out of Los Angeles, and eventually ended up in Decatur, Georgia, teaching animation and film history at the Savannah College of Art and Design. More important, the scope of the book evolved from a simple memoir to a personal history of anime in America.

At first, the writing process involved my interviewing Fred and editing the transcripts, which he then fashioned into the opening chapters. However, he soon started writing without the aid of interviews while I mainly acted as an editor, trying my best not to mangle his wonderful conversational style. After all, this is Fred Ladd's story, the behind-the-scenes story of how anime came to the Americas, told by one of the men responsible for bringing anime to the West, a story that I hope you will enjoy.

Preface by Fred Ladd

An old vaudeville sketch, I've heard, began with a little guy in an out-landishly colored plaid suit declaring, "I was born of normal parents in 19-aught-5 in Podunk, Iowa, in a little log cabin I built myself."

This writer, yours truly, was born Fred Laderman in February 1927 of parents who emigrated from Russia to Toledo, Ohio, and were remarkably patient with their nonconformist son — right from the start. (Not till thirty years later, in New York, would I become the *lad* in *Plad* Productions; the pen name, *Ladd,* stuck.) As an eight-year-old, I was doing impersonations of cartoon star Betty Boop (singing "*When I Grow Up, In a Year, One, Two, or Three*"...), Swedish film star Greta Garbo ("*Eh vant to be alone!*"), and actress Katherine Hepburn ("*The calla lilies are in bloom again; I love calla lilies, really I do*"), I'd beg a quarter from my mother (who, in those Depression days, really didn't have a quarter to spare) and walk miles to downtown Toledo where I'd buy a Kewpie hamburger (15 cents) and sit in the balcony of a movie theater (10 cents) watching feature films — at least twice. I loved show business — in particular, the feature films of Walt Disney, whose dramatization of *Snow White and the Seven Dwarfs, Pinocchio,* and *Bambi* remain fondly in my memory to this day.

In Scott High School, I wrote an ongoing humor column for the Scott *Thistle,* coauthored annual variety shows, and decided in my junior year that I'd pursue a career in writing, directing, and producing children's radio programs. The look of wonder on children's faces when they hear an engrossing yarn has always delighted me.

From there, it was "onward and upward!" to Toledo University, then to Ohio State University, where I concentrated on radio programming, as unaware as everyone else that *television,* in 1947, lay just over the horizon! In 2004, Ohio State would bestow upon me its coveted Distinguished Alumnus Award, but not for radio programming; by then, the broadcasting industry was hailing me as the man whose (English) adaptations of *Astro*

Boy, Gigantor, Kimba the White Lion, 8th Man (pilot), *G-Force,* and *Sailor Moon* had launched the amazing tsunami wave of anime from Japan to the Americas.

By the arrival of the twenty-first century, anime and its ancillaries in the West — manga, videos, merchandise, computer games — had become a multibillion dollar industry. The conventional wisdom was that — if not for the spectacular success in America of the pioneering *Astro Boy*— there'd have been no *Gigantor,* no *Kimba,* no *Speed Racer,* no *Sailor Moon,* no *Pokémon,* no *Dragonball.*

"Anime" (pronounced *AH-nee-may*) is what the Japanese call animation. Literally, the word applies to any screen image that's animated: TV programs, product commercials, feature films; as used in this book, the term refers most often to animated television programs *in series.* And much space in these pages is devoted to introducing to Western observers the trail-blazing artist/animator Osamu Tezuka, hailed and revered by the Japanese as *manga no kamisama*—the "God Comics," and the "Walt Disney of Japan." Indeed, without Osamu Tezuka, anime might very well *not* have come to America and, subsequently, to the entire West! Quite a man was Tezuka!

Undoubtedly, without Tezuka this book would not have been written. The question arises: why now? Why write a book now about events that occurred nearly a half-century ago? To understand why, the reader needs to feel the twinge of shock this writer senses when a caller from Tokyo apologizes, "Sorry to bother you with these questions about the beginning of *Astro Boy* in the U.S., sir, but [*embarrassed little laugh*] you are the only one left!"

The caller is right. The division of the National Broadcasting Company, namely, NBC Enterprises in New York — the U.S. distributor that imported the world's first anime series and sold it to independent TV stations across the country — is gone; its executives are either retired, working elsewhere, or dead. Its successor is, as of this writing, a unit of NBC-Universal based in Los Angeles and staffed by a younger generation with no first-hand knowledge of what transpired in New York City a half century ago.

Fan sites on the web, run by well-meaning but under-informed enthusiasts, proliferate reams of misinformation. Earnest authors and columnists write articles and books about the appearance of anime on Western television in the 1960s, yet their accounts are necessarily written from the point of view of reporters looking in from outside. None are written from the point of view of an insider who was actually an integral part of the phenomenon itself and was central to, and instrumental in, making it happen.

Still, with all these compelling shortcomings virtually begging to be remedied, nothing probably would have been done had not Harvey Deneroff, himself a distinguished author and recognized authority on animation, come to this writer and said, "Look, for posterity you have to set the record straight."

This book is an attempt to do just that. I have tried not to make it an historical tome. I view many events of the past fifty years with the humor I saw evident in those events at the time. The one great moment of sorrow in those fifty years came when Osamu Tezuka, the man who literally invented series anime, died on February 9, 1989.

I met his widow in Tokyo in the summer of 1997 at the studio her husband had built. It was an unplanned, chance meeting. In the few minutes we had together, I told Mrs. Tezuka what I had come to realize many years earlier: that her husband had that rarest of talents: not only was he a fine artist but also a true visionary; he correctly foresaw the day when robots would replace men at work — and men would resent it.

Did I foresee the day when anime would become a tsunami wave of culture from the Orient? In 1963, I did not. Fifty years later, I am glad to have been an integral part of it and I welcome the opportunity — in Harvey Deneroff's words — to help to "set the record straight." Here, then, is the hitherto untold, complete, inside story of how anime came to America, to the West, and, eventually, to the rest of the world outside Japan.

CHAPTER 1

Astro Boy: Japan's *Tetsuan Atom* Lands in New York and Starts the Anime Tsunami

Who would have believed that a phone call to my Times Square office that cold February morning in 1963 would not only change my career, but would also launch a multibillion dollar industry and change the (pop) culture of the Americas, forever?

When the phone rang, I was told "NBC's on the line." "NBC?," I wondered, "Who do I know at NBC? George Heinemann?" Heinemann was then the head of children's programming at NBC-TV; he had come to New York from Chicago. I knew he was interested in doing something with the *Stuart Little* character — and, indeed, he got Johnny Carson to narrate a simply made, inexpensive version of the *Little* tale for television, but Heinemann certainly wouldn't remember me just from a brief conversation we once had. I took the call. "Hello? This is Fred."

The caller was not George Heinemann. He identified himself as Jim Dodd, from NBC Enterprises. He was familiar with some of the work I'd been doing on a series, he said, a series called *Cartoon Classics*. I was pleased. That was a series I adapted from European animated featurettes, typically 30-minute or 40-minute tales, that I reversioned for American television. Mr. Dodd said he'd like to meet me at his office at 30 Rockefeller Plaza; he had some foreign animated programs he'd like to show me.

From our conversation I thought that NBC had acquired some foreign-made animated featurettes on their own (from *where,* I wondered) and they wanted me to adapt those, just as I had adapted *Cartoon Classics.* I foresaw that as possibly a good way to generate some handsome fees and establish myself as a writer-director on national television. (I soon learned that I was to be wrong on both counts.)

9

Soon after that fateful call, I was in an NBC elevator, heading for Enterprises. The company, I would soon discover, was a division of the National Broadcasting Company, a division that distributed NBC TV Network series to independent, non-network TV stations after their network run. In addition, Enterprises operated as a kind of venture capital company that invested in such varied projects as Panavision camera lenses and the original Broadway production of *My Fair Lady.* What they were contemplating now, I would find, was the acquisition of animated children's programming that could be licensed and repackaged at prices low enough to make it attractive to the country's independent stations.

Jim Dodd came to meet me as I stepped from the hallway into NBC Enterprises' executive offices. Dodd was a tall man, in his 60s, who turned out to be quite delightful. We hit it off right away.

What he wanted to show me was the first few episodes of a new children's television series being animated in Japan — *What? Was there such a thing as a Japanese animated series?*— a series that Dodd and his colleagues were considering taking on; its title, he said, was *Tetsuan Atom* (sometimes anglicized as *Tetsuwan Atom),* meaning "Mighty Atom." I remember thinking that the first thing that had to be done, if we went forward, was to change that title.

I had a number of questions I wanted to ask — questions that Dodd said he'd answer after the screening. The screening room would be tied up later, he explained, so would I mind seeing the films first, then we could sit and talk afterward? Done. I was ushered into the screening room. An hour later, after I had seen episodes one and three of *Tetsuan Atom*—*The Birth of Atom* and *Expedition to Mars*— Dodd asked, "What do you think? Can that little boy robot be another *Pinocchio?*" (At the time, I was shuttling between New York City and Brussels, co-producing *Pinocchio in Outer Space,* an animated feature for which I had written the story and recorded the tracks.)

Tetsuan Atom is indeed the story of a Pinocchio-like boy *mecha* (robot) in the future, the creation of famed Japanese artist Osamu Tezuka. It's based on a comic strip (or *manga*) character that Tezuka created and which first appeared in *Shonen,* a boys' magazine, in April 1953.

Another Pinocchio? I wanted to think about that a bit. While I was thinking, I asked Mr. Dodd if he could tell me how NBC came across this most unusual series. He did so, gladly. He explained that, at the time, NBC had a representative in Tokyo who was sitting in his hotel room one day watching TV when, suddenly, he saw a new cartoon character performing incredible feats of strength — incredible even by cartoon standards. The rep thought, "What the heck is that?" He didn't recognize the little robot character with the funny hat and rockets in his boots. Since there was no TV animation coming from Japan in those days, he thought that, because of its extremely limited animation, the new show must be something out of Hanna-Barbera Studios, in Hollywood. (Hanna-Barbera, in those days, was producing TV series noteworthy for their economical, limited-action animation.) The rep's curiosity was aroused. He tracked the show down and found that, No, this was not something from Hanna-Barbera, or from some crummy little studio in the States, but a local show called *Tetsuan Atom* made right there in Tokyo.

The rep also realized that, Gee, this show could have some potential back in the States. So he sent word of the show to headquarters in New York and to "Get in touch with Fred Ladd," because the rep was aware of what I had done with *Cartoon Classics.*

At about the same time, Dodd continued, one Kazuhiko "Ken" Fujita, a seasoned Tokyo-based agent, got permission from Mushi Production, which was making *Tetsuan Atom,* to represent it in the USA. (He may have received that permission largely because of his erudite manner and his ability to speak fluent English; no one at Mushi did.) Fujita found his way to NBC Enterprises and there he showed them 16mm prints of *Tetsuan Atom.* Dodd and other top men there — Bill Breen, Bill Schmidt, and chief

Pinocchio in Outer Space. Carlo Collodi's famous puppet wrestles with his conscience in the 1965 feature-length production.

Morris Rittenberg — did not really grasp what they were seeing, they didn't understand Japanese; but still they had a good feeling about the show. They felt that — properly adapted and economically dubbed — the series could quite possibly succeed in the U.S. market.

They made K. Fujita a cautious offer — one that he promptly rejected. "Too low," he complained to me later. "Very good deal for American side, but poor for Japanese side." NBC did not expect that; they thought Fujita would go for it. And, indeed, when Mushi Production heard of the offer, they *wanted* it! So did the Fuji Television Network, which was broadcasting the series in Japan and bankrolling its production.

Then, in a surprising turn of events, a young hustler whose name, coincidentally, also happened to be K. Fujita (Kiyoshi Fujita, head of a company he called Video Promotions) persuaded Mushi Production and Fuji Television that he, Kiyoshi Fujita, could strike a deal with NBC. And he did! Kiyoshi Fujita went to New York, met with Rittenberg, Schmidt, Breen, and Dodd and accepted the same basic offer from which Kazuhiko Fujita had walked away! The deal was done! NBC optioned the property with the guaranty that they'd produce a pilot film and, if the pilot was successful, NBC would go ahead and commit for an entire series of 52 episodes. (If the pilot failed, NBC would have lost little, and cut bait.)

Now came the job of finding a writer-director-producer in the West who could properly adapt and economically dub a pilot — and maybe the entire series of 52 episodes, if the pilot was successful. Where does one look for such a person?

Jim Dodd decided to take the NBC Tokyo rep's advice. He got "in touch with Fred Ladd." Dodd was also aware of my work on *Cartoon Classics* and *Pinocchio in Outer Space,* and agreed that I might be "Just the right guy for this project."

Meeting American Tastes

The question was, "Could *Tetsuan Atom* be another little *Pinocchio*?" I thought about it for a moment and saw some obvious resemblances to Pinocchio (creator Osamu Tezuka acknowledged that he got the idea for *Tetsuan Atom* from *Pinocchio*); but, while *Tetsuan Atom* initially seemed to be another *Pinocchio* — he was a mechanical boy created by a Geppetto-like father figure and was later sold to a circus — *Atom* actually was different from Pinocchio in a very significant way: Pinocchio did not know right from wrong. Tetsuan Atom *always* knows right from wrong, and he does something about it, that is, he gets rid of the bad guys and helps the good guys.

Historic moment: Osama Tezuka, bare-headed in New York offices of NBC in October 1963, shakes hands with NBC's William "Bill" Schmidt, far left, upon signing of contract to deliver 52 *Tetsuan Atom* programs to NBC Enterprises for distribution worldwide (outside Japan). This act would launch the wave sweeping anime to Western shores. Beaming, second from right, is agent Kiyoshi Fujita (flanked by assistant) whose Video Promotions, Inc., accepted NBC terms previously rejected by rival agent.

Jim Dodd and I chatted a bit longer about the series. He liked what he heard, and he saw that he had piqued my interest. Now he asked: "Do you want to do a pilot?"

How *Tetsuan Atom* Became *Astro Boy*

Do a pilot? I did not answer Jim Dodd's question immediately. Before undertaking a pilot, and certainly before committing to an entire series, I had to know more: how soon did NBC need the pilot? how much did they think the pilot film would cost to adapt and dub into English? who would pay film laboratory costs, once the English soundtrack was delivered? how long a trial

Pinocchio in Outer Space. **Pinocchio and Nurtle the Twurtle, from the planet Twurtle Dee, on Mars watching Martian creatures attack their spacecraft in the 1965 feature-length film, animated in Belgium and released in Japan by Toei and in North America by Universal Pictures. The picture, which Fred Ladd co-produced with Norm Prescott, was an official entry in the 1966 Venice Film Festival.**

"sales period" would be needed before NBC decided to go ahead with (or quit) the series? These and more questions needed to be answered. Dodd, Schmidt, and Rittenberg all considered the questions. It was Morris Rittenberg who spoke the answers. Happily, they were all "in the right ball park."

Later, after screening Episode 1, *The Birth of Atom* again, I pointed out to Jim Dodd some story problems I felt needed to be addressed if the shows were to meet American tastes. For example, in Episode 1, the brilliant director of the Ministry of Science (we renamed it the "Institute of Science") is a certain Doctor Tenma. His young son, Tobio, who is clearly not driving carefully, is killed in an automobile accident. It is difficult for an American audience to sympathize with a reckless driver. So, in my version (modified solely through dubbing), I'd have a narrator say that Tobio is driving his car on an electronic highway of the future; the highway, not the boy, is actually controlling the car. Suddenly, there's an electronic glitch!— the highway control breaks down! Tobio's car crashes and poor Tobio is an innocent victim! American audiences sympathize with innocent victims; we can understand the father's grief when his good son is lost in an accident that never should have happened! Dodd and company were pleased with that approach. From that moment on, the NBC team of Dodd, Breen, Schmidt, and Rittenberg were convinced that Ladd probably was indeed "the right guy in the right place at the right time."

There were other situations too in the initial episodes, incidents that were considered nonviolent or quite appropriate in Japan but which in fact were perceived as violent or inappropriate by NBC's Department of Standards & Practices. Issues such as cruelty toward animals, cartoon nudity, and insensitivity toward race and religion were all nonissues in Japan, but no-no's in the West. For all these no-no's, I proposed what I knew to be quick, inexpensive fixes, for example, by trimming a shot of gunplay before the action went too far over-the-top, I and others on my team could save a show from expensive retakes or outright rejection.

Initially, NBC had considered dubbing this series on-the-cheap in San Juan, Puerto Rico. Their reasoning, in effect, was, "Look, TV animation is in its infancy, Hanna-Barbera 'owns it' and they're not cheap. While programs such as *Cartoon Classics,* made from existent, repurposed and reedited foreign animation have had some success in syndication [i.e., non-network stations], the idea of us releasing a whole new series made overseas, let alone in a country (Japan) which has no track record for this kind of thing — it's never been done! It's risky! If we bomb with this, at least we'll have kept our losses to a minimum."

But now NBC, feeling better about the familiar *Pinocchio* aspect of the series, yet realizing that the problems I'd identified would probably make dubbing in Puerto Rico problematic (i.e., *risky*), decided that dubbing a series in San Juan wasn't such a great idea after all. They wondered, could I supervise production of the English version in San Juan? My answer: No. Well, could I do the show in New York at a price competitive with San Juan? Wise, gray-haired men at Titra Sound Studios, the facility I used at 1600 Broadway (the National Screen Building), estimated that dubbing a typical *Tetsuan Atom* episode would require two days of studio time. I was certain from my experiences with *Cartoon Classics* that each *Tetsuan Atom* episode could be dubbed into English in one day (half the time required in Puerto Rico) with more experienced cast, crew, and recording techniques. The deal was agreed in principle: my production company would write the adaptation, pick the voice actors and produce the English version entirely in New York, at a studio within walking distance of NBC's offices, for about the same price as doing it in San Juan.

NBC Enterprises was now satisfied that 52 half-hour episodes of this unique Japanese series was worth going for — especially since the Fuji Television Network was guaranteeing completion of all the programs.

Producing the Pilot

In March 1963 NBC Enterprises flashed a green light: "Go ahead with the pilot, *Birth of Atom.*" And that is what I did. Working hand-in-glove with Titra, I began laying out the initial episode of what was to become a series of 104 programs — the most massive project of its kind ever undertaken, and 52 more than anyone ever contemplated.

With NBC now ready to proceed with an English-language pilot for *Tetsuan Atom*, a "magic" English name for the little robot had to be found. In *Pinocchio in Outer Space,* which was then in production, the whale in space was named Astro. Everyone agreed that Astro was a good word. My recollection is that NBC sales executive Bill Breen then noted that, in the world of American comic books, there was always a *This-boy* and a *That-boy* (as in Superboy) — "How about Astro Boy?" (A recent report has it that William "Bill" Schmidt's young son first uttered the words "Astro Boy." Remarkably — whatever its actual origin — the name *Astro Boy* has become today, in twenty-first century Japan, nearly as popular as *Tetsuan Atom,* with the Japanese pronunciation being "Astoro Boy.")

Once I began actually writing the pilot, *Birth of Astro Boy,* in March 1963, I, of course, had to give English names to all the other characters in the film. I've always liked humorous, characteristic names, and so Dr. Ochanamizu, because of his long, elephantine nose, became Pacydermus J. Elefun; the self-important, pompous Mr. Higeoyagi became Mr. Pompous (that was Tezuka's favorite name; it always made him laugh, for reasons I've never completely understood); the police in New York were largely Irish, so I named the chief of police Chief McLaw; the not-too-bright detective who dislikes Astro Boy became Inspector Gumshoe; Astro Boy's sister was, of course, Astro Girl.

Somewhat more difficult was explaining, in the pilot, how the name Astro Boy came to be. (If only we could have just said, "Fred and the NBC team dreamed it up!") Actually, I started with the name Astro Boy, which was now a given, and worked backward: Doctor Tenma, the scientist whose son would perish in the auto accident, became "Doctor Boynton"; his son, Tobio, became "Aster Boynton III"; and the robot built by Doctor Boynton to replace Aster Boynton III became "Astro Boy." That seemed logical enough and it worked for me.

When a foreign film is dubbed into another language, the original producer supplies (1) a print of the film in its original version, (2) a duplicate negative, (3) a copy of the music-and-sound effects track(s), (4) neutral title backgrounds (no writing superimposed), and (5) an English translation of the original dialogue. However, I had considerable difficulty in trying to under-

Astro Boy. The world's most beloved robot was created as *Tetsuan Atom* (Mighty Atom) by Japanese artist Osamu Tezuka in 1951, but given a fictional birthdate of April 7, 2003. Pinocchio-like in many ways, Astro Boy differs from Geppetto's famed wooden puppet in that Astro Boy inherently knows right from wrong.

stand the translation of *Birth of Astro* provided by Mushi Production. The translator they hired, I am sure, knew little English. A phrase like "glass broken before your hand" would actually mean, I deduced, "broken before you received it." And I actually checked a world globe looking for the "Himiraya Mountains" before realizing that many Japanese pronounce the English letter *L* as an *R*, so the "Himirayas" were in fact the Himalayas.

When I acted out that first pilot script to the NBC executives, they laughed and thoroughly enjoyed it; this was fun, they had never done anything like this before. But when I finished, I pointed out that *Birth of Astro Boy*, which chiefly introduces the main characters, has a lot of dialogue and a lot of background (exposition), but not much action; I felt that, if I were a station buyer, I probably wouldn't be too excited about a show with so little action — children, after all, want to see action! So I recommended that we also dub program #3, *Expedition to Mars,* a great space adventure with sparse dialogue and lots of action — big action! What's more, that episode features something that really tweaks kids' — and adults' — interest: Mars, the mysterious red planet. (*Pinocchio in Outer Space* also features the lead character, a mechanical boy, braving a trip to Mars.) I did not have to belabor the point — we, the NBC team and I, all agreed.

Dodd's Due Diligence

We were now approaching the recording date set for dubbing the two pilot films of what would become *Astro Boy,* a new children's series to be released under the imprimatur of NBC. Jim Dodd called to invite me to join him for lunch at a little, nearby French restaurant he favored, on Manhattan's West Side. I agreed, sensing that Dodd was understandably concerned about venturing into deep waters with which he and his associates were totally unfamiliar. I expected this would be Dodd's final step of due diligence, his thorough research of a new industry before becoming heavily committed.

After opening pleasantries and ordering our entrées, my host looked at me, shrugged his shoulders, and explained that this was his first foray into "children's programming"; he knew that I was experienced at it, and wondered how I happened to gravitate not only to creating animated "programs for kids," but foreign-produced animation, at that. "That is so unusual, so specialized. What started you on that path?"

I smiled. "That's a long story, Jim. Are you sure you want to hear it?" He assured me that he did; he had plenty of time, that's why he selected this little French restaurant where everything takes time to prepare.

I took a deep breath. "As a kid growing up in Toledo, Ohio [Dodd lived in Connecticut], I loved doing impressions of animated cartoon 'stars' — Betty Boop, Popeye, Mickey Mouse [later in life, I would learn that the voice of Mickey Mouse belonged to none other than Walt Disney himself]. I did those impressions at shows in grade school and, by the time I entered high school, knew that I wanted to pursue a career in animation — not as an animator [I can draw stick figures, nothing more], but as an author of children's stories to be rendered in animation for *television* [in the early 1940s, television was a dream on the horizon]. As for the *writing,* I've always had a love of language; in 1945, I was one of nine champions in an annual, statewide High School senior English exam.

"Want me to go on?" Jim Dodd nodded *yes.* "Go on," he said.

"I graduated (cum laude, Phi Beta Kappa) from Ohio State University four years later, with a degree in radio programming, hoping to land a job at powerhouse radio station WLW, Cincinnati. But ... never made it to Cincinnati; went to New York, got a job as continuity director at an FM station that folded when television hit big a year later, then landed a job at an ad agency through the decade of the 1950s. That's where — and how — I met famed animator Shamus Culhane. I had written some TV commercials that called for animation; Shamus was famous for his animation of the character 'Dopey,' the endearing little mute dwarf in Disney's feature *Snow White and the Seven Dwarfs.* Shamus wound up doing the animation for those network commercials I wrote."

"Was he still in Hollywood?" Dodd wanted to know.

Shamus had opened a shop in Manhattan to be near the giant ad agencies on Madison Avenue. He was one of the first to "cash-in" on the demand for animated TV commercials.

"Did he get you started in foreign animation?"

No, what actually happened is that I had put together a series of nature documentaries called *Jungle,* showing animals in their natural habitats all over the world. Most of the film was, in effect, stock footage purchased, nonexclusively, from old-time photographers. I intercut the shots into a new story. But, at the same time, and using the same technique, the Disney Studio was turning out feature-length, live-action productions with titles like *The Living Desert, The Vanishing Prairie,* and *Seal Island,* shot by people who were primarily naturalists and, secondarily, photographers. They thought nothing of setting up a camera in a field and spending weeks photographing a flower bursting into bloom — in exquisite time-lapse photography. I was acquiring film from some of those photographers, just as Disney was and I thought I was paying a very low rate. Later I discovered that I was paying five times more per foot than Disney was paying!

Yes, Dodd said, but Walt was probably buying ten times as much footage.

Sure he was, I gladly conceded; his features ran over an hour in length, our shows ran only fifteen minutes, each. In any event, the *Jungle* series played Europe; but, at that time, some of those countries had blocked funds (their dollars could not be exported), so we took payment in the form of animated cartoons — in effect, barter. That's when I had to learn how to dub, in a hurry!

"That's one of the things I want to talk to you about," Dodd said: "the quality of the dubbing." (*Aha!* I thought, that's the real reason for this lunch; Jim Dodd is doing a little due diligence before making a major commitment.) He said that he and his associates had seen some awful dubbing out of Puerto Rico, Canada, and other places. The prices were good but he said, "look, we're NBC, we can't put out a product with inferior dubbing."

"You've seen my dubbing, Jim," I started to say, somewhat on the defensive.

"That's why our man in Tokyo said to call you, and that's why I did," Dodd interrupted. He had seen some of the animated cartoons and live-action features I had dubbed. His next remark surprised me by its unusual wording: "Those dubbed voices look as though they're coming out of those mouths on the screen."

What a relief! For a moment, I thought my host was going to say "Nice try, but...." Instead, he was, in my view, putting me on notice that NBC Enterprises was going to accept no less quality in *Astro Boy* than had been seen in earlier productions that came from my shop. Further, the last episode in the series would have to show no less quality of workmanship than was shown in the pilot.

I smiled and nodded in agreement. "Jim, did you happen to see the TV Academy Awards show the other night — the part where Robert Young (late star of the television series *Father Knows Best*) showed a clip from an episode dubbed in German?" Jim had seen the clip, thought the dubbing was wonderful. I did, too. Everyone did. The dubbing was so perfect that Robert Young then quipped, with a smile, "Now you know: the series is shot in German, and dubbed into English."

What makes the dubbing so wonderful, I added, is that, (a) the voices are perfectly cast — the German actor playing Robert Young *sounds* like Robert Young — and (b), the adaptor who wrote the German dialogue knows how to track labials. What are labials? I asked rhetorically, in reply to a puzzled look on Dodd's face. Labials are prominent lip shapes made when a speaker produces a specific sound. For example, say, "Miriam picked a pint bottle of bum brandy." Jim, you can't say "Miriam" without bringing your lips together twice to form the two letters *M* in Miriam. Try it. (He did try, and couldn't do it.) *Nobody* can do it, I assured him; and the letters *p,* as in "picked," and *b,* as in "bum brandy" — what we call the "explosives" — cannot be formed without pursing your lips and, at the same time, expelling a little air between them. A good adaptor is a writer who can write natural-sounding dialogue, while keeping all the labials in the adaptation, and keeping them in the same places in which they occur in the original dialogue.

Jim Dodd smiled and nodded his understanding. Regarding casting, he recalled that his associate Bill Schmidt thought that Astro Boy's mentor, our "Doctor Elefun," should sound like Sam Jaffe, a popular character actor of the day; and another associate recommended that his friend, Mary Lou Foster, a character actress noted for her ability to create children's voices, be cast in the role of Astro Boy. I had worked with Mary Lou Foster, agreed that she might very well make a good Astro Boy, and said that I would use her in that role.

Jim Dodd's final comment: "We [meaning NBC Enterprises] don't plan to advertise the fact that the series is being animated in Japan. We're not going to deny it, if anybody asks, but we're not going to publicize it, either. First of all, there are probably some buyers at stations out there who still haven't gotten over the fact that Japan was our enemy in World War Two. Second, if a buyer hears that the show is of Japanese origin, he's going to think it must be cheap ... shoddy ... and, even if he likes it, he's going to try to get it for two dollars an episode. So we're just not going to mention anything about Japan. Maybe they'll think that, since the show is in limited animation, it's probably coming from Hanna-Barbera Studio."

When Jim Dodd and I had finished our entrées, topped-off with the French restaurant's famous flan dessert and coffee, we walked back to Broadway. I sensed that the man from NBC was satisfied with this aspect of his due diligence; he could walk back to his office, feeling confident and reassured. "Do a good job, Fred," he said.

In April 1963, with just two performers — actress Mary Lou Foster in the title role of Astro Boy and Cliff Owens playing the narrator, Doctor Elefun, scientist Aster Boynton, plus a number of other, lesser, characters — we recorded/dubbed pilot #1, *The Birth of Astro Boy*. Owens was wonderful; an experienced dubber and skillful actor who could convincingly portray many disparate roles, he sailed effortlessly through his lines. Foster, however, turned out to be a major disappointment: she could not easily synchronize her lines, required numerous retakes, and struggled to create more character voices than Astro Boy's alone. All of us in the studio that historic day knew that we could not record an entire series with Mary Lou Foster.

The next day, with Gilbert Mack added to the cast mainly to play an arrogant, spaceship's commander, we recorded/dubbed program #3, *Expedition to Mars*. The men were strong and confident in their roles; once again, however, Mary Lou Foster struggled through her parts. (*Note:* Within months of these recording dates, Ms. Foster was hospitalized and would be unable to return to work.) Nevertheless, by running into overtime, we did complete the day's schedule, and I felt confident that we were delivering to NBC a worthy, highly salable product.

Bill Schmidt walked from his office to watch a few minutes of the first dubbing session (his comment: "amazing!"). His associates at NBC Enterprises would wait several days to see the pilots in their finished, 16mm print form, just as prospective buyers would be seeing them.

Synced Up

After recording *The Birth of Astro Boy* and *Expedition to Mars,* we synced up our English negative of the soundtrack (yes, a soundtrack *negative* is required) with the picture negative and sent it to Byron Laboratories in Washington, D.C., to strike prints. When those first prints of the two pilot episodes arrived at NBC, all of us — Jim Dodd, Bill Breen, Bill Schmidt, Morris Rittenberg, and I — looked at them intently. The lights went on after the screening and Rittenberg spoke first. Quietly — he was always soft-spoken — he expressed great satisfaction with what he saw and heard, especially with Cliff Owens as the "eloquent" voice of the Narrator. Schmidt, appreciative right from the start, simply repeated "Amazing!" Dodd remarked: "Didn't Fred do a great job with the *voices!*" Breen rose and said, "If I can't sell that, I can't sell anything!" He was right. Eventually, he sold the initial 52 *Astro Boy* episodes to scores of stations across the United States, beginning with WNEW-TV, Channel 5, in New York. (Incidentally, the Spanish-language version, which I understood was made in Mexico, was adapted from our English version, rather than from the original Japanese.)

The initial sale, to WNEW-TV, was virtually a giveaway. Breen explained that he made the station an offer they couldn't refuse just to get the show on the air and build an impressive ratings history. Only one program a week was broadcast, for a planned 52 weeks. NBC's owned-and-operated Channel 4 would not, and did not, run *Astro Boy.*

The show did indeed prove to be popular with audiences in New York. And because of that track record, NBC could go to other stations and say, "Look at these fantastic ratings in hardboiled New York with its seven outlets!" The show subsequently sold well in markets all across the country and in Mexico. By the summer of 1963, Enterprises knew they had a hit on their hands. Morris Rittenberg confirmed NBC's pickup of its "Option for the Series" and spoke of dubbing throughout the summer to meet several stations' September start date.

Kids Don't Count Cels, the Play's the Thing

From the outset, there was concern about the very limited amount of animation in the programs coming from Mushi. By way of comparison, a typical seven-minute Hollywood theatrical cartoon, such as a Mickey Mouse or Bugs Bunny short subject, utilized some 6,500 animation cels, while a typical half-hour *Tetsuan Atom* episode used only 4,000! That meant many shots contained no animation at all and were mere stills, in which the only action was a camera move, such as a zoom-in or a spin. My oft-repeated feeling, though, was that the storylines coming from Tokyo were compelling, zingy, and the editing, fast and snappy. As Shakespeare said, "The play's the thing!" meaning, in my lexicon, "Kids don't count cels"; if a story is great, kids will watch.

The limited animation used in *Tetsuan Atom* and subsequent Japanese cartoons was mandated by the small budget provided by the networks there. Japan is, after all, a relatively small market with relatively small audiences. Advertisers, such as the candy company that sponsored *Tetsuan Atom* in Japan, did not pay the enormous license fees that American cereal sponsors, for example, pay to sponsor American cartoons on national television. As a result, the Japanese studios had to seek economical ways to achieve the *look* of animation. And those ways, including the inventive ways in which the artists struggled with the rigors of necessarily limited animation, became synonymous with anime *style*. So, what everybody later thought was a matter of style was actually nothing more than a studio's desperate way to try to save yen!

It was natural for audiences in the USA to compare Mushi's animation with that of Disney or Hanna-Barbera (and suffer in the comparison). The burden on us as adaptors of the Mushi cartoons was to make the American viewer think he/she was seeing more animation than was actually on the screen! How to do that? By bombarding the senses, that's how; by playing to the ear, if not to the eye.

Coming from a radio background, I knew we could "sweeten" the soundtracks to make the viewers think they were seeing more than they actually were. For instance, we added traffic sounds (cars whizzing by, horns honking, etc.) to visually static street scenes to "bring them to life"; similarly, we might add the sound of a dog barking in the distance or the lonely howl of a far-away train to a night scene. And, where feasible, we added off-screen "dialogue," usually grunts and other sounds of assent, to fill voids in otherwise still shots. All these touches helped add a sense of life, briskness, energy, and "drive" to the action.

And We Added an Opening Theme Song

Tetsuan Atom shows arriving from Tokyo opened with an orchestral version of the now-familiar march music. That's the way the series was broadcast in Japan. But I grew up in America in an era when every kids show on radio and on early television opened with a theme song. *Not* to do so would have been unthinkable! (On my own U.S.-made cartoon series, *The Big World of Little Adam,* each of the 104 episodes opens with the song "Oh, It's the Big World of Little A-dam." Kids like to sing along with a song that they know and love.)

I recommended to NBC's Jim Dodd that we do the same with *Astro Boy.* We could keep the same catchy melody — just add words. Dodd agreed and commissioned his friend Don Rockwell to write lyrics to the original theme composed by Tatsuo Takai in Tokyo. It was Rockwell who wrote the now-famous words, "There you go, Astro Boy...." And that's the song that opened and closed all 104 *Astro Boy* programs.

When Osamu Tezuka, on a visit to New York, first saw our English version, he was stunned — literally, *stunned*— to hear each program open not with the orchestral version of Takai's theme, but with music and lyrics! He had not expected or even contemplated such a thing. He immediately ordered that Japanese lyrics be written to Takai's melody and had all *Tetsuan Atom* shows open with it. That was a switch: instead of the English version following the Japanese lead, the Japanese version in this case followed the American lead! Today, all Japanese animated programs open with a vocal group singing a theme song. The first five *Tetsuan Atom* episodes in Japan still open only with Tatsuo Takai's lyric-less march.

"S'all right! S'all right"

I tried to Americanize the show in other little ways, too. For instance, Tezuka had a character very much like the Shmoo in Al Capp's *Li'l Abner* comic strip. I'm not sure where Tezuka got it, but that character would just pop in and out, and was put in strictly for laughs; it was just a little bit of nonsense stuck in strictly for comic effect. It delighted Tezuka to do that.

In one of the scenes in the pilot, Dr. Elefun is speaking to somebody lying down in a bed when — all of a sudden — the Shmoo-like thing pops up from the side of the bed, then just pops right back down again. I didn't know what that meant, but I understood its purpose, though I didn't know it was going to become a running gag.

At the time, the late ventriloquist Señor Wences, a very popular regular on *The Ed Sullivan* TV show, would have his little hand puppets constantly say, "S'all right! S'all right," which always brought great laughter from the audience. So, when the little Shmoo-like character in our *Astro Boy* pilot popped up from beside the bed, I had him say "S'all right!" before he disappeared. While that was probably the farthest thing from Tezuka's mind, the Americans who saw it got a kick out of it. The point is: My aim was not just to *dub* the show, but to *American-ize* it.

Adapting and Dubbing

The deal with NBC Enterprises to adapt and dub each episode of *Astro Boy* amounted to something like $1,800, which was certainly not lucrative, even at that time. The figure had to be lowball because of the possibility of NBC sending the work to Puerto Rico for about the same price. Titra Sound Studios, where I did virtually all my dubbing work, had at one point considered bidding for the job, but Titra told me, "Fred, with our setup and production philosophy, we have no way of bringing in a show that inexpensively." They, like the studio in San Juan, were budgeting two days to record a typical half-hour cartoon show.

In those days, one would dub a film into English by using short pieces of film cut into loops that would be individually threaded into a projector and run 'round and 'round, over and over, until an acceptable performance was recorded. There might be as many as 133 loops for a half hour TV show — far more than Titra or a conventional recording studio could handle in a single day.

But the techniques I had developed over the years were not conventional. One of the ways I sped things up was by making some of the cast members writers. They were not ordinarily writers, but the job wasn't that tough to do when they were handed a translation of the Japanese dialogue and a writer's guide ("bible") I had prepared, defining the interpersonal relationships of the characters in English. It helped enormously that the cast knew the show and the characters well. What's more, the actors/writers would soon be in the studio performing the very lines that they, themselves, had written. And if I, while directing, had a question or comment, the writer/performer was right there in the studio with me to resolve the matter immediately.

There were only three members in the cast, each of whom had "a thousand voices"; they were incredibly talented performers: Billie Lou Watt (who replaced the ailing Mary Lou Foster), Gilbert Mack, and Cliff "Ray" Owens. (I picked those two particular male actors because one, Owens, had a warm, low, fuzzy voice, while the other, Mack, had a higher, brighter, sharp-edged voice. The two men complemented each other.)

Mack would not, and claimed he could not, write. But Owens and Watt (Watt became the voice of Astro Boy and, later, Jimmy Sparks in the *Gigantor* series and Kimba in the *Kimba* series) did agree to write. I gave each a 16mm projector and said, "Here's the picture; go home and write it." They did, they enjoyed it, and the method worked very well, indeed.

Before going into the studio and actually recording the English voices, I first read and corrected the dialogue. Then, if any questions arose in the studio, the writer was right on the spot to explain, performing his or her own lines. All three performers were crackerjack dubbers. We became a kind of small, extended family and developed a sort of "studio shorthand" among ourselves, as well as with the projectionist and recording engineer. We thought of ourselves as "a lean, mean, dream machine." As often as not, a reading intended as a rehearsal was in fact so good, it became a "keeper." That way, we would knock off a show a day, often calling the date "a wrap" well before the 5:30 P.M. deadline.

A studio day meant from 9:30 A.M., when the union projectionist showed up, until 5:30 that afternoon. If you weren't out by 5:30, or if you started before 9:30 A.M., you were on overtime. I would always get the cast into the studio at 9:00. We would sit there while they would sip their coffee and munch on their English muffins. I took that half hour to tell them the story in context — of course, the writer knew what it was all about, but the other two actors did not — so we could hit the ground running when the projectionist came in at 9:30.

Today, in California, a producer can pay a dubbing actor by the hour — and not necessarily by the day. Under that condition, the dubbing producer finds it most cost-effective to record one actor at a time; the actor lays down ("splits-out") all his lines, and leaves. Then, the second actor comes in and does the same thing, and so on. But, in New York in 1963, Screen Actors Guild rules were very different: All performers had to be paid a minimum for a day's work — even if a performer had only one or two lines to record, that actor received the same daily minimum wage as an actor who had a hundred lines to record.

Once the recording session began, the studio in 1963 would typically record a loop of, say, three or four lines of dialogue. Then the engineer would stop, play back the recording to check for quality, then copy the sound from quarter-inch tape onto a sprocketed film medium — usually 35mm soundtrack film. But we didn't have time for all those niceties! The cast was competent, the crew was competent, and if none of us heard anything wrong during the recording, we went right on to the next loop.

Our studio had two 16mm projectors. The projectionist would thread a loop of film on Projector #1, then — while we were recording dialogue for that loop — he would thread-up the next loop on Projector #2. Then, back to #1, and so on. Every minute had to count!

At first, the studio crew were not all that happy with the way we were working, feeling that we were going too fast; the crew simply weren't accustomed to this kind of "lean, mean" efficiency. They'd call out, only half in jest, "Hey! You got to slow down, you're killing us! We're not used to this kind of breakneck speed. You guys leave at the end of the day and you're gone for a few days, until the next picture, but we're here every day, and you're killing us."

I was the new kid on the block. I didn't know we had to follow old, established rules, so I was developing new techniques — and learning that people are reluctant to change. They're accustomed to the old ways. However, the cast was energized by the spontaneous, straight-ahead, steady pace we were setting, and they urged the crew to keep up with us. After a few more brisk sessions, the crew, like the cast, grew to favor the lively tempo. They were finishing early. Soon the crew also began to push us to speed up, so they could leave early to go shopping, keep dentists' appointments — whatever!

Another thing I did to hold costs down was to go into the studio only on its dark days. Someone at Titra typically would call and say, "We have a dark day Wednesday, next Tuesday is open, and next Thursday is open." And I'd say, "Good, put us in all those three days." That helped a lot; we could get the facility for a lower fee and, even if the studio made little on our "dark-day" sessions, it came out ahead, and so did we.

I would also try to book my cast at times when they had no conflicts with other jobs, or else permit an actor to work in the morning on his loops in order to be free that afternoon to go elsewhere. This built a feeling of camaraderie among "the family"; the actors, in effect, had the best of all worlds: They could dub their running roles in a cartoon in the morning, then, in the afternoon, dub a role in a live-action foreign feature in a studio down the hall and thus "double-dip their fees!" When one of our cast left to go to another job, those remaining behind would "sing the departing actor off" with a line from a popular old song, "Nice work if you can get it...." There was no bitterness in that good-natured teasing; all three cast members were so serenaded at various times, and we might just as well have been singing "For He's a Jolly Good Fellow."

All this helped keep spirits high, costs low. Dubbing the series was not a high-profit venture. On the contrary, we were pinching everything that was pinchable. At the end, there would be money. But, from the word "Go," the New York production of the original *Astro Boy* series was one hell of a bargain for NBC Enterprises.

Television Animation 1963: Climate of the Times

Harvey Deneroff notes the status of TV animation, circa 1963, as it appeared to NBC executives seeing Japanese animation for the first time:

When *Astro Boy* debuted on New York television in the fall of 1963, animation for TV was still in its infancy. Unlike the landscape today, where cable networks, such as Cartoon Network, proliferate, showing animation 24/7, there was actually something of a shortage of animated programming for kids in 1963. It was this gap in programming that NBC Enterprises sought to fill by taking a chance on a science-fiction series animated not in the United States or in Europe, but in Japan.

Animation for TV actually dates back to a time before World War II, but the honors for producing the first animated TV series in the United States goes to *Crusader Rabbit* in 1949. Produced by Jay Ward and Alexander Anderson (nephew of animation pioneer Paul Terry, creator of Mighty Mouse), the *Crusader Rabbit* show was sold into syndication. The program's format, which consisted of four-minute cliffhangers, was to become standard for TV animation over the next decade.

Despite the popularity of *Crusader Rabbit*, the bulk of animation on early American TV was supplied by theatrical cartoons, some of them dating back to the very beginnings of animation early in the twentieth century, including Earl Hurd's *Bobby Bumps*, Max Fleischer's *Out of the Inkwell,* and Paul Terry's *Aesop Fables* cartoons. These were followed by cartoons from Hollywood's Golden Age (1928 through the early 1950s) as seen on CBS's *Mighty Mouse Playhouse* and ABC's *Disneyland* and *Mickey Mouse Club* shows.

There was some original programming produced for the major networks in the 1950s, including segments of UPA's *The Gerald McBoing Boing Show* and Hanna Barbera's first TV series, *The Ruff and Reddy Show*. When the CBS Network purchased Paul Terry's Terrytoons Studios, the network made five-minute episodes of *Tom Terrific*, which were shown as segments of the popular *Captain Kangaroo* morning show. However, most early production was aimed at the syndication market, including Hanna-Barbera's *The Huckleberry Hound Show, Quick Draw McGraw*, and *Yogi Bear*.

It was in the early 1950s, before the big Hollywood studios started granting television licenses to their film libraries (including their animated cartoons), that television producer Bill Cayton took advantage of this standoff.

It was with Cayton and his ad agency, Cayton, Inc., that Fred Ladd first started working in television; at the time, Cayton was producing a series of prize fight films called *Greatest Fights of the Century,* which were televised on the fledgling NBC TV network.

At the same time, Cayton amassed a collection of films that photographed animals struggling to survive in their natural habitat. To Ladd fell the job of editing and scripting this raw footage into a coherent television series that came to be called *Jungle Macabre*—later, *Jungle*—that bowed on WABC-TV, Channel 7, in New York in the early 1950s and was later distributed to stations across the country. This was Ladd's introduction to TV production and paved the way for his entrée into the world of animation.

Cayton understood the value of using existing and available, that is, foreign, animation, in much the same way as he had used stock footage of animals to make *Jungle*. So he sought to amass great quantities of European animation, and, again, the task of mounting a cohesive, consistent series of shows for American television fell to Ladd.

Together, Cayton and Ladd scoured European animation studios looking for well-made films that were suitable for children, and which were based upon well-known tales (e.g., *Beauty and the Beast*). The films also had to be long enough to sustain serialization as six-minute cliff-hangers, in the style of *Crusader Rabbit*. For this, the typically European 30-minute cartoon proved ideal.

Ladd's way of working was, first, to dub the foreign cartoon in its entirety and, afterward, divide the English version into six-minute episodes. It was by watching the way in which live-action foreign films were dubbed into English in a Manhattan studio that Ladd learned the art of lip-synching foreign-language films.

Titled *Cartoon Classics* and distributed by Radio-TV Packagers, Inc. (another Cayton company), the series sold well to stations hungry for wholesome quality kids' entertainment. Eventually, over 300 six-minute *Cartoon Classics* episodes were produced and delivered to non-network–affiliated stations. And it was this work that would lead Ladd in 1963 to garner the assignment to produce the English-language version of *Tetsuan Atom/Astro Boy*.

The success in national prime-time television of *The Flintstones* in 1960 created a huge demand by networks for original, half-hour animation programming. However, none of the 11 shows made for network TV in the wake of *The Flintstones* succeeded in prime time; however, several shows such as *Top Cat* (1961), *The Jetsons* (1962), and *Jonny Quest* (1964), went on to become early classics of Saturday morning animation.

While the most successful of these new Saturday morning shows would eventually find their way into syndication, independent stations still had to scramble to find suitable product. Thus, when NBC Enterprises took on American distribution of *Astro Boy,* there was a huge pent-up demand for animated programming, which studios like Hanna-Barbera were not able to fulfill.

CHAPTER 2

A Trip to Japan

Of the first batch of nearly a dozen shows Mushi delivered, NBC rejected six episodes! Standards & Practices (euphemism for Department of Censorship) cited excessive violence and/or otherwise objectionable material. The news of these rejections was devastating — a *disaster* for the Japanese! The outright rejections represented an enormous financial hole for Mushi; thousands and thousands of dollars were seen as going down the drain, and they would have to eat the costs of replacing those six episodes! Imagine, if you can, the consternation running through the halls of NBC Enterprises and the outright *panic* sweeping the offices of Mushi! Their reasoning was, "If NBC is rejecting six episodes out of the first batch of shows, how many are they going to reject from the next batch ... and the next?" To make matters worse, the creators did not understand *why* their shows were being rejected in America; after all, those shows were accepted and broadcast by Fuji Network in Japan — and had even received excellent reviews from a doting local press. Surely the creators must have been thinking, "What's wrong with those idiots in America?"

I was not surprised when Jim Dodd said, "Fred, you have to go over to the studio and straighten this out." I had never been to Japan, and the idea of visiting that exotic land, expenses paid, did have appeal. But the proposal could not have come at a worse time. I was in the process of launching my own series of 104 short, space-themed television cartoons called *The Big World of Little Adam,* was writing and directing the approved episodes of *Astro Boy,* besides keeping tabs on progress in Brussels of the animated feature *Pinocchio in Outer Space* and following up on a problem-plagued production in Yugoslavia of my second animated feature film, *Journey Back to Oz.*

Nonetheless, the urgency of the Mushi situation prevailed and, days later, at the end of Tokyo Olympic Week 1964, I was on a Northwest Airlines flight to Tokyo. My wife Eileen was also on a separate Northwest Flight to Tokyo, due to arrive at Haneda Airport a couple of hours later (we had two young children and, as a precaution in the event of an airplane accident, never flew together). The Japanese reception committee, three young men at Haneda Airport, had prepared a charming greeting for me when I first set foot on Japanese soil. There, on the tarmac, was a waist-high, smiling wooden cutout of Astro Girl holding a little sign that read WELLCOME TO MY COUNTRY, MR. FLED RADD [*sic*]. Astro Girl was, I realized, a second- or third-grader who was still working hard on her spelling. What a warm, friendly greeting!

The all-male welcoming committee had not known that my wife would be arriving separately. They seemed mildly astonished. When I asked "Why?," one young agent replied with a broad smile, "Here in Japan, we have an old saying: 'When you go to a fine restaurant, why take along your lunch pail?'"

Eileen landed a short time later and was as pleased as I was by the happy reception. We were whisked to the Ginza Tokyo Hotel where we would spend the night. The hour was late (11:00 P.M. local time) and we were fatigued. After brief showers, we climbed into bed, adjusted our watches to reflect Tokyo time, turned off the bedside lamps, and wondered if we'd feel sluggish the next day because of jet lag.

Suddenly, there came a knocking at the door. Must be the bellhop delivering something, we guessed. It was not the bellhop. Standing in the doorway, grinning pleasantly, were our three hosts, to whom we had said goodnight in the lobby. They had said then that they would see us soon, but we had not expected to see them *this* soon. They entered the room, one carrying a 16 millimeter film projector, one carrying a large can of film, one carrying a long electric cord. In minutes they had set up their equipment and were projecting, on the hotel room wall, a 16mm film print of one of Tezuka's animated feature classics, *New Treasure Island*.

Eileen and I had heard that Japanese businessmen were workaholics who often put in workdays running 18 hours and more; this was affirmation. An hour after arriving, the three gentlemen packed up their gear, thanked us for our courtesy, hoped we had enjoyed Osamu Tezuka's great masterpiece, and backed out the door. We bid them goodnight one more time, then crawled into bed, wondering how we would ever awaken in time to be driven to Mushi Production in the morning for a meeting with Osamu Tezuka.

Osamu Tezuka. Osamu Tezuka. Who's Osamu Tezuka?

Osamu Tezuka was an extremely prolific and popular manga artist known in Japan as the *manga no kamisama,* or "God of Comics." He was born in 1928 in Takarazuka, a little town near Osaka. He loved to draw, beginning at a very early age, and — even while enrolled in a university as an 18-year-old medical student — he made his debut as a *cartoonist* with a 4-panel cartoon strip that he called *Ma-chan's Diary.* Soon thereafter, paperback compilations of his longer stories —*New Treasure Island, Lost World,* and *Next World*—appeared and became overnight sensations. To Tezuka's own astonishment, copies of those compilations sold an amazing 400,000 copies *each* — an unthinkable amount for comics — making Tezuka nationally famous!

He did eventually receive his physician's license, but put it aside choosing, instead, to devote his life to creating manga and (later) animation.

The young manga artist's success caught the eyes of program executives at the Fuji Television Network Here, they agreed, was a way for Fuji Television to begin broadcasting *Japanese* children's cartoons — not just American-made cartoon programs *adapted* for Japanese children. They put their idea to the surprised young artist and, to the delight of all, Tezuka was thrilled at the idea of animating his manga characters; he had, in fact, just opened his own small animation studio. Now, suddenly, here was the opportunity to produce animated children's programs funded by, and broadcast on, the Fuji Television Network. His first series, he decided, would be based upon his popular manga character, Tetsuan Atom, the little boy robot inspired by the puppet Pinocchio.

From Printed Ideogram to Spoken Dialogue

In his manga, Tezuka's characters spoke to each other with words printed in ideograms (pictographs assembled into printed Japanese writing called *kanji*).

(*Note:* Kyoto University Professor Tetsuji Atsuji, speaking in the Japan Foundation's 2007, five-city tour of its presentation "Forest of Words," demonstrated how ideograms can appear in horizontal and vertical lines. [Tezuka's characters spoke to each other with words printed mainly in vertical lines.] Further, Professor Atsuji surprised his audiences by revealing that modern-day calligraphers use over 200 different shades of black ink applied to paper with brushes made of hair from elephants' ears, mouse whiskers, ostrich eyebrows, and human hair from a child's first haircut.)

Osamu Tezuka, a life-long lover of insects, had named his first animation studio Mushi Production; *mushi* are insects, and the artist incorporated the ideogram for insects in his name. But at Mushi, Tezuka would have to forget about having his characters speak in kanji on a printed page. He would have to learn how to have them communicate in recorded dialogue painted as lipsynch on animation cels.

In point of fact, the artist had always been greatly interested in animation and admired the works of Walt Disney and Max Fleischer. (Tetsuan Atom's signature exaggerated eyes were inspired by Fleischer's famous wide-eyed character, Betty Boop.) In the late 1950s, Tezuka agreed to allow his name to be associated with an early Japanese animated movie, *Saiyu-Ki* (1960), which was released in the United States in 1961 as *Alakazam the Great.* Tezuka was given screen credit as codirector, but his actual involvement seemed to be little more than ceremonial.

(*Alakazam the Great,* along with two other Japanese animated movies — *Shonen Sarutobi Sasuke [Magic Boy]* and *Hakuja Den [Panda and the Magic Serpent]*—were released in the United States at almost the same time. All three disappointed at the box office.)

Tezuka's association with *Saiyu-Ki,* though, inspired him in 1961 to set up his own animation studio, Mushi Production. The following year, he was approached by the Fuji Television Network to produce a *Tetsuan Atom* television series to be sponsored by Meiji Candy Company. The first *Tetsuan Atom* half-hour adventure went on the air on January 1, 1963, launching the first half-hour animated television series in Japan, and certainly one of the most — if not *the* most — important of all.

On our first morning in Japan, my wife Eileen and I were driven to the studio of Mushi Production (we would translate that as "Busy Bee") Production. Osamu Tezuka was waiting. I could tell that the studio had been swept clean. It was spotless. I would learn later that Tezuka had ordered the studio cleaned from top to bottom because he did not want me going back to New York, telling damaging tales about any lack of neatness, cleanliness, or orderliness in the studio.

In fact, I would later learn, Tezuka actually was concerned that I might be a *spy* for NBC! He seemed to be on his guard. After a brief cup of tea in his office, we got down to work. What about those six rejected films? Was it I, in fact, who rejected them?

I explained about NBC's Standards & Practices Department and what their concerns were — the good news and the bad. First, the good news — I could *save* three of the six rejected shows! I could, and in fact had already left instructions for the editors in New York to trim the end of a few problematical shots. That would eliminate the *threat* of over-the-top violence by removing gunplay that, if left intact, was going too far. I also explained that nobody ever *died* in *Astro Boy.* Yes, *Tetsuan Atom* had Atom, in the Mushi version, while bent over a slain victim lying prostrate in the street, saying "He's dead"; but, in the English version, Astro Boy kneels over the victim and says, "He's unconscious; get him to a hospital!"

Tezuka laughed! His attitude toward the *spy* changed perceptibly, at once.

Staff of newly formed Mushi Production in Nerima-ku, Tokyo, October 1963, shortly after NBC Enterprises contracted for 52 *Tetsuan Atom* programs. Osamu Tezuka, in beret and posing near street entrance at far right, was flush with success, expecting it to go on forever. Courtesy of Tezuka Productions. © Tezuka Productions.

I could see that he understood immediately that Mr. Ladd was, in fact, not a spy, but a *friend*; in the course of a few minutes, I had already saved three of the six rejected shows, simply by cutting away from a shot of a crook holding a gun — before the crook could shove the gun against his victim's temple.

To a group of young writers that joined us — none looked more than 23 years old — I demonstrated that it's OK to show a criminal brandishing a gun, but *not* OK to show the criminal pressing that gun against someone's temple. We (Americans) consider that to be violence. With that, I pushed my raised index finger to within an inch of one writer's temple and looked around, to see if I had successfully made my point.

One young fellow said, "It is hard for us to understand this. You probably think that our samurai, protecting their masters, are cruel and violent. But we look at your western gunfighters killing a complete stranger in cold blood for no good reason. We think *that* is violent and cruel."

The "kid" had me. That took me by surprise; I had no glib answer for that. I muttered something about "Yes, well ... cultural differences between our two societies. What is acceptable in one society may be *taboo* in another."

The remaining three shows that had been rejected were unsalvageable, I explained. One show dealt with a scientist's experiments on living animals. Vivisection. I could not save that show. Nor could I save a show about a young bachelor whose pad had pictures of naked women plastered all across the walls. The third reject was a story (*Christ's Eyeballs*) about a criminal, while running from police, taking refuge in a church. To let his henchmen know

Osamu Tezuka surprised his guests, on occasion, by revealing himself to be an accomplished accordionist. Photo courtesy of Tezuka Productions.

where he, the criminal, is hiding, he scratches a secret message on one of the eyeballs of Christ on a crucifix. In Japan, that action was no problem; of course, no such scene can be shown on U.S. television.

Tezuka understood that the three rejected episodes could not be salvaged for NBC's market. But he also understood that Mr. Ladd had saved three episodes from the scrap heap and that the man from NBC was not a spy or adversary, but a friend. Indeed, our friendship endured till the day Tezuka died of cancer in 1989.

On the second day of my visit, Tezuka and his top production man, the late Kaoru Anami, had lined up a stack of episodes for me to screen in the studio's little screening room. The intent was for me to screen the prints and comment on them to Mr. Anami *in the screening room,* so that any necessary changes could be made immediately, before the prints were shipped to New York. But I explained that it is not my practice to select shows and have them screened for me at normal projection speed. That takes too long. I asked for, and received, a cutting table equipped with a viewer and a pair of rewinds. So equipped, I whizzed through the shows in less than five minutes each.

That's my training—to size-up a show's plot and counterplots very quickly and without benefit of sound. (I do speak Spanish, and a bit of French, but virtually no Japanese, so nothing was to be gained by playing the sound-track.)

Tezuka watched skeptically and without any noticeable appreciation. I understood his feeling: he had labored weeks, months, on an episode that finally became a reality and here was this stranger from New York zipping through it at whirlwind speed, totally ignoring the compelling music and dra-matic performances on the soundtrack! I knew what I had to do: I changed reels, put on the next show in the stack, began winding through the story at brisk, but respectful speed, and narrated the story aloud (in English, of course) as I watched events unfold on my tiny 16mm viewer. As it turns out, I called all the shots and plot twists correctly (score one for the stranger from New York). Tezuka realized that my method was working—and *I accepted every single show in the stack!* That did a lot to smooth any ruffled feathers. Tezuka even agreed, in the future, to draw all signs in English, such as Bank, Hotel, Police, etc.

Tezuka, Anami, and I had a delightful lunch together at a little sushi bar near the studio, and all was well with the world.

A Happy Countenance

Tezuka was about my size, 5'9" or 5'10", bespectacled, nicely dressed and always wearing a beret, which was his trademark. At first I thought that beret was his way of proclaiming himself an artist. Not until many years later did I learn that the man was, in fact, bald—or *nearly* bald. In any event, he had little hair. That was revealed to me one day by a young lady who had worked in his office as secretary and translator.

Tezuka always seemed to have a happy countenance. He enjoyed laugh-ing and enjoyed having company; he was known to sleep only four hours or so each night, yet his staff and associates never saw him irascible or testy. In-deed, it's hard to picture Osamu Tezuka as anything but jocular and smiling.

Tezuka spoke little English, but knew enough so that we could go out and have lunch together and communicate. I would speak very slowly and try to explain things graphically. I could tell by his reply that he understood. Then he would ask me questions. Typically, he would ask why I had done something in a certain way at a certain point, indicating that he understood I had sometimes added humor at a point in the action where there was none in the Japanese. He wondered how I had selected English names for his char-acters, in particular the name of Mr. Pompous, an old gentleman with a white, walrus-type moustache. (That character struck me as being so pompous, I called him Mr. Pompous.) As I noted earlier, that name delighted Tezuka for reasons I never understood. Tezuka would say "Mistah Pompous," then toss his head back and roar with gales of laughter.

In the beginning, I worried that he would not like the English versions we made in 1963–64. (It is normal for an artist to dislike derivative versions of his work. Frankly, I was not pleased with the Japanese version of *Pinocchio in Outer Space* released in Japan by Toei in the 1970s.) But in fact, Tezuka *did* like *Astro Boy*. He *understood* that we were adding humor in places where originally there was none; he laughed and thanked me. He was also greatly impressed with *Pinocchio in Outer Space,* he said, even in Toei's imperfect version.

My trip to Tokyo was a big deal at Mushi and in Japan, due in no small part, I knew, to the fact that I had the NBC imprimatur behind me. I did not know in advance that Mushi had arranged a press conference, where both Tezuka and I were questioned by a phalanx of reporters. The story they sought was that of the historic, "First Japanese Cartoon Series Sold to the United States" and the "Arrival of Famed Japanese Icon *Tetsuan Atom* on American Shores." They asked me about the ratings of *Astro Boy* in the States, why we picked the series, and what did Americans think of all this?

I was in Japan for only a week. My hosts urged me to extend my stay, and indeed I would have enjoyed remaining there longer, but I knew I had to get back. I was growing restless about delaying the *Little Adam* series any longer, and I was aware that another trip to Brussels was imminent.

As for sightseeing, we (Kaoru Anami, a few other studio staff members, and I) — Tezuka himself remained behind to meet deadlines — had squeezed in a brief trip to Kyoto, ancient capital of Japan, where we visited historic shrines and temples. Japan's famed bullet trains, still new and novel at that time, whisked us from Tokyo to Kyoto in a record-shattering three hours. Looking out the sleek train windows, one saw farmers and their families bent over their crops, working their rice fields entirely by hand, much as their ancestors had done for centuries.

My hosts also wanted to show me how *modern* Tokyo had become. They drove me along their new superhighways, highways just like those in New York, and pointed out several tall buildings, all just like those in New York and erected in the international style of the time with lots of glass-and-steel facades. Tokyo? The reality is that I might as well have been in New York — or even Brussels. Kyoto, in its preserved ancient state, had been a joy. Much of ancient Tokyo, however, had already disappeared in 1964. I understood my hosts' enthusiasm to show me how up-to-date the city had become, but felt an unspoken touch of sadness, too, at Tokyo's rapidly vanishing architectural heritage. What a loss! And what a pleasure to see young women attending Tokyo's Kabuki Theater on a Sunday afternoon, clad — not in modern Western dress — but in kimonos.

In a short time, Kaoru Anami, the head of production at Mushi, and I had become friends. We were both "production guys" and understood there was that bond between us; Anami saw that I had come to help, not hinder or hassle, the studio. And he was appreciative.

Another guide in that party making the trek to Kyoto with me, my wife, and Kaoru Anami, was one Fumio Suzuki. Suzuki-san was a young employee of Video Promotions, the firm that finally signed the deal for *Astro Boy* with NBC Enterprises. On our return to Tokyo, Fumio, as he asked us to call him, did something really unusual. He invited us to visit his home—something that Japanese businessmen normally do not do. They take clients to a restaurant, a club, a bar, or other commercial establishment, but not to their home. So, my wife and I were made to feel special. We relished the occasion.

The first thing we did, before entering Fumio's house, was take off our shoes and set them upon a mat outside the door. The senior Suzuki, Fumio's father, was in the house, visiting, and his wife was there, too, as was Fumio's toddler son, Masayuki. Eileen wondered, half aloud, what the kitchen was like. Surprisingly, Fumio invited Eileen to see the kitchen, which of course delighted Eileen — but sent the young housegirl/cook running from the kitchen, her hand covering her mouth to stifle embarrassed laughter. She needn't have done that. The house was typically small but neat, pots of vegetables were in the wooden sink, being sprayed with forcefully running water. The scene charmed Eileen.

At the time, Suzuki was in the throes of a divorce; his young son, Masayuki, was just learning to eat with a kind of training spoon that Japanese children use before they can manage chopsticks. The boy's grandmother was kneeling down beside him, helping him to eat a bowl of rice, probably topped with a little bit of veggie or meat. (Twenty years later, Masayuki, then living in Los Angeles, came to visit me in an office not far from his apartment. He had turned into a very ingratiating young man.)

Before we left, Fumio's sister arrived and, as is the custom in Japan, she presented Eileen with a gift — a Noh mask that had been hanging on a wall. The mask was made from thin, hammered copper, and portrayed the theatrical face of sorrow. The mask may or may not have had great monetary value; that did not matter. The fact is that Eileen was reluctant to take the mask, feeling that Miss Suzuki probably treasured it. Still, Eileen knew that she could not refuse the gift — that would be perceived as rude. Reluctantly but gratefully, she did accept the Noh mask, thanked her hostess profusely, and carried the gift back with her to New York when she left Tokyo a few days later. Today that mask hangs in a place of honor on a wall where we can see it every day. Neither Eileen nor I will ever forget that act of extraordinary kindness in a neat little house in Japan.

The Next 52

In the United States, programs such as *Astro Boy* were, and are, usually distributed to individual stations on what is called a "library" basis, that is, a station would get an entire series of, say, 52 shows all at once and was licensed to keep showing them over a three-year term. This necessarily involves repeating episodes again and again "from library."

That is not what's done in Japan. The Japanese do not repeat shows; instead, they keep making new episodes. *Tetsuan Atom*, as noted earlier, was sponsored on the Fuji Television Network by Meiji Candy Company, which underwrote most or all of the cost of a total of 193 episodes. NBC initially committed to 52 programs and had no expectation of ever taking any more. But when Mushi was finishing the last of these episodes, an emissary showed up in New York to negotiate with NBC for the next 52!

Executives Rittenberg, Schmidt, Breen, and Dodd were startled. They explained the American library system to Fumio Suzuki, Mushi's new emissary, and expressed their regrets that they could not commit for any additional *Astro Boy* programs. Suzuki then explained that Mushi had no choice but to keep making new episodes, and, since NBC was refusing to accept any additional ones, the Japanese would have to offer their upcoming episodes to other distributors.

That was an impossible situation for NBC. They could not be selling *Astro Boy* to one television station while rival outlets were being offered essentially the same show from a different distributor — to say nothing about use of the name *Astro Boy!* And, in Japan, Osamu Tezuka had come to depend upon NBC royalties to pay for the increased quality of animation *demanded* by NBC! How was he to pay for that higher quality without guaranteed U.S. royalties?

After considerable negotiation and enormous pressure, the parties finally reached a compromise: NBC would take another 52 programs, but Mushi had to agree not to require NBC to accept any additional episodes beyond the 104, and, Mushi would not offer any other episodes to any other party.

Fortunately for NBC, there was still a shortage of popular cartoons on the air in the mid–1960s; *Astro Boy* had proved to be a ratings winner and Bill Breen's sales team was able to go forth and easily sell all 104 finished episodes. That massive series — a record for a Japanese animated series in the

American market and one that stands to this day — made money for both NBC and Mushi.

I initially saw producing the English-language version of *Tetsuan Atom* as simply another project; something to do to help pay the rent while I was busy, working on other things. I had no idea that this was to be the beginning of a whole tidal wave, a tsunami, of anime that would eventually sweep the country! Soon thereafter, however, opportunities came along that made me start to realize that the project at hand was to be a lot more than "just another job."

Word of the American success of *Astro Boy* spread through Japan like wildfire. Many other Japanese artists and producers felt that, if Osamu Tezuka could do it, so could they. Literally overnight, animation studios began to spring up, and a whole new industry was being created in Japan. I was lucky enough to play an ongoing role in what was to become the worldwide phenomenon of an art form that we today call *anime*.

The respite for Tezuka and his Mushi Production, however, was short-lived. By 1965, he had already laid the groundwork for a major new series that would come to be known as *Jungulu Taitei Leo* (Jungle Emperor Leo). Our name for the series would be *Kimba the White Lion*.

NBC would distribute only 52 of a far bigger series, and both NBC and the Fuji Television Network informed Tezuka that the days of producing cartoons in economical black and white were over. Color television had come to Japan and, henceforth — for the first time — all animated series would have to be shot *in color!*

CHAPTER 3

Tetsujin 28 and *8th Man*

The success of *Astro Boy* in America launched a new industry in Japan: animation for television. (The Japanese call it *anime*.) Overnight, new animation studios — instant studios! — began popping up all over Tokyo! One such overnight wonder was TCJ, Television Corporation of Japan. Another was Tatsunoko Production, a small studio that opened its doors just outside Tokyo. Yet another was Nippon Sunrise. Tokyo Movie Shinsha was born.

The outlook of these new players, clearly, was "Ah! Here is a whole new industry for Japan! Tezuka has started it with his Mushi Production; if *he* can do it, surely *we* can do it too." And they did. There being no seasoned animators hanging around, the new studios hired kids just out of art school. They even raided other new studios — particularly Mushi — for talent with at least *some* experience. For famous comic characters to animate (like Tezuka's *Tetsuan Atom*), the new animation studios looked to *manga* (popular comic strips and books).

One successful manga hero of the day was a most unusual character called *8th Man,* written and illustrated by the team of Kazumasa Hirai and Jiro Kuwata. Animated by TCJ Studio, *8th Man*'s lead character was a gifted super detective, cut down by a ruthless killer; then, miraculously "restored" by the brilliant "Doctor Genius" (yes, that was my name for him), Genius kept the detective's incredible mind alive and functional, but transplanted it in the metallic body of a robot, thereby creating a cyborg — part human, part machine. That series, I believe, became the progenitor of the live-action television series called *The Six Million Dollar Man,* which was based upon the same premise. So was the feature film, *Robocop.*

TCJ also went into production of an animated television series known as *Tetsujin 28* (*Iron Man 28*, which I re-named *Gigantor*). As luck and fate would have it, I became involved in producing the English-language versions of both these enduring shows.

8th Man

Our name for the lead character was "Tobor" (read it backward). In Japanese, he was called Hachirô Azuma, the 8th Man, because he was the eighth man in his squad of the Tokyo Metropolitan Police. What struck me most about this part-man, part-robot, was the stunning Japanese notion of a "robot who can cry"! That is a memorable idea — memorable because it is so offbeat, so moving, so emotionally disarming, so *human*. To this day I regret having adapted only the series pilot; the remainder of the series, while retaining my nomenclature and angles for humor, was dubbed in Florida at a price far too low for us in New York to match.

Gigantor

TCJ, the same Tokyo-based studio that animated the manga adventures of *8th Man,* also animated the manga adventures of a giant robot called *Tetsujin 28*. That character, 50-feet tall and remotely controlled by 12-year-old "Jimmy Sparks" (*Shotaro* in Japanese), first appeared in the boys' magazine *Shonen*; the manga was written and illustrated by Mitsuteru Yokoyama.

Earlier, I mentioned a sales agent headquartered in Tokyo — one Kazuhiko ("K.") Fujita. He was the man dismissed by Mushi after failing to make a deal with NBC Enterprises for what became the *Astro Boy* series, thus paving the way for a second agent to step in and accept the very same deal from which he (K. Fujita) had walked away! K. Fujita learned his lesson from that bitter experience and wasn't about to make the same mistake twice! (And, after all, he reasoned, it was his idea to go to NBC in the first place.) So, when TCJ began working on the *8th Man* and *Tetsujin 28* series, K. Fujita went to TCJ and succeeded in convincing TCJ to give him the rights to represent both those series abroad (that is, not only in North America, but also the entire world outside Japan). In the case of at least *Tetsujin 28,* Fujita also convinced producer Dentsu to allow Fujita to act as agent for that behemoth of advertising agencies.

Then, rather than go back directly to NBC Enterprises, where he felt he had probably "poisoned the air," Fujita went to NBC's competitor, ABC Films; that division of The American Broadcasting Company was to ABC what NBC Enterprises was to the National Broadcasting Company. He offered *8th Man* to division head Henry ("Hank") Plitt — and Plitt liked it! The year was 1964, *Astro Boy* was already a hit, and Plitt felt that, if he could get the same *Astro Boy* team (Ladd and company) to adapt/dub a pilot of *8th Man,* he had a pretty good shot at bringing in a winner for ABC.

Plitt called me; it was history repeating itself. I found myself speaking with ABC's Hank Plitt, very much as I had spoken earlier with NBC's Jim Dodd. Instead of *Astro Boy,* it was *8th Man.* I said we'd call the lead character ("Azuma" in Japanese), "Tobor" ("That's 'robot' spelled backward, Hank"); the brilliant doctor ("Tani") would now be "Doctor Genius," the bumbling chief of police ("Tanaka") would now be "Chief Fumblethumbs," and so on. Peter Fernandez, a talented writer-director who had worked with me extensively on *Astro Boy,* wrote much of the script for the pilot, which we recorded using the same performers that we were using on *Astro Boy* (Cliff Owens, Billie Lou Watt, Gil Mack); and the entourage that Plitt brought with him to screen the finished pilot called the English soundtrack "really good!"

Apparently, Hank Plitt knew about K. Fujita's other robot show — *Tetsujin 28*— too. Plitt must have passed on it, turned it down, on the basis that *one robot show for now is enough, thank you;* NBC certainly knew of it and would not consider it, either, for the same reason that Plitt had offered: they had the robot series *Astro Boy* and, in their words, *we don't want to compete with ourselves.*

When I learned that NBC Enterprises had no interest in *Tetsujin 28,* the giant robot controlled by a 12-year-old boy, I thought they were making a mistake, and said so. "Every 12-year-old boy in the world wants a giant protector," I argued, "and every boy that age wants to control a big, powerful *machine* like a car or a truck or a fire-engine." (It's a macho thing.) It was all to no avail; NBC's collective mind was made up. Then came the surprise question: "Why don't *you* take it, Fred?"

"*Why?*"

I thought about it. Soon, "*Why?*" became "*Why NOT?*" After all, *Pinocchio in Outer Space,* the animated feature I was making in Belgium, was virtually completed, and production of *The Big World of Little Adam* animated television series similarly was winding down. So, *why not* began to make more and more sense. The more I thought about it, the more I liked the idea.

I talked it over with my partner at the time, the late Al Singer. Singer's background had been as a game show director-producer (he had directed the successful *Name That Tune* program) and he knew little about *Astro Boy;* but as he felt that I was at the core of the "action" on Japanese animation, and he trusted my judgment, he backed my decision to *go for it!*

Using whatever monies were available from distribution of our television series, *The Big World of Little Adam,* we formed a new corporation, Delphi Associates Incorporated, and on December 22, 1964 we contracted for *Tetsujin 28* with K. Fujita, acting as agent for Dentsu. After exercising our option for a pilot, we committed to take 52 episodes of the 96 that TCJ Studio expected to produce.

Almost immediately, we were handed a number of surprises: The first was that TCJ did not want to sell us the first 26 shows! The reason, they explained, was that the young animators on the series were inexperienced and were just learning their craft; so, though the poor quality of animation on the first 26 episodes was OK for forgiving Japanese audiences, it was *not* OK for international audiences.

I did not see how we could show the origin of the robot, or the human characters that surrounded him, without any of the explanation inherent in the early episodes, but K. Fujita was so insistent that we finally capitulated. Our Program #1 (*Struggle at the South Pole*) was actually TCJ's episode 27; but our series pilot was TCJ's episode 28 (*Battle at the Bottom of the World*). The two episodes actually constituted a two-part adventure set in Antarctica.

Not many programs in the series were components of such multipart adventures, thank goodness, but our pilot film *was*— and that partially explains why I picked episode 28 to be our pilot: it's a great adventure set in a vast, little-known locale, it *ends* (there is no "To Be Continued" notice at the finale) and the great, sub-freezing adventures in that story end spectacularly with a heartwarming note of triumph! Those are the things that successful pilots were, and are, made of.

Multipart tales, whose action is spread over two or three episodes, are all right *when they're being broadcast on national television;* there, the producer can control and schedule the ways in which the programs can be seen coast-to-coast. Of a certainty, Part I will be shown first; then, Part II; and, finally, Part III. That is not necessarily the case in syndication. There, individual stations are free to play the programs on hand in any order that pleases them. In general, individual stations prefer *not* to schedule programs in any particular order; they want to be free to mix-and-match programs, for the sake of variety.

In the *Astro Boy* series, each episode was complete unto itself. No story was continued over two or more episodes. Unfortunately for Al Singer and me, that was not the case with *Gigantor*. The adventure in Antarctica, as televised in Japan, was shown as a two-part story. The adventure with "Captain Spider" actually spread over three episodes! The villains "Lurks" and "Professor Envee," with their nefarious plot to build 10,000 fake Gigantors, spread their dirty work over three separate episodes. In all, the Gigantor series of 52 programs in English actually contained 15 such mini-series!

Our solution to the problem posed by the multiparters was to have TCJ in Tokyo *re-shoot* the ending to any episode that did not have its own natural ending. We instructed the studio as to exactly which shots to re-shoot from earlier episodes; then, in New York, we edited those retakes into a sequence that was compatible with the show at hand. In so doing, we were replacing TCJ's "cliff-hanger" (i.e., incomplete) ending with our own new ending. That

Gigantor. Created in 1956 as *Tetsujin 28* (Ironman 28) by Mitsuteru Yokoyama, this giant robot (sometimes 50 feet tall, sometimes 40, at the whim of the artist) was designed by its fictional creators to be the ultimate weapon for use against the Allies in World War II. At war's end, however, the robot was repurposed, its great power used to fight for peace and justice. It was remote-controlled by a bright 12-year-old boy, the son of its slain inventor. Characters, from left to right: Inspector Blooper, Dick Strong, Jimmy Sparks, and Bob Brilliant. ™ and © Entercolor Technologies Corp.

done, we scripted the new ending in such a way that it hinted of more action to come, but still seemed to put an end to the story at hand. That took some doing, but we did it—and now every *Gigantor* program that was originally "to be continued" comes to its own natural end.

Music was another matter entirely. In the *Astro Boy* series, all the music seemed contemporary, timely and catchy. That was not the case with the music from *Tetsujin 28*. As tape recording after tape recording arrived from Tokyo, each roll proved to be more disappointing than the previous one; the music was neither Oriental nor Western, but an amorphous blend of both, sounding like neither. Indeed, our distributor, Trans-Lux, actually *insisted* that we get rid of the original music and replace it with something more to the liking of all.

Al Singer's brother was the late Lou Singer, a well-known composer who had penned "One Meatball!" a popular novelty song of the time. Lou reteamed with lyricist Eugene Raskin (the pair had previously written the theme song for *The Big World of Little Adam*) and we were soon ready to record what has become the enduring-and-endearing *Gigantor* theme song, "Gigantor, The Space-Age Robot!"

My first thought was to record the song at Empire Sound Studios, the same facility we had used to record the theme song for *The Big World of Little Adam*. That was not to be. My old friend Alan Abel (later to become a famous hoaxer) was percussionist in the Radio City Music Hall Orchestra. *His* friend was the band's arranger, Norman Beatty. Norm agreed to write the arrangements for the *Gigantor* theme song and variations (cues), then suggested that we record the music—the band and the singers—right in Radio City Music Hall itself! In so doing, we could get band members to perform for us between shows, without leaving the building.

(Upstairs in the Music Hall, far removed from public areas, is an enormous room in which Arturo Toscanini at one time rehearsed the NBC Symphony Orchestra. Those days had ended long before I was made aware that the room existed. It had been kept dark and unused for a number of years—until, one day, a group of musicians in the orchestra got the idea to use it as a recording studio. They struck a deal with the Hall's management, and opened the room as Plaza Sound Studios. The acoustics and facilities were, as one would expect, superb.)

Three sessions were required to record all the music for *Gigantor*: In ses-

Opposite: **Fred Ladd welcomes opening-day crowd to Japanese American Cultural and Community Center's Postwar Japanese Anime/Manga Exhibit, in Los Angeles' Little Tokyo, April 6, 2003. The author co-curated the event, which ran all summer long, with over 6,000 school children visiting. Photo: Jed Laderman.**

sion one, we laid down the band track for the calypso-like version of the theme song, plus several short variations, plus a number of very short "bridges" used to segue from one sequence to another.

In session two, we attempted to record the singers — performers from the Radio City Music Hall Choir and Glee Club — for the theme song. That, unfortunately, did not work to my satisfaction; the high, soprano voices of the women overrode the tenor and bass voices of the men, and I thought that was the wrong sound for a powerful robot five stories high! We scrapped that session, and came back to the studio soon after for session three, this time armed with baritones and basses. They delivered the deep, rich tones for which the theme song is noted and remembered to this day.

Thoughts from the Twenty-First Century

Astro Boy, Gigantor and, to a lesser extent, *8th Man,* achieved astonishing success upon their release to television in the Western Hemisphere. Osamu Tezuka, creator of *Tetsuan Atom/Astro Boy,* also produced a series known in the West during the 1960s as *The Amazing 3,* and TCJ made a series known here as *Prince Planet.* Neither of the latter two series met with any significant success. Yet, all were made in an Eastern (Japanese) culture radically different from that of the West (no Western culture has produced anything to rival anime) and all Japanese television animation at the time was produced in black and white during an era when no Western studio would shoot animation in anything but color.

As popular as *Astro Boy* was at the time, with 104 episodes playing repeatedly in television markets all across the United States, the popularity of that series did not endure. By the end of the decade of the 1960s, *Astro Boy*'s popularity had been eclipsed by *Gigantor* with only 52 episodes — perhaps largely due to its catchy and memorable theme song.

The lack of any episode describing the origin of Gigantor never seemed to hinder the series' popularity; the concept just seemed to explain itself. Years after the series was in release, I would learn that TCJ was correct in admitting that much animation in its first 26 episodes was of poor quality — some characters appeared to be "on steroids" — but the real surprise came when I discovered that *Tetsujin 28,* our wonderful *Gigantor,* was invented by a pair of scientist-engineers to be the ultimate weapon, a kind of robotic B-29 aircraft, for Japan to use in World War II against the Allied powers, including the United States.

That tidbit of information never made it to the screen in any *Gigantor* program. In the words of one of our young licensees, "*Tetsujin 28* is not *Gigantor.*"

CHAPTER 4

Quixotically Comes Kimba

As surely as the year 1963 saw the arrival in the West of *Tetsuan Atom* (*Astro Boy*) and 1964 saw the arrival of *Tetsujin 28* (our *Gigantor*), 1965 saw the arrival of *Jungulu Taitei Leo* (our *Kimba the White Lion*). *Jungulu Taitei Leo* translates literally as *Jungle Emperor Leo*. In English-speaking territories around the world, we might say *Leo, King of the Jungle*. Osamu Tezuka, the artist who created *Tetsuan Atom* in 1953, lived in Japan, a country ruled by an emperor, not a king, so he would naturally think of a lion as being "Emperor of the Jungle."

Jungulu Taitei Leo began as a graphic novel (manga), started by Tezuka in 1950 (actually predating *Atom)* and running over 500 pages. The artist considered *Leo* his major work; *Tetsuan Atom* initially appeared as a minor character who "took off" from a longer work, much as *The Simpsons* "took off" from a short vignette in *The Tracy Ullman Show*. The concept of *Leo* was that a cub born to Panja, King of the Jungle, and his mate Eriza, was the newest member in a dynasty of intelligent white lions. Both his parents perish early at the hands of Man (in the very first episode of the television series, as a matter of fact) and the cub, our Kimba, is left to fend for himself.

And, as surely as *Astro Boy* is a little reformer, believing that human beings and robots should coexist in harmony, each respecting the other, so Kimba becomes a reformer of jungle society, believing — as his father did — that the ancient, violent law of the jungle should be disavowed; that all animals should live together in peace and harmony, settling their disputes as human beings aspire to settle theirs — by a council of wise and seasoned elders. (Kimba, setting out to reform the law of the jungle, always reminded me of Don Quixote battling windmills)

Tezuka's plan for *Jungulu Taitei Leo*, as detailed in these pages, is the plan that the artist proposed to the Fuji Television Network in Japan. He envisioned developing the storyline through 26 "pieces," as he called them (we would say "episodes"), devoted to the lion cub's boyhood; then, 3 transitional pieces devoted to the "Young Days"; and, finally, 49 pieces devoted to the "Prime Days," during which Leo's two children would enter the narrative. But that plan was not to be.

Television graduated from black and white to color in the year 1965. In the United States, the National Broadcasting Company (NBC) was the first to announce that, henceforth, its daily schedule would be transmitted entirely in color. The Columbia Broadcasting System (CBS) and American Broadcasting Company (ABC) followed close behind. And in Japan, the Fuji Television Network informed Osamu Tezuka that Fuji would indeed accept Mushi Production's plan for *Jungulu Taitei Leo,* but not in black and white — the series would have to be produced *in color.*

For Tezuka, this amounted to a double whammy! The Fuji Network and NBC were *both* insisting on color production of any new series! Certainly the artist had worked with color before, but never on a project of the magnitude of the projected new series. Mushi Production cel painters had each been working (according to veteran Mushi animator Sadao Miyamoto) with 11 bottles of paint, graduated from white to black. Now Tezuka was wondering if, in the future, each painter would need 11 bottles of red, 11 bottles of green, 11 bottles of blue, 11 bottles of orange, 11 bottles of violet ... ad infinitum. The idea was staggering!

And, whereas the Fuji Network seemed amenable to the concept and plan of *Jungulu Taitei Leo,* NBC Enterprises was skeptical — indeed, *leery*—of any concept whose premise was based on the law of the jungle. (Would children see beasts battling each other in bloody combat? Would jungle clearings be strewn with the corpses of dead animals? Would we see vultures feeding on rotting carcasses?)

Kaoru Anami, Mushi studio's 39-year-old head of production, was not concerned with the concept of *Jungulu Taitei Leo;* he worried about the fundamental issue of how to produce the series in color. Anami saw the task as enormous. Thinking that perhaps I could be of help, he asked me for any advice I could give. My answer was that I was certainly no expert in how Hollywood's animation studios handle color, but I knew someone who was: Preston Blair, veteran animator for Disney Studios. Blair had animated the "Dance of the Hours" sequence of Disney Studios' classic film *Fantasia* and was known in animation studios around the world, including Mushi, as the author of the respected handbook *How to Animate Film Cartoons.* My connection to Blair was all Anami had to hear! Within weeks, Anami and a small contingent from Mushi arrived at my office in the building adjacent to Radio City Music Hall for a meeting with the recognized master.

Preston Blair was a tall man, with a head of thick white hair; his bearing was erect, his cheeks glowed healthy red, and his blue eyes seemed always to twinkle. When he strode into my office to meet the contingent from Tokyo, the Japanese rose to their feet, bowed in respect, and softly said "Sensei! Maestro!" They were clearly thrilled to be in his presence.

Blair's advice, after a session of some two hours' duration, seemed to boil down to two basic but overriding principles: (1) *simplify,* and (2) *stylize.* Asked about subtle color variations in objects such as flowers — not an insurmountable problem in a feature film — Blair recommended that, in a television series, all petals of the flower be painted the same color ("You don't have the luxury in a series of painting petals in multiple shades of delicate colors") and, as for how to render shadows, the advice was, "You have to stylize; you can't paint shadows on grass (for example) in blue or darker shades of green, you just have to make all shadows black."

(*Note:* Sadao Miyamoto, then animating *Tetsuan Atom* at Mushi, later claimed that the studio's palette eventually swelled to 360 individual colors!)

Osamu Tezuka accepted the inevitable: He would produce *Jungle Emperor* in color. And, at that point, he did something he did not have to do before — he submitted to NBC Enterprises a complete "plan" of exactly what he intended to do in the new series. (NBC was taking no chances; they were skittish about the overriding theme of violence in the jungle and, if they were going to help finance the new series, they wanted to know exactly what they would be getting!) So, a finely detailed plan of *Jungulu Taitei Leo* was prepared and submitted.

Fortunately, copies of that plan, translated into English for NBC, survive to this day. They show how thoroughly Tezuka had envisioned the upcoming series. Because that document is historic and because it was pivotal, Tezuka's plan, now a museum piece, is reprinted here in its entirety.

But, the Best Laid Plans of Mice and Men...

The same team at NBC that acquired Tezuka's *Astro Boy* series in 1963 liked the idea of acquiring his *Kimba* series in 1965; *but,* in his plan, they found certain provisions that they just could not accept: (a) they could not accept that the star of the show, that cute little lion cub, was scheduled to *die* in the final episode; (b) they could not accept that the cute little cub should die, *at all!*; (c) they could not accept that the cub was slated to grow up, halfway through the series, and have cubs of his own (that would change the little star into a father-figure and audience identification with the cub would be lost); (d) Mushi would need to script each episode so that the episode came to an end — not be continued in a subsequent episode (as would be implied if the cub were permitted to grow up); and, finally, (e) NBC could not accept a series — *any* series — slated to stretch to 78 episodes, 26 more than were economically feasible. (Tezuka was politely reminded that NBC really had wanted only 52 episodes of *Astro Boy*.) Even 52 episodes would be too many if the overriding theme was to be the worrisome *law of the jungle*.

Osamu Tezuka, meanwhile, was busy assuring NBC Enterprises that he was not insensitive to their expressed need to tone down the level of violence. He would show bulls or stags, for example, locking horns and butting each other about, but any implied gore would take place only off-screen; no blood would be shed in plain sight. In addition, he agreed to NBC's insistence that *Leo* remain a cub throughout the entire initial series of 52 episodes — a variation of Tezuka's original proposal to have the little lion mature after the thirtieth episode. One thing more: Tezuka understood that NBC would commit *only* for those initial 52 episodes. They would not commit to any additional programs portraying the white lion maturing into an adult. NBC's rationale was that *Astro Boy* was, in effect, "another *Pinocchio*" and the little white lion was "another *Bambi*."

That rationale was extremely important in NBC's sales strategy. Enterprises, after all, sold its wares to station buyers and program directors throughout their territory. Buyers were usually men constantly being solicited by salespeople eager to sell their programs; buyers are skeptical. So NBC sales personnel, offering children's programs that were perceived as "another *Pinocchio*" or "another *Bambi*," had a tremendous edge.

(Incidentally, the Japanese origin of these programs was neither promoted nor denied; buyers, accustomed to seeing children's programs produced in the United States, simply assumed that all these programs coming from NBC were made in America too.)

Now, with all the pieces in place to NBC's satisfaction, Enterprises gave the word to go ahead. And I wrote the dubbing script for Program #1, which I called *The Birth of Simba*. (That title did not survive.)

First, film cans arriving from Tokyo were labeled with the English words "Go White Lion," an English translation of the Japanese title; that is how Episode 1 still is known today. Second, Jacques Liebenguth, the head of sales after Bill Breen departed NBC, asked where I got the name "Simba." I explained that Simba is an African name for lions (the name is Swahili, I thought), and I did not favor the name Leo. (I am aware that *Leo* and *Leon* derive from the Romance languages' word for *lion,* but am also aware that *Leo* is the name of the familiar MGM Pictures lion.) Besides, I like the word *Simba*. That sounds strong. Virile.

Jacques Liebenguth listened, then shook his head "no" His reasoning was that if *Simba* is a generic word, a word in common usage, then that would give NBC a problem with their merchandising efforts. Merchandisers want a name that is unique to their product, he explained, and if *anybody* can use the name *Simba*, then that's no good. On the other hand, a member of Jacques' family was named Kim, so how about calling the little white lion *Kimba?*

Frankly, I did not want to call the character *Kimba*. I thought that didn't sound masculine enough. Not strong enough. But Liebenguth was insistent, a compromise was made, and the character has been known as Kimba ever since.

Recording of the English dialogue for the pilot began on November 9, 1965. Cliff Owens and Gilbert Mack, stalwarts of the *Astro Boy* and *Gigantor* series, developed voices for the new characters appearing in the *Kimba* series. Billie Lou Watt, the voice of Astro Boy and of young Jimmy Sparks in the *Gigantor* series, had little difficulty in honing yet another voice for the character of young Kimba. Still, progress in recording the new pilot was going slowly; Cliff Owens was settling into using the voice of an old codger for the mandrill character that we called "Dan'l Baboon," and Gilbert Mack was hard pressed to avoid sounding raucous as the voice of the parrot "Pauley Cracker."

By late afternoon, we all knew that we would be going into overtime (i.e., past 5:30 P.M.), but we did not. All the lights in the studio suddenly went out. We were plunged into total darkness!

At first, the three performers in the studio and I thought that the technical crew was playfully telling us that it was time to go home. But, no — this was the beginning of the massive power failure that struck the entire eastern seaboard. Times Square had gone dark, Manhattan had gone dark, all of New York City had gone dark, every state from Florida to the Canadian border had gone dark.

All of us in the National Screen Building at 1600 Broadway groped our way to the street and somehow managed to get home.

Sabotage?

Next day, in section after section of the city, the lights came back on. That afternoon, our unit of performers and crew returned to the studio where we had been interrupted the day before, we finished recording the remainder of the dialogue on November 10, and the pilot film — episode 1 of *Kimba the White Lion* — was completed.

An Outline for Jungle Emperor
[our *Kimba the White Lion*]
As Submitted to NBC Enterprises by Mushi Production in 1965.

Original Work

This proposed television series is based upon a long-running manga, by *Osamu Tezuka*, which ran in serialized form in the Japanese magazine "*Manga*

Kimba the White Lion. Osama Tezuka's first anime series in color, *Jungulu Taitei Leo,* 1965. Initially broadcast on Japan's Fuji Television Network, then distributed in the West by NBC Enterprises, which committed for the series only after securing Tezuka's assurance that no law-of-the-jungle violence would be portrayed onscreen. Kimba, at his caged mother's urging, leaps to safety from a doomed transport ship.

Shonen," published by the *Gakudosha* Company. The manga, begun in 1951, ran continuously for approximately seven years.

Premise of Television Animated Series

a) The television picturization should be handled with modern sensibilities so as to appeal to today's children and adults.

b) To confine the story to a life history of Leo [Kimba]. Not to dance around the event, but always stand in the whirlpool of the event, be influenced mentally and develop its character.

c) Make the most of those elements and develop them. The elements are: the theme of original work; the impression of a grand epic; action and thrill of adventure; the humor and pleasure of a cartoon; vitality to do what is right and achieve the Ideal; and also a pure love for all creatures.

d) all pictures should be in color; 4 quarters (78 episodes) of 30-minute programs.

The detailed contents are:

[Kimba's] Boyhood: 26 episodes

His Young Days: 3 episodes

His Prime Days: 49 episodes (During these Prime Days, Leo's [Kimba's] children enter into the story; they are [to be] named Rune and Rukio.)

Theme

From the standpoint of admiring life and loving all creatures, living things are divided into an animal group and a human group. Though there are historical conflicts between those two groups, the ideal community is sought where all will be happy. This series will describe efforts made to achieve the ideal community and hopes for its future.

Whole Story

The age is the modern time. The chief stage is Africa; in particular, Uganda, Leopoldville, Congo, Central Africa adjoining Sudan. The "Mt. Moon" mentioned later is an imaginary mountain, not the real Luvenzori mountain range. The hero is a white-haired lion named Leo.

[Kimba's] ancestor, Androcles, drank a brain-empowering elixir provided by a scholar named Kupton in the days when Egypt flourished. By drinking the elixir, Androcles acquired great wisdom. He helped the pharaoh make the country prosperous, and the people happy. Later, chance turned

Kimba the White Lion. Kimba, under guardianship of his father, proud King of the Jungle, descendant of a line of intelligent white lions.

Androcles into a "guardian deity of a native" — after which, Egypt went into a period of decline.

Civilization shifted to the far reaches of Europe, Asia, and America; Africa entered a long dark age, wherein it became known as "The Dark Continent." In recent years, however, the light of civilization has begun to shine on the Dark Continent, and a new Africa began to emerge, making for an epoch in 1960 which was called the African Year, the Year of Africa.

Turning our eyes from the world of human prosperity, we see that the animal world is still controlled by the human race; animals are still serving mankind. For instance, human beings take the lives of animals in a "sport called hunting." They wear animals' hides and eat their meat.

Leo's father, Panja [our Caesar] was a descendant of Androcles. He had white hair, was brave, wise, and strong. To resist man's hunting as a sport, and his preying upon animals for meat, Panja did everything he could to raise man's conscience. He challenged not only the human race, but [also] all creatures who disturbed the happiness of the jungle.

Carnivores preying upon herbivores — the law of the jungle was loathsome to Panja. To keep weak animals from being preyed upon, the tenderhearted Panja stole cattle from the corrals of natives who lived nearby, and gave those cattle to the carnivores of the jungle. All this was to little effect; Panja's intended goodness merely heightened the confrontation between Panja and mankind. In the end, mankind was the winner: Panja, relying upon his bravery and strength, was no match for man's wisdom and weapons. Panja was killed. Eriza, his wife, was then caught by the men who killed her husband, placed aboard a ship, and sent sailing away to a zoo. Aboard ship, Eriza gave birth to a son — Leo. But soon thereafter, the ship sprang a leak. Eriza, knowing that the ship was sinking, let her child leave. She told him to be brave; to inherit his father's willpower; to return to Africa and fight for the sake of Peace and Happiness of the jungle.

Leo arrives at Africa, swimming through the raging waves of the Atlantic Ocean; but, in reality, it was Portugal, where Leo was picked up by Ken-ichi [our Roger Ranger], an 18-year-old boy, and his uncle. While being raised by them, Leo deepens his true understanding about humans, and human society and power.

Leo finds that it is wrong to indiscriminately regard humans with hostility; that the goal of human society is to harmonize individual happiness with that of the whole; and that man, in developing science and knowledge, is happy. In other words, man is happy by civilization.

By chance, Leo returns to the home of his parents, the jungle. There he finds a world of uncivilized savagery and egotism. He establishes a theory that a happy life for animals should be based on civilization. Then, burning with the ideal of his theory, Leo starts leading the other animals. But that is a very difficult thing to do.

Some animals persist in the old law of the jungle; some agree to follow Panja's way, while others are indifferent. In addition, there are backward animals, incapable of understanding new ways. There are natural disasters. Evil people come along. The age-old way in the jungle of carnivores eating herbivores cannot be changed. There is a mental blind side to wish for negligence. There is a hesitation, too, about ways of leadership.

The whole television series of "Jungle Emperor" [*Kimba*] will progress by taking these conflicts and making them basic elements of the developing story. In time, Leo falls in love, and marries. He begets two children; that further increases his life experiences, improving his character. Under a scorching sun, Leo carries out his ideal — his plan — step by step, thereby displaying the unique and strong vitality of the African-born. In this way, the civilization level of animals gets higher and higher.

Some sensible men changed their view of animals, and gave Leo a helping hand. But that is still far from human civilization. Furthermore, there were obstacles to prosperity in human civilization: one was the elusive remedy for *purpura* [*sic*] which was spreading among the animals; the other, exploration of Mt. Moon.

A group of scientists one day try to explore Mt. Moon looking for the Moonlight Stone, which is composed of super energy and which once caused continental slides. Mt. Moon has a bad air current; prehistoric animals, such as dinosaurs and wooly mammoths, live there, making scientific expeditions impossible. But, inasmuch as Leo was familiar with *Ofukurosan*, a mammoth living on Mt. Moon, he cooperated with the expedition, made contact with *Ofukurosan*, and led the scientists to discover a great vein of moonlight stone — this, in return for the expedition's rewarding him with a cure for *purpura*.

Through this event, Leo came to realize the importance of cooperation between animals and humans. He learned that, by cooperating with each other, humans and animals complement each other; each group makes up for the other's deficiencies, so that both will be happy and more civilized.

Suddenly a snowstorm swoops down upon Mt. Moon, 5000 meters above sea level. The party carrying the expedition records starts descending the mountain. But on the way, one person falls down ... and then, another. Finally, the last man is going to break down. Leo kills himself and gives his own body to save the last man in the expedition from hunger. In this way, Leo does not die, but lives on in [ideal].

The expedition records reached the world of humans. After the death of Leo, his son [Rune] inherits his father's ideal, which he will develop more.

It is expected that the cooperation between animals and humans will increase, and the world will prosper more and more.

Division of Story

In view of the television features and producing conditions, which we should not force the television viewers to see repeatedly, this story cannot be made in such a way that the hero grows up gradually.

Therefore, we first divide the story formally into three steps, *viz* boyhood, young days, and prime days. In the prime days, we [introduce Rune], Leo's son, who is a character equal to the boyhood Leo.

The rate of these three ages, three steps, in quantity, is as follows:

Boyhood: 26 pieces [episodes]
Young days: 3 pieces
Prime days: 49 pieces

Because of the nature of the story, telecasting order of some pieces will necessarily be fixed.

At the beginning of boyhood, Pang's death and Leo's birth are placed, and we place Lie — as Leo's friend — in the early time. [Note: Pang elsewhere is also referred to as Panja.]

The marriage comes in the young days. He begets two children in prime days. The last is Leo's death and a suggestion of his future.

The first quarter describes the establishment of Leo as leader, the second quarter depicts the dynamic fight to realize the ideal, and the third quarter delineates a developing energy for the future....

Characters

A) LEO

Lion, male, almost white hair over the whole body in the first and second quarters; he corresponds to about a third grade boy in primary school. In the 3rd and 4th quarter, he grows up from youth to prime days. Establishes animal civilization in the jungle in order to build a happy animal life like human beings, inheriting the will of the late Pang, his father. Though cute in appearance, he has a strong will inherited from his father, brains, strength, and speech, as well as vitality. His way of thinking is reasonable and scientific, while at the same time he is tender and amiable and also has a sense of humor. A young noble, full of a sense of justice and courage.

B) LEI

Lion, female, nearly as old as Leo. In the 1st and 2nd quarter, she lives in a jungle not far from Leo's, but in the 3rd and 4th quarter, she becomes Leo's wife. Her parents were killed by hunters, so she stays with a lion uncle.

Her family line is also distinguished in her part of the jungle. She gets on well with Leo because neither has parents; they are orphans.

C) PANG

Lion, male. Leo's father. About 30 years old (by human standards). Devoted his life to the animal world, and was killed, dashing against hunters with all his might. Has a combination of sturdy vitality and prompt action with strength and tenderness. Wise and elegantly noble.

D) TOMMY

[Our Bucky] is a Thomson gazelle. Male. Leo's friend. About 20 years old. A fall guy and optimist. Capable of running very swiftly.

E) KOKO

A parrot (our Pauley Cracker). Male. Leo's friend. About 30 years old. Though once kept by humans, later settled in the jungle at Pang's instruction.

Short-tempered, fast, and big in motion, misjudges in making hasty conclusions. In reality, he is good natured.

F) MANDY MANDRILL

Male. [Our Dan'l Baboon] A substitute for Leo's parents, he is sympathetic to Leo. Well advanced in years — a senior in the jungle, and adviser to young Leo. Familiar with things in the jungle, Mandy knows the difficulties facing Leo in the young lion's dream of reforming the jungle. The old-timer has a warm heart, is loved and respected by all animals. Shows strength in emergencies.

G) BUBU

Lion. ["Claw," in our version.] Male. About 35 years old. Yellow hair, black mane. A villain's part. Filled with controlling desire, always aiming at the boss-seat in the jungle, stops at nothing for the purpose. Orthodox violent lion having mighty strength and pride. Hated by animals. Feeling inferiority complex against Panja's family, a feeling of which he is not aware.

H) TOT

Black leopard, male. About 27 or 28 years old. Clever and evil character considering himself to be a counselor of Bubu. Cunning and cold-blooded. A stranger, originally from another place.

I) DICK AND BOW

Both are spotted hyenas. Followers of Bubu, they are so-called punks. There are, in addition, many hyenas that act as Bubu's followers.

J) KEN-ICHI

Human, male. A Japanese, 18 years of age. Chance makes him become a counselor of Leo's. Humanist, kind & tender, and also sympathetic to animals. Has a strong sense of justice, and likes adventure.

K) MARY

Human, female, 18 years old, Japanese, Classmate of Ken-ichi [our "Roger Ranger"]. Fond of curious experiences, she is on the way to Africa, and is a little beside herself because of some shock. She loved Ken-ichi at first sight, married him, and basks in Ken-ichi's pure love. She regards animals as man's natural servants.

L) MR. BEARDED

Human, male. Ken-ichi's uncle. About 40 years old. Native Tokyoite, having a clean personality, but rugged in feelings. Young-bald. [*Note: The same character appeared in Astro Boy as Mr. Pompous.*]

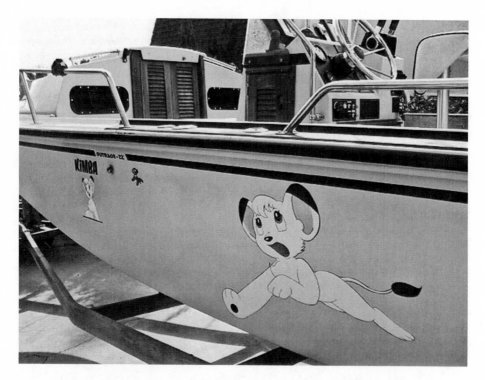

Ahoy Kimba! Boston Whaler named and decorated in honor of the little white
lion by super fan Stephen Daratsos. Craft is moored in Marina del Rey, California. Photo by Stephen Daratsos.

M) HAMEGG

Human, male. Englishman. World-famous hunter, but cunning. [*Note:*
The name Hamegg was a favorite of Tezuka's, it amused him and he used it
here as a joke; the same character — with the same name! — appeared in the
very first episode of *Astro Boy* (*Tetsuan Atom*) as a circus master. Picking up
on Tezuka's humor in *Astro Boy*, I named the character Cacciatori and gave
him an Italian dialect; here, in *Kimba*, I named him Viper Snakely and, as a
concession to Tezuka, Viper does sound vaguely British.]

N) CHEETAH

Male, 20-year-old cheetah. Fastest runner in the jungle. A rash fellow,
he is on Leo's side.

O) BACCHUS

Hippo, male, about 40. Boss of the hippo group. A peace lover who,
though strong, doesn't like fighting. Humorous and dexterous, despite his
figure. Cooperates with Leo.

P) SAMSON

Buffalo, male, about 35. So-called Japanese Samurai (ancient soldier). Loves solitude. Admirer of Panja's way of living, also accepts Leo's way, and helps Leo in emergencies. But he does not change his own Panja-like conservative character.

Q) OFUKUROSAN

Prehistoric woolly mammoth. Female. Age unknown. Influential animal on Mt. Moon. Friendly toward Leo.

R) PAGOOLA

African elephant, male. Boss of the elephants, a conservative group in the jungle. Opposed to Leo but, because of his migratory ways, meddles little. Samurai-like character.

S) RHINOCEROS-BOSS

Black rhinoceros, male. Simple-minded Boss of the rhinoceroses, abhors humans. Fights ferociously against anyone who has a human name or imitates human behavior. He is, therefore, Leo's enemy.

T) GABUGA

Crocodile, male. Weak-minded, but has strong feelings. Has enormous appetite. Evil, wicked fellow. Leo's enemy.

U) ERIZA

Lion. Female. Panja's wife, Leo's mother. About 25 years old, she is a good, understanding wife. Beautiful, strong-willed.

V) OTHERS

Numerous children and female characters.

[Note: The points above represent the key elements of Tezuka's "Plan" for *Jungle Emperor*.]

Footnote to History: Kimba versus Simba — The Uproar

Fast forward nearly thirty years, to 1994. The phone in my Los Angeles office rang with a call from the *San Francisco Chronicle*. The caller was a reporter named Charles Burress. He wondered what I could tell him about the massive protest being waged by a group of agitated anime fans outside a theater in town, where the Disney-animated feature film *The Lion King* had just opened. The fans were in an uproar, according to Burress, charging that *The Lion King* was little more than an uncredited "steal" of Osamu Tezuka's

Kimba the White Lion series seen on television thirty years earlier! I could hardly believe my ears. "I've heard nothing," I assured Mr. Burress, "I'm a long-time Disney fan; the Disney organization has a reputation for being squeaky-clean, untarnished. Tell you what, my wife and I are going to see *The Lion King* at the [Television] Academy Saturday night; let me see the picture, then we can talk Monday, and I'll have a better idea of what this is all about."

At the screening, I did notice, near the beginning of the film, the arrival on screen of a character that bore a strong resemblance to our "Dan'l Baboon," and he played the same dramatic role as Dan'l played in *Kimba*. That did not bother me, though; I thought "look, a monkey is a monkey, the jungles are full of them, no one has a monopoly on monkeys," and I dismissed the similarity as a nonissue.

A few minutes later, a talking bird arrived, a bird that may not have been a parrot, but played the same dramatic role as that of our parrot, Pauley Cracker, in *Kimba*. This, too, I dismissed as inconsequential and nothing to get excited about.

The third similarity, however, was one I could not simply dismiss. Hyenas appeared — like the pair in *Kimba* — sneaky, slinky, sinister; they were henchmen of the lion king's evil brother, Scar (Claw was the name for the evil lion in *Kimba)* and their vile, smarmy ways seemed to have been lifted directly from nearly identical scenes in *Kimba*. At this, I began to feel uncomfortable; the sameness of characters and situations between *The White Lion* and *The Lion King* was becoming unsettling.

But the coup de grâce, the "cincher," as I saw it, came for me when Disney's Simba, now grown, climbs onto a rocky promontory, silhouetted against the sky, and stands triumphant — a scene strikingly similar to one in *Kimba*. At that, I turned and whispered to my wife, "Now, don't tell me we're going to pan up to the sky, and see the dead father lion in the clouds." No sooner had I said that than we saw a pan up to the sky, and saw the image of the dead father lion in the clouds. I actually had to stifle a gasp: "I can't believe this!"

The following Monday morning, I called Charles Burress in San Francisco and told him in detail what my reactions had been. I told him that the image of the lion in the clouds was such a distinctive one, such a signature mark of the Japanese artist Osama Tezuka, that a viewer would be hard-pressed to believe that the concept in *Lion King* was not inspired by Tezuka's *Kimba*. Charles Burress' report appeared in the *Chronicle* soon after. Within days, the story was being reported in the *Los Angeles Times,* the *New York Times,* and other American newspapers from coast to coast. In London, Reuters picked up the story and distributed it abroad.

A spokesman for Disney Studios promptly defended their film by claiming that the story of *The Lion King* was not inspired by *Kimba* (indeed, the spokesman said, Disney animators had never seen the *Kimba* series on television); *The Lion King,* according to the spokesman, was inspired by Shakespeare's play *Hamlet,* in which a king's evil brother kills the king, in order that he — the evil brother — may accede to the throne.

Incredibly, with the series *Kimba the White Lion,* being restored and released anew in DVD box sets in 2005, and with live, stage presentations of *The Lion King* playing in theaters in the United States and abroad, the controversy of *Kimba* versus *The Lion King* persists to this day.

Mushi Production never initiated any action against the Disney studio. Tezuka Production's stated position was that Osamu Tezuka was a great fan of Walt Disney; Tezuka would have been honored to see that the great Disney studio was being influenced by the work of Osamu Tezuka.

Post script: Whether or not the Disney people knew of *Kimba* before production started on *The Lion King,* it taxes credulity to think that they knew nothing about it during production. Ex-Disney animator Phil Young, later a professor at the Savannah College of Art and Design, recalls that fellow Disney animator Shawn Keller, who was a huge *Kimba* fan (Keller had once emblazoned his car with *Kimba* stickers), complained rather loudly about what Disney was doing while the movie was in production.

By the end of 2005, *The Lion King* property had earned close to $500 million.

CHAPTER 5

Mighty Mushi:
The Decline and Fall

So now Osamu Tezuka's mighty Mushi Production was a juggernaut, cranking out easily a half-hour program each week — a remarkable achievement, equaled only by Hollywood's huge Hanna-Barbera Studio — and growing larger by the day. Mushi was the model for other studios in Tokyo to emulate; *Tetsuan Atom/Astro Boy,* its premiere series, was racing toward its target 193 episodes, *Jungulu Taitei Leo/Kimba* was on track to reach 52 episodes, or more, in which the young white lion would reach adulthood and sire his own little white cub(s).

Tezuka thought his studio was fiscally secure. And why wouldn't he? For many years before launching Mushi Production to produce animation, the artist had become famous for his manga, having introduced *Astro Boy* as *Mighty Atom* in comic books in 1952, and *Kimba* even earlier (1950) as *Jungulu Taitei Leo.* Publishers of comics were accepting everything that Tezuka drew, Fuji Television was broadcasting nationally every animated series that Mushi produced (paying only for broadcast rights in Japan), and NBC Enterprises was distributing Mushi-made series — that had already cleared the Fuji Television Network — in the rest of the world. From Tezuka's point of view, the plan seemed perfect; he had every reason to believe it would go on forever.

Tezuka was mistaken. He would soon learn that, contrary to what he knew of distribution of his works in Japan, NBC Enterprises would not accept every series Mushi proposed — they would "cherry-pick" from among its submissions, and accept only those series judged by them to be shoo-ins — surefire winners — properties that NBC salespeople in the field could show and sell with ease.

With *Astro Boy* and *Kimba* successfully launched, Mushi Production sent Enterprises pilot films of a new story called *Goku's Great Adventure.* This was a 39-episode series based upon a famous Chinese legend called *The Monkey*

King. I was asked to sit with Jim Dodd, Jacques Liebenguth, Bill Schmidt, and Morris Rittenberg at a screening. Anticipation was high — would this be another *Kimba?* We watched perhaps 10 or 15 minutes, then began to squirm uncomfortably and look at each other. The characters, which we expected to be cute and funny, were neither. The lead character, Goku, a boyish-looking monkey, appeared to be tough. He used foul language in Japanese. We could change that in the dubbing process, of course, but the angry look on his face would nonetheless dictate that we have Goku speak in rough and abusive terms. (Goku was obviously *not* a "nice guy"!) In Japan, the PTA was complaining about the foul language coming from Goku's mouth — remarkable criticism, given Japan's leniency toward children's programs. Another cast member is "the Buddha" — yes, the Buddha who is revered by millions of worshippers all around the world.

All of us in that NBC screening room concluded early that *Goku (The Monkey King)* was *not* another Kimba; nor was the storyline of *The Monkey King* another grand jungle adventure. Less than twenty minutes into the screening, our feelings were unanimous: thumbs down on *Goku.*

This was a major blow for Tezuka. Mushi's contract with the Fuji Network required the studio to produce an entire series for broadcast in Japan (independent of any action by Enterprises). But production of this new series in color, and animated to NBC's higher standards, meant that Mushi would have to produce *Monkey King* at a substantial loss. Unfunded cost overruns would deal the studio a crippling blow.

In the United States, an animation studio such as Filmation or DePattie-Freleng might have taken one of its series rejects to another broadcaster or distributor. But not Tezuka, not Mushi. Tezuka would not want to risk antagonizing NBC Enterprises by going "across the street to another shop." Mushi went ahead without guaranteed American dollars and, in the process, suffered a major loss.

Nor would that be the last blow to the studio. Osamu Tezuka had, in 1953, created a successful comic strip that he called *Ribon no Kishi (Princess Knight).* That, too, became a 52-episode color series from Mushi Production and it was also submitted to NBC Enterprises. This time I sat in the screening room only with Jim Dodd — Bill Schmidt, Jacques Liebenguth, and Morris Rittenberg did not join us. Surprised, I asked why not? Jim Dodd explained that the others had read advance paperwork submitted by Mushi and understood that the "Princess" of the title regularly masqueraded as a Prince! The Princess, named Sapphire, was the daughter of a king and queen who desperately wanted a male heir, because only a male heir, a prince, could accede to the throne of that ancient kingdom.

So the king and queen decided to raise Sapphire secretly as a boy. Her

NBC rejected the Mushi Production series *Ribon no kishi,* aka *Princess Knight* because Sapphire, a princess, was sometimes required to masquerade as a prince (seen here in princely garb with tiny sidekick Tink, and brandishing a sword). NBC feared that the theme of the series would be perceived as "sex switch." Courtesy of Tezuka Productions. © Tezuka Productions.

hair was clipped short. She dressed much like a boy, rode horseback like a boy, dueled like a boy — even vanquished villains of the court like a boy! No one in the court suspected that the young Crown "Prince" was in fact a girl — a *Princess* Knight.

But, in private, Sapphire yearned to wear dresses and have a boyfriend. That is when the men of NBC raised their eyebrows and moaned a low "*oh, oh!*" Even though Sapphire was born a girl, wanted only to be a girl and behave like a girl, the executives of Enterprises looked at each other and said, "Sex switch." That was enough to scare them away.

The only one in the room who said, "It's great, let's go with it," was this writer, yours truly. I found Sapphire to be spunky, blithe, rebellious; and the concept, perfect for the humor of mistaken identity. I saw no problem with the idea of a girl posing as a boy. I thought the stories, as executed by Tezuka and the writers of Mushi, were fun.

Tezuka had even written-in a tiny green-suited, yellow-haired sprite named Tink (after "Tinkerbell" in Walt Disney's feature *Peter Pan?*) to act as Sapphire's sidekick. None of this swayed the NBC sales team. Their fear was that the station buyers who would either buy, or reject, this series would reject it, on their perception that this series was all about "sex switch."

NBC Enterprises turned the series down. This series did not languish, however. It was acquired by an animator named Joe Oriolo, who had enjoyed considerable success in producing a new television series starring *Felix the Cat.* Oriolo, aware that Tezuka's comic strip had become a sensation among girls in Japan, changed the name of the Mushi's series from *Ribon no Kishi* to *Choppy and the Princess,* dubbed it into English, and licensed it to independent television stations throughout the United States.

Short shrift was made of yet another new series from Mushi. In it, the hero wore triangular sunglasses that gave him the appearance of a frowning, sinister antihero. Bill Schmidt took one look at the character design printed on a glassy presentation folder and remarked, "How can anyone cheer for a guy who looks as crooked as *that?!*" The project went no further.

Word began to spread in Tokyo that Mushi Production was "in trouble." Perhaps emboldened by word of Mushi's imminent demise, rival studios began knocking on NBC's door. Jim Dodd called to ask if I could attend yet another screening that week; a new studio, represented by a writer named Kohan, wanted to screen their pilot film of a new series called *Moon Masked Rider.*

When I arrived for that screening, I was frankly a bit surprised; Jim Dodd asked if I'd like a have an office in a room virtually adjacent to his. He was serious. I was pleased, not only because Dodd was acknowledging that I was spending considerable *time* in the Enterprises' suite, but because I seemed to have quietly become a de facto consulting member of the NBC team. I neither accepted nor declined the offer. Our guests arrived.

Kohan-San was the senior member of the studio delegation. He was conservatively dressed in black, as were two younger members of the studio staff. The producer of the series, however, was a man whom I judged to be in his forties, expensively dressed in very dark silk, set off by a white necktie slashed with brilliant splashes of red, blue and black. (I think I will never forget that necktie.)

Moon Masked Rider, it turned out, featured a man who was an ordinary worker during the day. By night, however, he donned a pure white, skin-tight costume, topped by a white mask; he hopped onto a souped-up motorcycle, pursued criminals at breakneck speed through the narrow streets of Tokyo, cracking a whip like a renegade member of Tokyo's Hells Angels on the loose. The violence level was maximum. This was no series for NBC.

Meanwhile, Mushi Studio, now struggling to survive under the staggering burden of needing to produce far too much with far too little, finally succumbed and went into bankruptcy in 1968. In fact, the studio was already moribund when my longtime partner, Al Singer, died of a coronary attack in 1967. Once again, I would be on my own.

ACT Now

Violence in children's television programming throughout the latter half of the 1960s was becoming an increasingly thorny issue for broadcasters. In Newton, Massachusetts, activist Peggy Charren led a highly vocal group known as Action for Children's Television (ACT), which portrayed itself as an association of parents, teachers, and other concerned individuals who pressured television stations, networks, and indeed the U.S. government itself to bear down on those broadcasters and advertisers who promoted violent kids' shows. ACT's position was that television had a *responsibility* to help *educate* children — not incite them to violence — and, if television stations and networks and distributors of children's programs (like NBC Enterprises) did not comply, then the violators should lose their licenses and/or charters.

Incredulously, at the same time in which American broadcasters were being pressured to eliminate violence from their children's programming, Japanese animation studios were *increasing* the levels of violence in their new shows! *Moon Masked Rider* was evidence of that.

NBC Enterprises would go on to produce Spanish-language versions in Mexico of *Astro Boy* and *Kimba* (based upon the English, rather than Japanese, versions), but never again had the occasion to screen a Japanese studio's new animated fare. Clearly, a corner had been turned — the climate for such programs had changed.

"Where Do We Go from Here?"

Shortly before he died, my partner Al Singer and I looked at each other and shrugged our shoulders. Film divisions of major broadcasting companies — NBC, ABC, CBS — were turning their backs on Japanese-made animated programs, declaring them "too violent!" Certainly there was a *need* for low-cost children's television programs among the nation's independent (i.e., non-network affiliated) stations, but the pressure against violent content was on. Japan seemed to have dealt itself out of the game, yet *only* Japan was cranking out series after series after series. No other nation on earth was as prolific a producer of children's programs. True, the *cost* of animation was rising in Japan, as in the West, but with Japanese networks picking up a substantial portion of the production costs, Western buyers could buy rights for territories outside Japan at relatively bargain prices.

As Mushi Production was declining in its fading days, a rival studio was actually gaining strength. That company was Tatsunoko Production, located in the outskirts of Tokyo. Accomplished Mushi animator Sadao Miyamoto, perhaps seeing the writing on the wall, resigned from the studio where he had been animating *Astro Boy* and joined the ranks of Tatsunoko. There, he helped to animate the adventures of a little boy character who bore more than a passing resemblance to *Astro Boy*; the youngster, who came to Earth from outer space, was called *Space Ace*.

Almost needless to say, the series was represented by none other than K. Fujita, the agent who sold Al Singer and me the series we called *Gigantor*. The comparison of *Ace* to *Astro Boy* was unavoidable; *Ace*, like *Astro Boy*, was an empowered youngster surrounded by human characters so similar to those in *Astro Boy* that they could have been related to each other! Situations in both programs were on the gentle side, there was a sweetness to both the concept and the characters, and violence was nowhere in sight.

Al Singer and I took a fresh look at some sample reels, and thought, "Maybe we can do something with *Space Ace,* after all!"

Larry White, then the head of children's programming at the NBC Network, had earlier seen some of the *Space Ace* material in our office and thought it looked "pretty good." He liked the idea that *Ace's* only weapons were glowing *rings* that acted much like boomerangs. He was also well aware that *Astro Boy* was a huge success on the local level, and thought this Tatsunoko series, being so similar to *Astro Boy*, could do well on the national level.

Problem: *Space Ace,* like the original *Tetsuan Atom/Astro Boy* series before it, had been animated in black and white, prior to the advent of color broadcasting in Japan. That would seem to exclude it from consideration right then and there. But, being long steeped in the animation process, I asked K. Fujita if perhaps Tatsunoko could get out the animation cels and *re-do* them in color. To my astonishment, Fujita thought that was a plausible idea!

Barely a few months later, Fujita returned with a *Space Ace* episode *re-rendered in color!* I was excited and happy — till I saw the episode title: *Ant Kingdom.* "Oh, oh," I thought, "that doesn't sound like an epic space adventure." It wasn't. *Ace* and company descended deep into the bowels of the earth, and did indeed encounter ants — ants that spoke, ants that had personalities, even ants that fought other ants in a kind of ant warfare.

My partner and I were, not surprisingly, lukewarm to the picture. If only Tatsunoko had delivered a picture about adventure in outer space — a picture that gave Ace a chance to show his stuff Big Time! What a pity the studio picked such a trifle!

Still, we needed *something,* this Tatsunoko series fit within ACT's guidelines, it was completed (so, no risk of Tatsunoko's default), the asking price was reasonable, K. Fujita could have the pictures reshot in color, and Larry White did express an interest in the series.

We changed *Ace's* name to *Ring-O* (based upon those incredible glowing rings he tossed in times of trouble), went back into the dubbing studio with our favorite voice actors, recorded new music for this series — as we had done with our *Gigantor* series — and, soon thereafter, delivered our pilot film, now retitled *Forbidden Island,* to White's office. With the film, we included a list of 12 or 13 additional subjects — all with great space-based adventures and sizzling-hot titles — subjects we would order in color from the studio as soon as Larry White committed to the series.

For several days thereafter, we held our breath. Finally, the day of decision arrived. White announced his "picks" for the new season! *Ring-O* was not one of those "picks." Instead of committing to *Ring-O,* White bought a Saturday morning show called *Cool McCool.* That series suffered from poor ratings at the onset, continued to do poorly in the ratings for the remainder of its run, and had a short life on the NBC Network.

Al Singer had been on friendly terms with Larry White for several years before this incident. After White turned down *Ringo-O,* Singer spoke with White only when there was no way of avoiding it, and he kept avoiding it till the day he, Singer, died in 1967.

CHAPTER 6

More from Mushi

In a way, Osamu Tezuka "lucked out" with *Tetsuan Atom*. To summarize: the artist, while still a young man who had chosen to draw rather than practice medicine, had been approached by two publishers of quality manga: *Manga Shonen* and *Shonen* (Boys) magazine, in whose pages he began the serialization in 1952 of *Atomu Taishi* (*Ambassador Atom*, later changed to *Tetsuan Atom*, or *Mighty Atom*). The little robot had actually been introduced early as a minor character, but — to Tezuka's surprise — the robot "clicked" and caught the public's fancy. A manga star was born! Ten years later, the Fuji Television Network would come to Tezuka, explain that Fuji wanted to star the robot in a new series of children's programs, and would give the artist money to help start an animation studio. Tezuka was overwhelmed; he had never contemplated any such thing.

He had started drawing while still in school, working toward his doctor's degree. When tapped by the Fuji Network, he hired other artists and production people, ensconcing them in housing no more than a stone's throw from his home in Nerima-ku (Tokyo). Finally, when the demands of production grew so great that the "cottages" in his cottage industry began bursting at the seams, Tezuka erected a building next to his home, and that became the offices of Mushi Production.

Big Time came for Tezuka and Mushi Production when NBC Enterprises optioned, then acquired, *Tetsuan Atom*, turned it into *Astro Boy*, and released it to the entire world outside Japan.

Yet, in fact, Tezuka's dream project, his great vision, was not *Tetsuan Atom* at all — it was *Jungulu Taitei Leo*, the series that, with NBC's backing, became *Kimba the White Lion* and, like *Astro Boy* before it, became a huge international hit.

If only all the studio's output had been so successful! But that was not the case.

Wonders 3 (W3)

This 1965 series of 52 black-and-white episodes was the first original television series produced by Mushi; the entire animation staff participated in developing the characters and story. Customarily, Tezuka's works appeared first as manga, then were adapted later into serialized form for television; *Wonders 3 (W3)* was just the opposite — it appeared first as a television series, then was adapted afterward as manga.

The premise of *W3* is that three aliens from outer space, dispatched by a galactic authority, come to Earth and assume the forms of a rabbit (called Bokko), a horse (Nokko), and a duck (Pukko). Their mission is to decide whether Earth is worth saving, or, on the contrary, deserving of total destruction as a warmongering danger to the galaxy! The attention of the threesome becomes focused on a boy named Shinichi, and on his older brother Hoshi, who, as it turns out, is a secret agent in an international crime-fighting organization.

Before long, the boy Shinichi discovers that the three animals are, in reality, aliens from outer space. He persuades them not to destroy planet Earth, but to help improve it.

W3, the television series, being available only in black and white, was of no interest to NBC. However, Joe Oriolo, the same animator-producer who had acquired Tezuka's *Princess Knight,* licensed this series, too, renamed it *The Amazing 3* and distributed it with modest results to independent television stations.

It is interesting to note that *Wonders 3* is the first anime series in which the Disney style of production was used. Osamu Tezuka, an admirer of Disney, appointed a specific animation illustrator for each specific character.

Vampire

Disney's skill in combining live-action with animation was greatly admired by Osamu Tezuka. One of Disney's earliest works was the black-and-white *Alice* comedies, wherein a live little girl, Alice, threaded her way through sketched or animated "sets." That skill in combining live images with animated ones was demonstrated masterfully — and in color — in Disney's feature-length film *Song of the South,* wherein animated birds fly adroitly around a live actor. Tezuka, in his 26-episode *Vampire* series, decided that he, too, would try his hand at combining live action with animation — though the technology required for that procedure was not readily available in Japan in 1966. (The series was evidently produced 1966–67, and aired in 1968.)

This series is impressive, too, for its social themes. We find a minority tribe of vampires (live actors), whose members have the capability to transform into wolves; so it becomes a battle of wolves versus human beings who try to oppress them.

The oppressors, too, are live actors; but the wolves (werewolves, not unlike wolves seen in Toei's feature *Little Norse Prince*), into which the vampires transform, are animated.

As in *Dororo,* a Mushi series then in the planning stage, the main character is a boy, Toppie. But the character that drew the greatest interest at the time *Vampire* was being televised was none other than Osamu Tezuka in person, playing himself!

The Japanese public, knowing of Tezuka's interest in medicine, accepted the notion in the television series that the artist was investigating a new drug — a substance called "Mad PA" developed by a "Professor Atami." Vampires were known to be seeking that drug. In one scene, Tezuka appears on television to warn the public that the Vampires are meeting in secret to plot a revolution: they are planning to take over the world. They succeed in capturing Tezuka, but, being the decent vampires that they are, they release him. As Tezuka is driving back to his home, his car plunges into a canyon! Fortunately, the artist is rescued. He returns to his home and studio, and lives to create more wonderful anime.

Clearly, Tezuka was having fun with this show. No real attempt was made to present this black-and-white series to NBC; nor, so far as is known, did any other producer or distributor come forward to adapt and distribute it.

Dororo

This short series (just 26 episodes) is virtually unknown in the Americas. Probably for budgetary reasons, it was shot in black and white as late as 1969. Like other Tezuka-created series, this one stars a little boy — the boy's name is Dororo and the setting is Japan in the 1470s, the middle of the Muromachi period.

Dororo comes to realize that he is not like other boys; he is actually missing 48 separate body parts! Determined to set things right and become a normal boy, Dororo obtains a fake body; then, encased in that fake body, he sets out to find 48 monsters that were made from his real body, years before. One by one, Dororo meets and defeats all 48 monsters and retrieves his missing body parts. By the end of the series, Dororo is whole again!

This series was unusual for Mushi Production in several respects. Not only was it a short series at only 26 programs, but the series was based on an original tale too thin to sustain for even 26 episodes. The 14th, 15th, 18th, 19th, 20th, 23rd, and 25th programs were based on stories written especially for television and were not part of the original tale. Next, the title was changed halfway through the series. Dororo was not an average little boy, nor would he have been average even with 48 more body parts than he had — Dororo was a boy *thief!*

He traveled in the company of an adult fellow named Hyakkimaru. And, because Hyakkimaru was more prominent at battling monsters than Dororo was, viewers came to regard Hyakkimaru as the main character. So Mushi Production changed the title of the series to *Dororo and Hyakkimaru.* The studio also made sure to keep plenty of animated body parts floating through the air!

Neither NBC Enterprises nor Oriolo Productions nor any other U.S. distributor stepped forward to seek distribution rights to this series. Signs of bleak times ahead for Mushi were already starting to appear.

CHAPTER 7

Marine Boy and *Astro Boy*

Marine Boy: Risky but Rewarding — for Some

Shortly before Al Singer's demise, K. Fujita returned once again with a new series — this time, he brought with him a color print of a new half-hour show, *Kaitei Shonen Marine* (*Marine Boy*), starring a winsome-looking, red-headed young boy who rode to adventure on the back of a happy, broadly smiling dolphin! I liked the show immediately, with the exception of a let-down ending (a small band of musicians on camera, playing a nondescript tune) and wanted to pursue a deal with Fujita. To my surprise, Singer was negative about all this. He saw the weak ending as a tipoff that the writers were in trouble: They did not know how to end a story. I felt that we could *work* with the writers (as I had worked years earlier with the writers of *Astro Boy*) and come up with a highly salable new series, one reminiscent of *Flipper*. But Singer would not budge.

I suspect that he thought the "weak writing" was symptomatic of a larger problem with this studio, namely, the operation, Japan Telecartoons, was new, K. Fujita was understood to have a personal stake in it, and this new series was being produced on the risky premise that Fujita would not only distribute the show in Japan, but also *pre-sell* it abroad to raise the necessary financing. (Recall that *Astro Boy* and *Kimba* were produced by Mushi Production with guaranteed financing from the Fuji Television Network, and *8th Man, Gigantor,* and little-known *Prince Planet* (*Yusei Shonen Papii*) were produced by TCJ with a similar guarantee by giant Dentsu Advertising).

I understood Singer's reservations about the stability of the studio and deferred to him. I also saw unmistakably that, in a 50–50 partnership, where both partners must agree on all major actions to be taken, the partners are equal *if they agree;* but if the partners do not agree on an action, then the one who says "No" is the boss.

Officially, Delphi Associates, Inc., turned down *Marine Boy*. Unofficially,

I directed K. Fujita to two editors (Pablo Zavala and Sheldon Riss) whom I had set up outside my editing room in Times Square. Stanley Jaffee, of Seven Arts Television, was attracted to the project and took it over, with Peter Fernandez handling the adaptation. Eventually, as though to prove Al Singer wrong, the series stretched to a remarkable 78 episodes, though the National Association for Better Broadcasting was reported at one point to have cited the series for excessive violence. Seven Arts eventually merged into Warner Bros. Television, where *Marine Boy* was later groomed for release on DVD. (Ironically, Seven Arts was headed by one Eliot Hyman, who would become my partner a few years later in an animation-coloring enterprise.)

Speed Racer: The Big One That Got Away

Al Singer had been dead for only a few days when K. Fujita returned once more, this time with a pilot film made by Tatsunoko Studio, producers of *Space Ace,* our *Ring-O*. Tatsunoko was working on a color series, which they called *Mach Go Go Go; go* means "five" in Japanese, so the title in English would be *Mach 5*. That was the designation for a racing car and the explanation for the number 5 being emblazoned on the side of the car. This series is about a teenage boy named Go Mifune (the English letter *M* appears on the boy's helmet and jacket) born into a family with auto racing in their blood. It sounded like a great idea for a series, a series I'd have liked to acquire for Delphi Associates, but, sadly, with the death of my partner, who had been with me when Fujita arrived in New York, and with my taking over Al Singer's work in addition to my own (we were then in production of a series of live *harness-racing* films being shot nightly), my plate was full. I simply could not get involved, anytime soon, in yet another major project.

So, reluctantly, I once more walked Fujita across the hall, where he and I sat with editors Zavala and Riss and we screened the pilot. How unfortunate, I thought, that this series didn't come along <u>before</u> *Marine Boy!* Al Singer would have liked this; the story line about auto racing fit in perfectly with our penchant for shows based on racing, and Tatsunoko Studio, under respected founder Ippei Kuri, was a well-established, successful organization.

The pilot film, I thought, had the earmarks of a winner. I wondered aloud about the possibility of calling Seven Arts/Stanley Jaffee about this series, but the editors quickly pointed out, and Fujita nodded agreement, that Seven Arts had its hands full with *Marine Boy*. I called Trans-Lux, distributors of *Gigantor*. Indeed, they were doing well with *Gigantor*, even in black and white.

They screened the *Mach Go Go Go* pilot, liked it, trusted the team of adapters — Peter Fernandez and others — who had worked with me for years on *Gigantor, Astro Boy et al.,* and Trans-Lux took on the series. Quickly, *Mach Go Go Go* morphed into *Speed Racer* and became an instant hit.

True, the series was not without violence (after all, the year was 1967 and violence seemed to have become the order of the day for all anime; Tokyo broadcasters had no reservations about airing such content for Japanese boys and girls). But in *Astro Boy* and *Gigantor,* we learned how to turn *apparent* violence into *comic* violence. We would, for example, have one criminal — when shot by a rival criminal — call out, "*Ouch! That smarts!*" Chim Chim, a cute monkey in *Speed Racer,* was played for laughs by veteran voice actress Corinne Orr, providing welcome comic relief.

Personally, I was intrigued by one element in particular in *Speed Racer* — the shadowy character whom the Japanese called Masked Racer. That character popped up from time to time in the series as Racer X to save Speed's life. Finally, well into the series, we learn that Racer X is, in reality, Speed's older *brother!* What an idea! This older brother, Kenichi, had been forced (for a complex variety of reasons) to leave the rest of his family; yet, his love for his kid brother led him to reappear at critical times when Speed's life was threatened by (a) corrupt competing drivers, (b) high-stake, big-time criminals, and even (c) foreign spies! (No such intricate plots were coming from any American studio engaged in the production of children's programs.)

Adventures like these, combined with sure-fire race-the-clock pressures, are fun to write, fun to record in a sound studio with savvy, seasoned performers, and fun to watch. Small wonder that *Speed Racer* emerged at the end of the 1960s as the most popular anime series of the decade, topping even black-and-white *Gigantor,* the undisputed champion till then.

By decade's end, I regretted the loss of the series *8th Man,* which I felt had great potential — potential largely unrealized by the start-up dubbing team in Florida — and by the loss of *Speed Racer,* which I consider a near-miss, "The Big One that got away."

And though I did not anticipate it at the time, *Speed Racer* was the last anime series I would consider for a decade to come! Increasing levels of violence in new anime from Tokyo, coupled with Trans-Lux's discovery of growing resistance to anime in a marketplace now glutted, made further acquisitions unattractive. I recall wondering at the time, "Is this the end of anime as we know it?"

CHAPTER 8

A Cinderella Process:
Turning Black-and-White
Animation into Color

From the day they started distributing *Gigantor* in 1965, the year in which leading U.S. television stations were converting to color transmission, Trans-Lux felt that they could get 25 percent higher prices if *Gigantor*, shot in black and white, was available in color. Doing the math, it became clear that color was now the way to go. The question was: how to convert the black-and-white images to color?

First, a check of TCJ, the animating studio in Tokyo, revealed that the studio did not save any old, black-and-white (*Gigantor*) cels, which, theoretically, could be re-rendered in color; the cels were tossed away after they were filmed, the rationale being that millions of cels were generated by the studio each year; the studio would need a warehouse just to store old, "useless" cels!

Tinting? Following NBC Network's turndown of *Ring-O*, my partner and I tried to save whatever we could of the project. We culled a number of additional *Space Ace* black-and-white prints, looking for great action shots of the young hero in space —flying, battling a space robot, confronting a human arch-enemy in orbit, hurling *Ace's* uniquely empowered rings, doing Big Things! We tinted the space sequences blue. The insides of space ships were tinted red, to simulate lighting aboard a submerged submarine. Shots of human arch-enemies were tinted green. The effects were interesting, but not compelling enough to result in a sale. Tinting was not the answer.

1968: Year of Color-Added Breakthrough

One Japanese friend I had met in New York believed that, as a practical matter, no studio in Tokyo would be able to re-render the artwork in a

Gigantor show for the small budget required to make the process viable. He suggested the possibility of performing the copying process in the country-side — "rural" Japan, he called it. Indeed, that sounded credible.

But the real "break" came one day when I had the good fortune to meet an artist living in New York, a Korean man married to a Japanese woman. When in Japan, the artist used the surname Toyama (his Korean name was Kim Ei-wan — my English spelling, not his), who, he said, had a brother living in Seoul, Korea. The brother, he said, was a camera expert who would surely know how to re-render and film the *Gigantor* cels at a price that would make the process viable! (Seoul prices, he said, were 50 percent of those in Tokyo.) Sounded good.

Mr. Kim, after he was given a trial roll of black-and-white *Gigantor* scenes, sent it to Seoul and, several weeks later, the trial roll came back — with a small roll of color film. With considerable anticipation, but actually not expecting to see anything great, I threaded the roll of color film on my office projector and started the projector rolling. The color images appeared on the screen.

The test was so good, the colors so vibrant, I could scarcely believe my eyes. Effusively, but cautiously, I praised Mr. Kim, complimented him and his brother, then asked if the minor flaws we saw could be corrected (the answer was "Yes"), and, very important, could the operation in Seoul be expanded to deliver a show a week — that's thirty minutes every week — at the agreed price, no cost overruns?

Mr. Kim was sure that it could be done, and suggested that we send his brother a complete *Gigantor* program to color, with payment to be made on a C.O.D. basis. *Agreed.* One complete program was handed to Mr. Kim.

Weeks passed. Then, months. Nothing had come from Korea. My feeling was that the brothers Kim had probably bitten off more *bulgaki* (popular Korean barbeque) than they could chew. But one day, Mr. Kim did walk in with the second test. Like the first one, this test was also quite good — not perfect, and only half the supplied program, but clearly a breakthrough in a process of re-rendering drawn, black-and-white images in color. The delay had come, Mr. Kim explained, from difficulty in obtaining 16mm color film in Seoul, and from working with only a few of his brother's employees — if full production were to follow, then the "plant" would need to be expanded and more workers hired.

This all sounded reasonable and encouraging. I took the two test sequences — the short first test and the longer second test — to our film laboratory near Times Square. Lab president Irwin Young had brilliantly (I thought ingeniously) solved unique problems for us in the processing of *Gigantor* black-and-white materials from Tokyo and in making multiple Agfacolor prints of our nighttime harness-racing series, where the racetrack's lighting was never intended for the shooting of color film.

Irwin Young and I screened the *Gigantor* color test films from Korea on a large screen in a client screening room. He instantly spotted some minor defects, defects that I had barely noticed before, and identified them as "processing" problems, that is, the Seoul laboratory that had developed the exposed 16mm film was not really well equipped to handle the task. Indeed, that laboratory had acknowledged that it was really geared to handle 35mm theatrical, rather than 16mm, film.

I actually found that comforting; flaws that I thought were inherent in the process were nothing more than foreign laboratory mishaps.

Young recommended that we use a positive, rather than a negative, film stock to shoot the color images being generated in Seoul. And, because the Korean laboratory could not, at that point, process the exposed positive-image film, the processing and final assembly would be done in New York City. (That was indeed what would become our modus operandi when we went into full-scale production soon thereafter.)

Meanwhile, word was quietly being spread throughout the laboratory that the boss, Mr. Young, was with a client in the large screening room, projecting dailies of a secret new film process — a process that *incredibly* transforms black-and-white to color!

That word did not escape the ears of Joseph ("Joe") Kotler, a Warner Bros. sales executive who was screening rushes in an adjacent room. He climbed the few steps leading to the projector in the large room, and was able to see past the projector to *Gigantor* on the screen *in color*, smashing a sinister, evil robot into a heap of multicolored rubble!

Joe Kotler knew that the *Gigantor* series, then being shown on WPIX, Channel 11, in New York, was in black and white. He waited until Irwin Young and I had bid each other goodbye, then approached me, introduced himself, and insisted that I join him for lunch. He would not take "No" for an answer. I did finally agree to be his guest and, over huge delicatessen sandwiches in a famous restaurant around the corner, he explained the urgency. Warner is all set with its Saturday morning, network schedule, he said — "Bugs Bunny, Roadrunner ... those are all in color — but the guys who sell in syndication (i.e., to local, independent stations) are crying that they've got nothing to sell for the kids' market. Warner has lots of other cartoons, but those are the old, black-and-white *Porky Pig* ones. They're great, but they're not in color!" Kotler raised his eyebrows. "Now, if those old black-and-white cartoons were in *color*...." He did not finish the sentence. He didn't have to.

"Joe," I explained, "this is still experimental. What I'm planning to do is color-convert *Gigantor*...."

"Forget *Gigantor!*" he interrupted. "Put *Gigantor* aside. Do it later! First you do *Porky!* Do you realize the story you'd have?" He raised his hand and swept it through the air, as though indicating a newspaper headline. "Warner Bros., the studio that brought you talking pictures, now brings you the world's first black-and-white cartoons ... *in color!!*" He leaned forward, as though to reveal a secret. "Do you know what that kind of publicity is worth?"

He did make a compelling case.

We hurried through the rest of our lunch. Kotler made a short phone call, then urged me to get into a taxi with him — there was one parked at the curb right outside the restaurant door — and return with him to Warner Bros. headquarters in the nearby Pan Am Building. I did, and in the Warner offices I was introduced to Donald Klauber, head of worldwide sales, and to Richard "Dick" Harper, an executive who seemed to be at least on Joe Kotler's level — maybe a bit higher.

Kotler briefly recapped the events that began in the film lab that morning; he then explained that he'd like to hand me a 16mm black-and-white print of a "typical" *Porky Pig* cartoon, running length about seven-and-a-half minutes, and have me convert the picture to color. Without question, the Warner executives were deeply interested. They wondered how I felt about this.

Frankly, I was more than a little interested. It had occurred to me, in that taxi ride from the restaurant, that a contract with Warner Bros. would provide the funding to build the capability needed in Seoul. We could lease the extra space we needed, hire more personnel, refine our technique (get the "bugs" out), and break the story to the press — at the proper time — that we had given Porky Pig a new lease on life! Porky was back — *in color!* Yes, this would seem to be a great opportunity, after all, *Gigantor* would be around forever (we had perpetual rights to the series), but I sensed that, with *Porky Pig*, it was imperative to strike quickly, while the iron was hot.

I thanked Joe Kotler for the lunch and, kiddingly, for the chance to have Porky stutter in color; then I assured Joe that I'd think it over and get back to him quickly. I understood that time was of the essence.

Before the day was over, I moved to form a new corporation — Color Systems, Inc. — and arranged with Mr. Kim, who was now back at his home in Tokyo, to meet him at his brother's shop in Seoul. Mere days later, the three of us were all standing together in that shop, which turned out to be larger than I had expected. There was room in the back for a handful of young girls to trace tiny, filmed black-and-white images magnified onto sheets of clear plastic, then paint the sheets with color, and photograph the painted sheets with an old 16 millimeter camera that belonged to Mr. Kim's brother. That is what I had understood would be the technique; I could envision that this might work in a boutique kind of operation, but now saw clearly that nothing like this, even if expanded, would be feasible for the kind of operation required to fulfill a substantial contract like Warner Bros. In my mind's eye, I could see the Warner deal going up in smoke.

But, surprisingly, the brothers Kim were aware of the problem, too. They brought in a man named J. H. Song, publisher of many government-sponsored books about tourism in colorful Korea. His arrival on the scene completely turned things around; he saw how he could photographically "explode" the images in a frame of film, then — as my wife Eileen, a graphic artist, had theorized —*separate* the *animated action* from the background, apply color to the separated elements with gels and other materials commonly used in publishing, then recombine the separations under a precisely calibrated color camera mount. Mr. Song not only had the equipment to do this, but he also had the organization and the *zeal* to do it — he was an animation buff.

Back in New York, with Warners' assurance that they would be forgiving of minor flaws, if any, in the first five or six pictures, Color Systems soon delivered the first color-converted *Porky Pig* cartoon. The subject was Porky's farm. Porky's straw hat was yellow, his flesh tone was pink, his vegetables were green, and his chickens were — blue! (Yes, blue!) I cringed when those blue chickens entered and began pecking their way around Porky's farm; I waited for harsh, even sarcastic, criticism from the half-dozen executives in the screening room. I waited in vain; no criticism came. Instead, to a man, they were euphoric with the color-converted version! (I had screened the black-and-white print beforehand, as a frame of reference.) Of a certainty, those men in the room felt they were "in" on an historic "first" — like seeing and hearing Al Jolson sing, for the first time, in the world's first "talkie," Warner Bros.'s *The Jazz Singer.*

In quick succession, we delivered five more subjects, each with a few discreet flaws. Then, in picture #7, *Porky's Ant* (originally animated in black and white by famed Warner director Chuck Jones) I felt we had finally hit it—a picture with no visible flaws, and rendered in rich, dazzling colors. Our client agreed. Chuck Jones himself was shown the color version; he called it "good clean work."

Color Systems patented the process, we signed with Warner to color-convert a total of 78 subjects, and we delivered all 78 with no retakes or rejections. We were off to a fine start.

Then, *Gigantor?*

Bill Cayton, the man for whom I had worked for ten years (1950–60) owned a group of vintage fight films, featuring such great boxing champs as

Jack Johnson, Jess Willard, Jack Dempsey, James Braddock, Max Baer, Joe Louis, Rocky Marciano, and more. All those films, without exception, had been photographed in black and white. Cayton was certain that Color Systems could somehow convert the boxing films to color, and he actually bought a short-term interest in Color Systems for that purpose. Alas, we could not get satisfactory color results from his negatives, all of which were contrasty, grainy duplicates of the originals, but I did acquire English-language rights to Osamu Tezuka's classic black and white anime feature *New Treasure Island* and we produced a color version. Bill Cayton purchased it, along with a few other black-and-white cartoons, and released them under his Radio & Television Packagers label. (In the process, Tezuka's *New Treasure Island* was renamed *Treasure Island Revisited*.)

Meanwhile, Eliot Hyman, once the head of Seven Arts Television (distributors of *Marine Boy*), as mentioned earlier, had acquired control of Warner Bros. and he was seeing spectacular profits accruing to Warner from sales of the 78 color-converted *Porky Pig* subjects. His ears perked up. Hyman had made huge profits during World War II from a process of miniaturizing (using microfiche) written correspondence sent to our troops overseas. The process was popularly known throughout the 1940s as "V-Mail." In Color Systems' new process of converting black-and-white animation to color, Hyman thought he might have come across "another V-Mail"!

By the time Hyman sold his interest in Warner Bros., each of the color-converted Porky Pig films had earned a profit of $15,000. From Warners' point of view, they had unearthed a buried, all-but-forgotten batch of obsolete shorts, given them a new lease on life, advertised them as "*new...in color!,*" and banked well over a million dollars, with no end to the profit stream in sight! As the year 1970 rolled in, Hyman bought out Bill Cayton's interest in Color Systems, Inc., then landed contracts to color-convert 18 *Krazy Kat* subjects, as an experiment for Columbia, and 100 *Betty Boop* pictures for National Telefilm Associates — the same NTA that had earlier assumed the distribution of NBC's *Astro Boy* series.

(Years later, as Entercolor Technologies in Los Angeles, — J. H. Song and Eliot Hyman had long since expired — we would convert to color, with the aid of a new team in Korea and using improved materials, 120 black-and-white *Popeye* cartoons for Turner Broadcasting, plus a group of old Warner subjects that would otherwise have lapsed into the public domain. Adding color to the black-and-white subjects made it possible for Warner to obtain a new copyright.)

All this activity marked the beginning of the huge animation industry in Korea, and it deserves a chapter by itself.

Land of Morning Calm

As surely as Japan is the Land of the Rising Sun, Korea is the Land of Morning Calm. My Korean Airlines jetliner landed not in Seoul, as I had expected on that first trip in 1968, but at Kimpo airport — Kimpo (pronounced kim-PO) is a village just outside Seoul. Fortunately, the flight arrived at night. After 36 straight hours of flying, New York–Anchorage–Seoul, I was exhausted — jet lagged-out. The brothers Kim met me and delivered me to a modest, but comfortable, hotel mercifully near the airport.

Next morning I arrived at the Kim camera shop, but I hardly recognized it as such. The "coloring activity" had taken every available inch of space. Two things struck me immediately: (1) the plastic sheets being used like animation cels seemed thick, crude, and not really clear; and (2) the camera stand was an improvised affair, consisting of a small table anchored to the floor (for stability), with a 16mm camera suspended above the table. That this makeshift arrangement was capable of producing such beautiful end product was amazing.

Seoul was certainly not Tokyo, in terms of animation capability. The small amount of professional animation being created in Seoul in 1968 was rendered at a firm called the Century Company, which was essentially a film distributor, not a production studio. There, two young animators sat in a corner of the company warehouse, drawing on paper. A theatrical feature called *Hong-Gil-Dong* had already been created in Seoul, and now Century Company proudly pointed to a newer theatrical feature, a Korean-animated version of Robert Louis Stevenson's *Treasure Island,* in which the character of young Jim Hawkins was a Korean boy.

Remarkably, no one in Korea at the time seemed to be manufacturing anything comparable to a professional animation cel. Such cels are made of fine, clear plastic, and they were being imported from a supplier in Osaka, Japan. For fine cameras and lenses, the brothers Kim looked to Zeiss in Germany.

As Osamu Tezuka in Tokyo had called his original studio Mushi Production (loosely translated as "Busy Bee Productions"), the Kims in Seoul, perhaps inspired by Tezuka, called their modest little operation Kaemi Production (loosely translated as "Busy Ants Productions").

J. H. Song, the publisher brought in later by the Kims, owned a three-story building that housed a substantial staff of office personnel, photographers, writers/translators, and darkroom technicians. Under the name of International Art Production, Song was printing government pamphlets, brochures, and handsome glossy magazines — many of which were printedin English. IAP's presses were unquestionably state of the art (such was the evaluation of my wife Eileen, herself a one-time participant in a print shop near lower Manhattan).

Song understood the need for precise registration of all color art elements that went before his camera(s). And he understood the need for ultra-cleanliness. He, himself, was fond of saying, "Dust is my enemy!" What emerged, in our search for a viable process of converting black-and-white motion picture images to color, was a fusion of two disciplines that ordinarily do not meet each other in the light of day — animation and printing. So effective was the process that, at its peak, Color Systems was delivering 16 color-converted *Betty Boop* cartoons each month. The average length of a *Betty Boop* subject is 7½ minutes, so NTA was receiving from Color Systems some 120 minutes of new color production every 30 days — a record!

Mr. Song was obsessed with secrecy. It was not enough for the publisher that he and I had successfully obtained a U.S. patent for the process that we developed; he forbade members of any IAP department from discussing their work with any other department, so that no one could "fit the pieces of the puzzle together" and figure out more than Mr. Song wanted any one person to know. In fact, friendly competition between departments was encouraged, in the belief that competitors are not likely to share their secrets.

Then, *Gigantor*?

Color Systems' heyday for converting black-and-white cartoons to color lasted from 1968 to 1976. Eliot Hyman, after a long illness, died at his home in Connecticut, and J. H. Song would die of a stroke in Seoul soon after. Their deaths would effectively mark the end of Color Systems in the United States, and the cessation of the color conversion process in Korea. *Gigantor,* the series preempted by *Porky Pig, Krazy Kat, Betty Boop*, and other black-and-white series looming on the horizon, never completed the trek from the United States to Korea. An anachronism, the *Gigantor* series reemerged on the airwaves via America's Cartoon Network in 2005 — in pristine black and white!

The color conversion work of International Art Production had come to an end, but several key employees of the firm would move on and set up their own animation shops in Seoul. By then, animation studios in Japan had become aware of the surge in animation activity in Korea, and now they saw the feasibility of establishing in Seoul what had previously been unthinkable in Tokyo — the *subcontracting* of their work to studios in Seoul, studios that could easily render lower-end animation there for a fraction of the cost of performing that work at home!

Indeed, the Japanese anime series called *The Golden Bat* (1966) was actually animated in Seoul, not Tokyo, and Japan's giant animation studio Toei Doga would actually take over Seoul's Dae-Won Studio to render animation exclusively for Toei.

Nor did all this activity escape the eyes of animation producers in the United States. Fred Wolf, the respected animator based in Hollywood and the producer of an American series of *Speed Racer,* began animating in Seoul. Soon, the makers of such American series as *The Simpsons, King of the Hill, Family Guy,* and other popular television series began flocking to Korea to have *their* series animated there.

Today, animation is a thriving industry in Korea. And to think: the industry really started in 1968 with an impromptu, makeshift little operation known as Kaemi Production, and an aged American cartoon star known as Porky Pig!

CHAPTER 9

Those '70s Shows

Toei Doga, the aforementioned giant animation studio in Tokyo, was in virtual simultaneous production of three or four animated feature films at the end of the 1960s. The studio could afford to be engaged in such expensive ventures — Toei Doga (Toei Animation) was and is owned by Toei Co., Ltd,, a huge conglomerate in Japan. Toei Co., Ltd. owns film studios, film laboratories, television facilities, an advertising agency, golf courses, resort hotels, and real estate holdings — an entire spectrum of diversified enterprises, including Toei Animation. Unlike American corporations, which are no longer permitted to own both the studios that make movies and the theaters that exhibit them (recall Uncle Sam's mandated split between MGM Studios and Loews Theaters), Japanese corporations have no such governmental restrictions; thus, Toei has its own movie production studios and the theaters in which to exhibit their movies.

Toei finances the production of animated features and books them into its theaters. So it was that, in the latter half of the decade of the '60s, Toei Doga was in production of its own versions of *Treasure Island, Little Norse Prince, Jack and the Witch,* and *Puss in Boots.* I was fortunate enough to be asked to create the English adaptations of those features. I turned down *Jack and the Witch* (I frankly disliked much of the styling, particularly that of Jack), but did adapt the other three, and found them a joy.

Treasure Island was superbly crafted, I thought — timed with American-style zest and full of visual humor. For example: a pirate, running at full speed along a cliff on Treasure Island, suddenly realizes that he's come to the edge of the cliff, digs in his heels as though applying brakes, and screeches to a grinding halt — complete with comic sound effects (standard in American cartoons, unusual in Japanese).

Little Norse Prince captivated me by its charming portrayal of village life in, or near, the Arctic Circle. I felt that the film generated a great degree of warmth, which, for reasons I never understood, the Toei staff did not appreciate. Toei's international sales department minimalized the film.

As to *Puss in Boots* (*Nagagutsu o haita neko*) (1969), which was directed by Kimio Yabuki, I regard this as one of the finest animated features I have ever seen. The graphics are complex and extraordinary — in particular, the ogre's castle, which is a marvel of labyrinthine chambers, winding stairways, ledges that dart in and out of turrets that rise perpendicular to jagged cliffs below! The film is a visual treat, as well as one rich in humor among its principal characters — especially Puss himself and the young lad he champions. (Even the ogre has certain endearing traits!)

Japanese timing, I learned early on, is remarkably — and surprisingly — like American timing. I could see that in Tezuka's first anime series (our *Astro Boy*) right from the start in 1963. I saw it again in the three Toei features described above. Whereas European animators time their on-screen actions somewhat slowly, introspectively, the Japanese pace their animated moves much faster — with zip and verve! That may help explain why anime has become so popular in the West: With snappy English dialogue applied in the dubbing process, a Japanese cartoon, like those above, can look and sound as though it were made entirely in Hollywood.

These feature films, which I do not regard in the strictest sense as *anime* (I reserve the term *anime* for Japanese-animated television series and direct-to-video), saw wide circulation in the early 1970s. Toei Doga in 1975 was also producing a series of short (10 minute) classic fairy tales, several of which I acquired and released on DVD in 2005 as *The World's Greatest Fairy Tales*. But were Tokyo studios producing *series* anime during the decade of the '70s? Indeed, yes — *Star Blazers* and *Captain Harlock*, to name two; what I saw was a lot of over-the-top violence, at a time when American television stations were refusing even to *look* at anime pilots known to contain violence.

The heyday of anime may be over, I thought. A revolutionary Japanese art form that landed like a starburst on American shores in 1963 has, in less than ten years, burnt itself out like a dying star! With that somber thought in mind, I accepted a challenge to adapt a number of foreign-made, foreign-language, live-action features for the CBS Children's Film Festival. These were films that portrayed children at risk — and not with happy-ever-after endings!

Case-in-point: A Czech film, *Captain Korda,* related the touching story of an orphan boy joyously adopted by a loving, childless couple who become real parents to the boy — until the boy's birth mother arrives with her surly new husband, and wants to take the boy back.

Another case-in-point: A Mexican story outside the CBS Festival, *Tuerto* (the term means one-eyed), recounted the tale of a boy born with just one good eye. He lives in poverty with his grandmother, who prays for a miracle for her grandson; he's constantly being tormented by neighborhood bullies who call him *tuerto*. One day, in a freak accident, the boy loses his other (good) eye. The grandmother, incredulously, gives *thanks* for that "miracle"; now, she explains, her grandson is totally blind, and the bullies won't torment him anymore and call him *tuerto*!

Pippi Longstocking was something else! *Pippi* was the brainchild of the late Swedish author Astrid Lindgren. The adventures — some would say "misadventures"— of Pippi and her two young friends were filmed as a co-production between Swedish and German studios. They produced four feature-length films, of which I created the English adaptations for three: *Pippi on the South Seas, Pippi on Board,* and *Pippi on the Run.* These gentle, humorous escapades were a welcome antidote for the often sad tales of the CBS Children's Film Festival.

Battle of the Planets: Anime from Out of the Blue!

Scarcely back from a 1979 trip to Manila to check on some animation facilities, I took a phone call as compelling as that momentous call from NBC's Jim Dodd, sixteen years earlier!

The call was from Sandy Frank, a program distributor based in New York. Sandy's office wanted to know if I would be interested in adapting a new anime series. (*What? Was anyone still thinking of adapting anime series — violence and all?*) "Tell me about it," I said.

The series was one being produced by Tatsunoko Production (of *Ring-O* and *Speed Racer* fame). The name of the new series was *Science Ninja Team Gatchaman*; it featured five teenage scouts who fight an ongoing battle, on the ground and in the air, with a masked supercriminal (called Berg Katse) and his cadre of guards. The series consisted of 85 half-hours. (This was too good to be true, I thought. After some 10 years of being distanced from the production of English versions of Japanese cartoons, I'm suddenly being offered a major series of what could perhaps be another *Speed Racer?*)

I asked several questions — about the size of the cast, nature of the dubbing elements to be supplied, expected rate of delivery, degree of violence contained in a typical episode — at this last question, the caller began to hedge a bit. He acknowledged that there was considerable violence throughout, but that *Gatchaman* was surely no more violent than *Astro Boy, Gigantor,* or *Kimba* had been.

That led to the matter of scripting and the tone of each script (recall that *Kimba,* with its principal theme of *the law of the jungle,* required extra-careful editing and scripting).

"Oh, don't worry about scripting," the caller was quick to reassure me, "the scripting will be done by our man in California!"

"*What?*"

"We have a friend at Hanna-Barbera. He's going to write the scripts."

I knew instantly, that meant trouble. The "friend" was an animator, not a writer, and certainly not a writer who had ever written *lip-sync dialogue.* He would be 3,000 miles away from our studio in New York and, if his lip sync did not work (as it surely would not), I would be running into overtime on every show, rewriting the dialogue "on the studio floor." I explained those anticipated "problems" to the caller, who saw no problems at all.

I could almost see the caller's shoulders shrug as he assured me, simply, "Cartoons are cartoons."

I thanked the caller, expressed my regrets, and told him that I regretfully had to pass; I thought he might be better off by doing everything in California.

As soon as I hung up, I wondered if I hadn't been too hasty. I had never turned down an entire series before! Eighty-five half-hours! Months and months — maybe years — of production: writers ... directors ... actors ... editors ... studios ... projectionists ... sound recordists. Had I let them all down? Why didn't I say, "Let me think about it. I'll get back to you in a few days"?

Indeed, I continued to think about that matter for years afterward. My only consolation — if any — was that *Gatchaman* needed major surgery to remove all the scenes unacceptable on U.S. television. "Sanitizing" the shows proved to be a Herculean task — more than the California team had anticipated. New animation had to be produced to replace all the footage excised from episode after episode. We were not really equipped to do that in New York. So, maybe I had made the right decision, after all. As things turned out, I would — like Moses — get a second chance years later.

Anime: *REanimated? Old Testament Tales* and *G-Force*

Going into the decade of the 1980s, when series anime appeared to be moribund, and I had moved our offices to Los Angeles, I spotted a news article in a U.S. trade publication: "Tokyo film studio creates series of animated *Old Testament (Bible) Tales* for Japanese schoolchildren." *Old Testament?* How unusual, I thought; if the studio were creating a series about Buddha, or about Shinto, that would be understandable — but tales from the Old Testament?

Home video was emerging as a major player in the entertainment industry in those days. I knew that a series of Bible tales, only 20 in number and

Abraham, obeying the Word of the Lord, prepares to sacrifice his son in the Old Testament tale *Abraham and Isaac.* © Video Japonica Films.

of varying lengths, would not be viable as a television series, but I believed it would be ideal for home video. I wired the studio, Video Japonica, and made them an offer that was high by any standard. The studio knew me by reputation — *Astro Boy, Gigantor, Kimba* — and thought the offer was fair, but they turned it down.

Months later, after turning a deaf ear to any proposal I put forward, they agreed to an eye-to-eye meeting in Tokyo. There, to my pleasure and surprise, they accepted the offer. What changed their mind, apparently, was the approach I suggested to the material — treat it respectfully, but with *warmth*. Since that meeting, they have applauded the English edition of their Bible tales and use it to teach English in Japanese schools. In the Americas, that series is available on DVD as *Bible Stories: Tales from the Old Testament.*

Later, in an unexpected development, I adapted a Video Japonica anime

Temptress for Philistines lures strongman Samson in Greatest Tales' production of Old Testament tale *Samson and Delilah.* © Video Japonica Films.

miniseries called *The Life of Buddha*—a project in which I thought I'd never be involved! That, in turn, led to an (again, unplanned) acquisition of the same studio's live-action miniseries — we call it *Animal Families*— short nature films so well photographed that they're distributed widely here to schools and on home video.

Animated Bible stories and the life of Buddha, dramatized in a mixture of peculiarly Japanese animation styles — did that suggest a revitalization of anime? I did not think so. Rather, a single studio, one focused on historical themes and events, was re-creating them in quasi-documentary style for distribution solely to schools and libraries; no thought was given to producing a line of fictional adventures in great quantities for television.

Was Anime REanimating?

Then, early in the decade, a veritable tsunami wave of anime rolled in from Japan to California. One Carl Macek, a writer-director based in Los Angeles, assembled three separate anime series —*Super-Dimensional Fortress*

Macross, Super-Dimensional Cavalry Southern Cross, and *Genesis Climber Maspeada*—and combined the three into an 85-episode series. Macek relabeled the series as *The Macross Saga, The Robotech Masters,* and *The New Generation.* The umbrella title for the over-all project became *Robotech.* All three subseries could be combined credibly because (a) all three were animated by Tokyo-based Tatsunoko Studio with the same visual style, same characters, same story elements, and (b) the precedent of an 85-episode series had already been established years earlier with *Battle of the Planets* (recall that this series, too, had come from Tatsunoko). Sales of *Robotech* to television were considered modest, but the series did rack up sales in home video and comic books.

Hard on the heels of *Robotech* came another 85-episode anime wonder—*G-Force!* I first heard of this in a startling telephone call from Turner Broadcasting System in Atlanta, Georgia. Henry "Hank" Gillespie, an acquaintance, was on the line, calling to tell me of a Tatsunoko series that Turner was in the process of acquiring. I interrupted him, "Hank, don't tell me that Turner is picking up *Robotech!*"

"No, not *Robotech,*" was the answer. "We're picking up a series from Sandy Frank."

I was stunned. For a moment, I was speechless. "You're not talking about *Battle of the Planets*—are you?"

"It *is Battle of the Planets.* But we're not calling it *Battle of the Planets.* Now it's *G-Force!*"

Again, silence. Then, "Wait a second, Hank. I don't get this. Sandy Frank has sold *the pants* off *Battle.* He's got it on a million stations."

"Yeah, but he can't get renewals. The series tanked. Kids won't watch it. *We* think it's a good show. We think that if it's *redone* ... and goes on the air with a new name...."

"So, you're asking me to redo it?"

"Well ... y'wanna redo it?"

Again, a pause. Then, slowly, "Hank, Sandy spent tons of money to adapt that series. If you're asking me to 'patch it up' ... to save what's good, and replace what's not so good...."

"I'm not asking you to save anything. We think the whole thing has to be scrapped—new animation and all. I'd like to see you take it back to exactly where it was when it first came in from Japan!"

It took me a while to digest that.

(*Note:* Recall that when Sandy Frank acquired one Gatchaman story arc [of three] from Japan, he did so at a time when Jimmy Carter was president, Action for Children's Television (ACT) was badgering Congress and the Federal Communications Commission [FCC] to revoke the license of any television station that did not eliminate violence from children's programs, and broadcasters were fearful of airing anything that could even be *perceived* as having overtones of violence. Frank knew that, in order to sell [the often violent] Gatchaman to broadcasters in Jasper, Wyoming, or Peoria, Illinois, or Des Moines Iowa, he would have to "sanitize" the shows by cutting out several minutes of extreme or threatening action from each episode. Beleaguered adapter Jameson Brewer, confronted with the problem in California, had no choice but to replace that taboo footage with innocuous material, some of which had little — if anything — to do with the story as it came from Japan. [Indeed, Brewer even had to find "excuses" to bring planets into the picture, because Gatchaman, as it came from Japan, had nothing whatever to do with outer space.]

(Problems of inherent violence all went away when Ronald Reagan became president in 1980. Reagan, in his vow to "get government off our backs," promptly dismantled agencies created to protect the public, and signaled to broadcasters that the FCC, which had bowed to the demands of ACT, would no longer be so stringent in its oversight.)

As with Moses, a Second Chance

Days after that momentous call from Atlanta, I called Henry Gillespie and told him that, yes, I would gratefully accept his exciting challenge to remake *Gatchaman/Battle of the Planets* into *G-Force*. I felt great satisfaction in that. Like Moses, I had been given that rarest of opportunities — a second chance — a chance to do what I really would have liked to do seven years earlier! How sweet it was!

Hold On There, Son — Not So Fast!

Gillespie reminded me of a line commonplace in television infomercials: "But wait! There's more!"

Before going ahead full speed, Henry cautioned, Turner had to be satisfied that my approach to the series would *work*— even on the hardest shows! They wanted to see two pilots. (They're spending a lot of money on this remake, Gillespie said, they're entitled to see what they're going to get.).

Gillespie and company selected 2 episodes from the 85 they intended to deliver — episodes 18 and 87 — "the two hardest shows in the series," they said. Why those two? Because, Henry explained, those are the talkiest, most complicated shows of all. If Ladd can handle those two successfully, he can handle anything! (Sounded formidable! But — if there were only 85 shows in the series — how can there be an episode 87? Answer: Frank Entertainment actually acquired over 100 episodes, only 85 of which made it to Western screens — *Battle* episode #85 is actually *Gatchaman #101.*)

Through our California company Sparklin' Entertainment, we recorded our version of how we thought *G-Force* episodes 18 and 87 should look and sound, and delivered them to Turner via Crawford Communications, Turner's production arm in Atlanta. Literally within days we were greenlit to go ahead with *G-Force* the series. Again, how sweet it was!

Full production of the series as *G-Force* began in the fall of 1986. During this same period, our sister production company, Entercolor Technologies Corporation, was converting the classic, black-and-white *Popeye* series to color. The work of Sparklin' Entertainment did not conflict with the work of Entercolor; both series were leaving our shops concurrently, with our particular stamp upon them, and we felt we were making genuine contributions to the genre of animation.

A New *Gigantor*

Mitsuteru Yokoyama, creator of the giant robot that he called *Tetsujin 28,* authorized giant advertising agency Dentsu, circa 1962, to produce an animated television series based upon his property. Dentsu did. The agency hired Television Corporation of Japan (TCJ) to animate the series, 96 black-and-white programs, 52 of which were later acquired by Delphi Associates, Inc., to dub and distribute — as *Gigantor*— in English-speaking territories around the world.

Less than twenty years later, in 1980, TCJ's rival, Tokyo Movie Shinsha (TMS) went to Yokoyama with a proposal that TMS be licensed to produce a *new* series based upon *Tetsujin 28*—but this new series would, first of all, be filmed in color and, in addition, would feature a new, updated robot, *Shin* (New, High-Tech) *Tetsujin 28.* The artist liked the idea, approved the new character designs, and TMS produced a series of 51 episodes. (Fifty-two would ordinarily be the number of episodes for network television, but the program was preempted for a week in Tokyo, so TMS produced no program for that week.)

As expected, the then-president of TMS, one Yutaka Fujioka, called me from his hotel in Los Angeles one afternoon, inviting me to join him for tea. I accepted, certain that Fujioka-San intended to pitch his new *Shin Tetsujin 28* series. Actually, I welcomed the opportunity; I was eager to see this new show, with the idea of acquiring English-language rights. After viewing an episode in the hotel, though, I was most disappointed. The redesigned robot now had a more human form — that was okay — but, instead of having a benign, friendly face, like its predecessor's, the new figure had a stern, *menacing* visage — threatening, and with eyes that had no pupils, just snake-like yellow slits! The new mecha looked like one of the sinister enemy robots that Gigantor always fights!

I thanked Fujioka-San for his hospitality and told him I'd think over the possibility of joining TMS in exploiting the new series. In fact, I knew upon leaving the hotel that I had no further interest in the new series at all. Fujioka himself may have sensed that disinterest.

During the next twelve years, the series languished as no one showed any interest in producing an English-language version. Then, in 1992, TMS's bright and ingratiating new sales manager in Los Angeles, Andrew R. ("Andy") Berman, began a low-key, but steady, campaign to win me over.

Apparently a born optimist, Berman pointed out the *positive* aspects of having a "new" color series with the famous name *Gigantor* in the title. He brushed aside complaints about the robot's cold, unfriendly stare. He saw compensating values in the characters that surrounded the robot. Finally, he started me thinking that maybe, *maybe,* if the robot's young master — "Jimmy Sparks" — kept addressing the robot in warm, friendly terms ... and if, every time the robot appeared, we'd hear his famous theme song — well, maybe we could recapture the *Gigantor* magic of old.

At last, Andy Berman wore me down. He, on behalf of TMS, and I agreed that we'd attempt a pilot episode. I selected episode 5, *Invisible Robot;* in that adventure, Gigantor takes on a robot that alternately appears and disappears at his inventor's whim! The inventor himself is an eccentric figure, but is whimsically, *humorously* eccentric. I thought that could be fun (and, indeed, it was fun to write flighty, sardonic dialogue for that character).

In the sound studio several days later, as we recorded the English dialogue and added music that had been created some thirty years earlier for the original *Gigantor* series, I was not at all certain that we were succeeding in our mission. I had doubts. Every time I saw the new robot's stern, intimidating face, I thought that *Shin Tetsujin 28* is *not* your "friendly, neighborhood robot," and is *not* Gigantor.

I was mistaken. Seeing the show afterward, in its completed form, with opening and closing titles, and with all the popular music cues in place, I was surprised to see how effectively the cold, stern-looking new robot took on the warmth, the friendliness, of the old Gigantor, the Gigantor that everybody knew and loved.

We — Andy Berman, TMS's top executives, and I premiered the pilot in January 1993 in New Orleans, at the annual convention of the National Association of Television Program Executives (NATPE). A young fellow named

Tom Vitale had been walking the aisles from exhibit to exhibit when he suddenly heard a theme song that he recognized — not only recognized, but cherished from the days of his childhood. It was the *Gigantor* theme song. Tracking the music to its source, he found it emanating from the TMS exhibit. There, he was confronted by a poster of a powerful giant robot staring at him. "That's Gigantor!" Vitale said; he explained that he would be creating a block of children's programs on the Science Fiction Channel in a matter of weeks and that *Gigantor* would be perfect as the locomotive that pulls that block along.

I thought, Vitale recognized the theme song, he knew immediately that *Shin Tetsujin 28*, a new robot on the horizon, was *Gigantor,* he wanted this upcoming series, not yet adapted or dubbed, as "the *locomotive*" for his train of children's shows coming to the Sci-Fi Channel... Andy Berman was right!

The New Adventures of Gigantor began running on the Science Fiction Channel in September 1993, and it ran till January 7, 1997 — a four-year run. The lesson, if any, is that, when it comes to reacting to drama on a screen, the ear can be as persuasive as the eye.

CHAPTER 10

Sailor Moon

DIC (pronounced *deek*) is a Hollywood-area animation studio, well known for television series such as *Inspector Gadget* and *Where in the World Is Carmen Sandiego?* Unlike its neighbor Walt Disney Studios, which animates its own shows on its own lot, DIC sends its shows to a studio in Japan to be animated. The resultant product is considered to be American animation rendered abroad; it is not anime.

One day, DIC president Andy Heyward came across a television series animated by Toei Co., Ltd., a new series that was not only anime, but *highly exciting, highly successful* anime. In Tokyo, a young lady named Naoko Takeuchi had created a manga called *Sailor Moon* (so-called because its young heroine sails to Earth from her home on the moon); the manga had already become a sensation and was generating millions of dollars in merchandising income in Japan and Europe. As DIC executive vice president Robby London noted at the time in an interview with Harvey Deneroff, "*Sailor Moon* is based on a toy line that is, without question, the hottest toy line that has ever hit Japan — $100 million just in Japan in the last year since it has come out. Subsequently, the show that's based on it has been sold in many territories, including several European ones, and everywhere it has been on, it has just been phenomenally successful."

Heyward acquired rights to the anime property through a huge publisher called Kodansha; he agreed to abide by their terms and thought that DIC — being accustomed to receiving animation from Japan — would have no difficulty at all in adapting *Sailor Moon* to Western tastes. That was inaccurate. Kodansha proved to be a strict customer to deal with, and the show, as elements arrived from Toei, had several built-in hurdles that DIC had never before encountered.

First, the shows were too long — more than a minute too long. The Japanese format allowed for two commercials to be inserted into each program's running length — DIC needed three. Next, many episodes contained scenes of extreme violence that, of course, had to be cut; but, by agreement, any material alteration to a program could be made only with the permission of Kodansha. Third, the series would be dubbed in Canada, a procedure that was new to DIC and not without its own special problems.

Recognizing that the studio needed help in coping with those unfamiliar conditions, DIC sought the assistance of Carl Macek, who had done a noteworthy job of adapting the *Robotech* series. Macek completed the first few episodes, then left; I took over the rest of the series of 65 episodes in April 1995, after seeing the engaging cast of characters created by Naoko Takeuchi and being thoroughly charmed by them.

"What great characters these are," I thought, "they are so *human*." Naoko Takeuchi understands *people*. She has created a group of young (14-year-old) high school girls that are *real,* with real passions for teen fashions, food crazes, real teen interest in their assorted high school classmates ("smart" vs. "dorky"), teenage interests in their maturing bodies, girls' interests in boys — the characters were three dimensional; they had depth. How different these characters were from those I had just seen in a pilot for a new series I was asked to join, a series to be called *Ronin Warriors*. Characters in that series, I felt, were typically two-dimensional *cartoon* characters, doing what they had to do in order to advance the plot, but lacking any real depth or humanity.

Sailor Moon came along like a tonic at the right time. The project, though challenging, was fun. Cutting the programs down to the required running length for U.S. standards was the easiest task. I had faced the same situation with *G-Force* and had developed a "feel" for where a moment of suspense, near a program's climax, could easily accommodate a final "word from our sponsor." Inherent violence at that spot — invariably, violence was implied there — then became easier to delete (without affecting the plot).

As for violence itself, I had never seen any to match that in *Sailor Moon*. I had been astounded from the start to see cruelty to children portrayed so graphically in what was, in fact, a kids' show! In one early episode, an enormous plant (ostensibly from outer space) grabs a child around the throat and begins choking her — deleted! In another episode, a similar choking results in a child being lifted into the air, eyes bulging — deleted!

By far the greatest incidence of implied violence came in two consecutive episodes — the now famous episodes 45 and 46. In these, our young heroine, Serena (who is Sailor Moon), lies on the ground at night, cowering while her beloved boyfriend, Darian (Tuxedo Mask) — while bewitched — holds a sword over Serena's head, ready to behead her! (This, in a children's show!)

So much screen time is taken in both episodes with that threatened cruelty that the only way to air the episodes in the Americas was to delete all the objectionable shots in both shows, then, combine the foreshortened shows into a single episode. DIC's editors thought that could not be done; the task was regarded as impossible. In fact, we *did* get it done; we cut or trimmed every shot showing the naked sword in the young man's hand; that did a lot to de-stigmatize the cruelty. Then we had the adapters in Canada craft the dialogue so that no mention — or even *suggestion*— of death was made by either character in the sequence. (With dubbing, that can be done.)

Kodansha was kept informed of our proceedings from the very start; after all, they would have to take a stand in any event. At worst, DIC would have had to reject episodes 45 and 46 as Not-Fit-For-Air, and seek some kind of remedy. As things turned out, Kodansha was quite understanding. They did approve, in principle, the merging of the two problem episodes, did approve the final cut, and did work out an adjustment with DIC.

The dubbing process for the series took place in Mississauga/Toronto, Canada. Rates are lower in Canada and, in addition, Canadian content (i.e., participation of Canadian talent) is essential for having one's programs broadcast in that territory. *Sailor Moon* did play Canada and was hugely successful there. *Sailor Moon* fans were — and are — ubiquitous!

Creation of the English-language version began when my cut of an episode, together with my notes as approved by DIC, were handed to Los Angeles–based writer Marcia Moran. Marcia would then write a continuity based upon the Japanese dialogue from DIC's point of view, which included use of current "hip" phrases and terms popular with North American teenagers. (The characters in the Japanese version were understood to use terms and phrases popular with teenagers in Japan). (*Altered by us: Serena, baby-sitting for a child that she thinks is a little girl, discovers it's a boy—"Eek! She's got a [penis]!" Changed to: Eek! This girl is a boy!*)

Next, the elements needed for dubbing were shipped to Toronto, to Optimum Productions, where Optimum's writers took over, writing the lip-sync version of the dialogue. DIC also sent several musical selections to be used in preparation of the soundtrack. Performers selected by Optimum and DIC personnel then recorded the dialogue, the dialogue was blended with music — and the final edition of the show was returned to DIC for distribution.

When *Sailor Moon* debuted on the local Fox station in Los Angeles in September 1995 those of us associated with the series felt that all had gone rather well. We were not happy, though, with the timeslot in which the program was broadcast — early morning, when children are in school or on the school bus — but we recognized that more favorable after-school timeslots had been committed many seasons earlier. What astonished us was that, schedules permitting, many mothers were watching the series along with their daughters; the show's demographics indicated that *Sailor Moon* was cutting across age lines — rare for a children's program.

For years after the series' premiere, teenage girls were coming to anime fairs and conventions dressed as Serena, their beloved Sailor Moon. And cadres of highly vocal fans were on hand to protest that — surprise!— they *did* know that episodes 45 and 46 had been combined! They knew, because they had the Japanese and Chinese home video editions of the series, and they saw the difference! (Our explanations of DIC's dilemma, the need for DIC to either (1) cut the violence, or (2) see the offending episodes rejected by broadcast-ers, helped defuse the fans' protest ... somewhat.)

As aforementioned, *Sailor Moon,* the anime series produced by Toei, actually consisted of three separate story arcs. The first (65 episodes) arc was acquired by DIC for television. The other two arcs, *Sailor Moon-R* and *Sailor Moon-S,* have been released to home video on DVD.

(*Note:* In *Sailor Moon,* as in *Astro Boy* fifteen years earlier, the classical Japanese mode of storytelling prevailed; characters — even Astro Boy and Sailor Moon—do not live forever. They are *mortal.* At the end of their tale, they die.)

So it was that, at the end of the mid-story arc, Serena (Sailor Moon*)* and her friends from outer space, all die. But fear not — all are miraculously restored, just in time for the next dramatic story arc!

CHAPTER 11

ANIMEnia! The "New" Industry Blooms — Overnight!

Much has been said and written about how Osamu Tezuka, *Manga no kamisama* (the "god of comics") and bearer of the title "The Walt Disney of Japan," originated the art form that today is hailed as anime. His first studio, Mushi Production, was the first in Japan to be erected and dedicated specifically to the production of weekly animated television programs for children.

The only other comparable producer in the world at the time was California's Hanna-Barbera Studios. William "Bill" Hanna and Joseph Barbara had been animators employed by the MGM Animation Studios to animate short subjects for theaters — at the rate of six a year. Their own cartoon "stars" were the famous cat-and-mouse team of Tom and Jerry. (They also produced another six or so cartoons directed by other MGM animators.)

With the mid-century U.S. advent of national television, and the concurrent decline of MGM animation, Hanna and Barbera set up their own studio in North Hollywood and soon were delivering animated children's programs at the rate of one half-hour show per week, per series! That is approximately the same as what Osamu Tezuka achieved a few years later in Tokyo: *his* cartoon star was Tetsuan Atom and his Mushi Production was built expressly to deliver thirty minutes of serialized animated adventure per week.

(*Note:* six months before *Tetsuan Atom* hit the airwaves on January 1, 1963, an animated series called *Otogi Manga Calendar* (*Calendar of Manga Stories*) had begun airing in Japan. But *Calendar* was a series of unrelated five-minute stories about great moments in Japan's history. The series did not compare in stature or in scope with Tezuka's trailblazing achievement six months later.)

An old saw in Hollywood is: "Let one writer sell an idea for a musical western and, the next day, a hundred writers are walking around out there with pitches for musical westerns." That is what happened in Tokyo when Mushi sold America's NBC Enterprises its *Tetsuan Atom* series. Japanese entrepreneurs who had never considered venturing into the film business before suddenly pounced upon the notion of latching onto "something new!"—animated children's programs! The scramble was on to get a new studio up and running before anyone else in Tokyo came up with the same idea!

Starting a new studio from scratch, in 1962, was a feat easier said than done. Japan was still struggling to recover from the devastation of World War II. Filmmaking in any era is not for the faint of heart; at that time, in Japan, the odds were especially heavy against the filmmaker. The Japanese government made it difficult to send dollars abroad ("export dollars") to buy equipment or supplies; every dollar was needed at home to help rebuild the country. Businessmen traveling abroad were required to obtain special visas. Not surprisingly, then, many would-be filmmakers turned to relatively inexpensive animation to express their visions, and the model of a strong American distributor (like NBC) guaranteeing substantial advances, plus ongoing royalties, enabled a few astute entrepreneurs to finance new animation studios.

Television Corporation of Japan (TCJ)

One of the first such studios to rise was TCJ, the Television Corporation of Japan. Its president, H. Murata, established strong ties with Dentsu, the huge advertising agency that not only had plenty of yen to invest — they had also, astutely, obtained licenses from the nation's leading cartoonists to produce animated versions of those cartoonists' manga.

All were eager to duplicate Tezuka's success. Tezuka himself, however, turned his back on Dentsu. He reasoned that he did not need or desire the manga of other artists; he would animate his own characters. (This was also the position of Hanna-Barbera Studios; they had their own characters to promote and had no interest in licensing characters from any other source.) So, with barely enough animators or animation trainees aboard, and pushed by Dentsu to get started, TCJ sprang into action. Their initial series included:

8th Man. From the team of science-fiction writer Kazumasa Hirai and artist Jiro Kuwata, Dentsu obtained rights to create an anime series based upon a manga that first appeared on a weekly basis in April 1963, just a few months after the debut of *Tetsuan Atom* on television. The manga, described earlier, was based upon the character Rachiro Azuma, eighth man on a metropolitan police detective squad — a super sleuth gunned down by a vicious criminal named Mukade. Left for dead, Azuma is painstakingly reconstructed by brilliant doctor Tani (our "Doctor Genius") as an unstoppable, indestructible humanoid robot that goes on to become a super powerful crime fighter.

Tetsujin 28. Created by the artist Mitsuteru Yokoyama, licensed by Dentsu through the artist's company, Hikari (in English, Light). *Tetsujin 28* literally means *Iron Man #28.* Our name for him is *Gigantor.* TCJ, starting in 1963, produced 96 episodes in black and white; however, seventeen years later (1980), the artist gave a different studio, TMS, the rights to produce a color remake called *Shin Tetsujin 28.* And, in 1992, the artist authorized TMS to make yet another color series, this one to be called *Tetsujin 28 FX.* The robot in the *FX* series is many times taller than earlier models, it can transform (in keeping with the trend at the time for transforming robots), but — if not for its distinctive Trojan helmet — FX is hardly recognizable as #28 or Gigantor. The boy (our Jimmy Sparks) is now an adult. This series has not been *Gigantor*-ized; it performed poorly in ratings in Japan.

Prince Planet. Yet another collaboration between TCJ and Dentsu (1965), this 52-episode, black-and-white series was televised in Japan as *Yuset Shonen Papii.* Papii is a preteen boy from a planet in the far reaches of outer space; he is sent to Earth by a galactic authority (shades of Tezuka's "W3!") to convince Earth to join a federation of peaceful planets. Papii's spaceship crashes in the American Southwest, but Papii survives, meets a girl with eyes as outsized as his own (both characters have enormous, button-like eyes, reflecting Tezuka's influence as demonstrated in *Tetsuan Atom*), and together they set out to fight against crime and evil on this planet. Papii's weapon is an atomic-powered pendant, which gives him great power, but in fact Papii eschews that power much of the time and, instead, tries to use his powers of *persuasion* to overcome his foes. U.S. distributor American-International Pictures made use of the letter *P* on Papii's pendant to coin the name Prince Planet. Distribution, though, was spotty. The series never seemed to catch on in the Western Hemisphere.

TCJ Studio has undergone some reorganization over the years and now is known as Eiken.

Tatsunoko Production

Artist Tatsuo Yoshida began his career as an illustrator in Kyoto, Japan, then moved to Tokyo and began drawing manga. One of his strips, *Iron Arm Rikiya* (recall that Osamu Tezuka's robot series *Tetsuan Atom* translates as "Iron Arm"), and another strip called *Ninja Squad Moonlight* soon rose to the top. Demand for Yoshida's work grew quickly; it swelled to the point where he summoned his two brothers, Kenji and Toyoharu (the latter uses the pen name Ippei Kuri), to help him. Together, the three brothers formed a studio that they called Tatsunoko Production, and a little seahorse became their logo.

The month was October, the year was 1962. Tezuka had formed his Mushi Production to animate his manga characters for television and Tatsuo Yoshida decided that Tatsunoko would follow Mushi's lead: Tatsunoko adapted its manga into moving images.

Space Ace. Tatsunoko's first anime as detailed earlier, this was clearly inspired by Tezuka's *Tetsuan Atom.* Its hero is a little boy, albeit a real boy from space — not a robot imitation of a boy. Ace's weapon of choice is a boomerang-like ring that delivers a glancing blow. Though as a (black-and-white) rerendered in color pilot renamed *Ring-O,* the show did not land a television commitment in America, the program did go on in Japan to become a 52-episode series that firmly establish Tatsunoko as a major player.

Speed Racer. Described in detail earlier, this 52-episode, 1967 color series will surely go down in history as Tatsunoko's pièce-de-résistance. Even fans of animation in the Americas, fans who are not particularly fans of anime, seem to look back on this series with affection.

Virtually unknown, though, even by the show's most ardent admirers, is its erratic pattern of distribution in the United States: (1) *Speed Racer* was initially distributed to independent television stations by Trans-Lux, distributors of *Gigantor* as well. In time, (2) Trans-Lux shut down its distribution and turned over all its series to a firm called Alan Enterprises. Thereafter, (3) Alan (Gleitzman) turned over all his properties (except *Gigantor*) to a "colorization" company called Color Systems Technologies; (4) they, in turn, sold out to Broadway Video, owned by Lorne Michaels, producer of NBC Network's *Saturday Night Live*; and, finally, (5) *Speed Racer* was acquired from Broadway Video by a licensing firm known as Speed Racer Enterprises! That, surely, is one labyrinthine chain of title!

Gatchaman. A top animator for Tezuka's Mushi Production, one Sadao Miyamoto, went from Mushi to Tatsunoko Production and became animation director for a new series then in the planning stage, *Science Ninja Team Gatchaman.* That series, planned initially to run for 53 episodes, premiered on the Fuji Network on October 1, 1972, and immediately became so successful, with its realistic styling, its portrayal of human characters, its fine animation, and its inventive use of color, that it was extended to 105 episodes by the end of its second year on the air.

Sadly, founder Tatsuo Yoshida died in September 1977. Brother Kenji took over, saw the *Gatchaman* television franchise extend into *Gatchaman II,* then, into a radio series, and, after that, into a feature film (made essentially of sequences made for television) and even a third television series of 48 adventures (October 1979) called *Science Ninja Team Gatchaman Fighter!* Series II and III were brought to America, not by Sandy Frank Film Syndication, Inc. (Frank had acquired only Series 1, his *Battle of the Planets*) but by a firm called Saban International. Saban combined all the acquired episodes into a single 65-program package and released it in the USA as *Saban's Eagle Riders.*

Tekkaman the Space Knight. As Tatsunoko's *Uchu no Kishi Tekkaman,* produced in 1975 — following *Gatchaman* by three years — this series was designed to show man's trek into the solar system, seeking habitable planets to conquer and colonize. The premise was that Earth, Mars, Jupiter, and Saturn were already overcrowded under man's dominion; now mankind had turned its eyes on the planet Uranus. To get there, a UN space agency appoints Joji Minami, a cocky teenage pilot, to command the spacecraft *Blue Earth.* Joji, in knightly fashion, wears protective armor made of "miracle" alloy Tekka (hence, he is dubbed "Tekkaman"); his lance-like weapon is the Tekkalance; and his knightly steed is a robotic vehicle named Pegase (probably after the mythical stallion Pegasus). So armored and equipped, "Tekkaman" goes where no "Gatchaman" has gone before!

(*Note:* the five scouts of *Science Ninja Team Gatchaman,* despite the spatial title *Battle of the Planets* conceived by its American distributor, never went into space — they were earthbound! Their ship, the Phoenix, was designed specifically to perform in earth's atmosphere; in space — if it could ever get there — the Phoenix would be a duck out of water.)

Trouble rears its ugly head when Joji Minami ("Tekkaman") and a crew member, the beautiful Miss Hiromi Amachi (whose father had sent Joji's father to his death!), learn that they are not the first to set foot on Uranus; evil Waldstar aliens, searching for an inhabitable planet of their own, confront them!

How this confrontation is resolved never becomes known. William Winckler, a young entrepreneur who acquired 13 (of 26) planned *Tekkaman* episodes, and who cowrote the English adaptations in Los Angeles with fan-author Fred Patten, learned that the series had been cancelled midway in Japan. Such cancellations, though not unusual in the United States, are extremely rare in Japan. Reports from Tokyo indicated that the *Tekkaman* series suffered from a lack of personnel and resources at Tatsunoko.

Tekkaman the Space Knight opened in Toronto, Canada, in September 1984, but it saw few sales after that. Tatsunono Studio, however, had more to say later about the concept and resolution of complex plot issues raised in *Tekkaman.* The studio followed up eighteen years later with a sequel of sorts — a series that was a sound-alike of *Tekkaman,* yet different enough to suggest its own American variation, namely, *Teknoman.*

Teknoman. Produced by Tatsunoko in 1992 as *Space Knight Tekkaman Blade,* this series acknowledged its predecessor, and it was clearly a continuation of series past (recall Tatsunoko's *Gatchaman* series evolving later into *Gatchaman Fighter*). In this sequel to *Tekkaman*, defenders of planet Earth are still called Space Knights and their spaceship is still the *Blue Earth,* but the hero of this epic is called D-Boy. He is a mysterious, shadowy figure (recall Racer X of *Speed Racer*) who appears in time to help Earth fend off an invasion by spidery space aliens (D-Boy, in this regard, is not unlike *Gatchaman*'s Red Impulse character who consistently arrives in time to help fight the enemy, Galactor. Unusual, mystery characters like these became a kind of trademark of Tatsunoko).

Nifty plot twists in this series include: (a) D-Boy arrives to help Earth in its epic struggle, but is mistrusted by Earth forces because they encounter more than one Tekkaman out there — and the others are evil! (b) The spacesuit/armor made of Tekka alloy turns out to have a Jekyll-and-Hyde split personality — a good side, and a bad side. He who dons it is well protected *for a brief period*, but, keep it on too long and the unsuspecting wearer becomes evil! (D-Boy's secret is that he knows, Cinderella-like, exactly when he must shed that armor.) In battle, however, he may not be able to shed it in time! (c) D-Boy, like Joji Minami before him, has an emerald crystal that he uses to change into his armor but, when that crystal is broken in a struggle with an *evil* Tekkaman, D-Boy uses backup protection built into his robot steed Pegase and dons the armor.

Another intriguing concept: Earth in the future has an orbital ring like Saturn's. Space aliens use the ring as a platform from which to rain destruction down upon Earth!

Teknoman was distributed in 1995 to independent television stations in the USA not by William Winckler, who had handled the foreshortened *Tekkaman* series, but by Saban Entertainment, Inc., distributors of Tatsunoko's earlier *Science Ninja Team Gatchaman Fighter*.

(*Note:* Many talented voice actors in New York City and in Los Angeles typically perform in various animated productions without their voices being easily recognized. Barbara Goodson and Tom Wyner, for example, both heard in *Tecknoman,* also played very different roles in *The NEW Adventures of Gigantor*. Miss Goodson, the voice of beautiful Star Summers in *Teknoman,* is also the voice of young master Jimmy Sparks in *NEW Gigantor*; and Tom Wyner, the comic voice of Inspector Blooper in *NEW Gigantor,* is also *Tecknoman*'s mechanical Teknobot.)

Also from Tatsunoko Production were the aforementioned *Robotech* (1985) (all three chapters) and *Samurai Pizza Cats* (1996), plus home video titles *Casshan Robot Hunter* (1995), *Tekkaman Blade II* (1998), *Generator Gawl* (2000), and *Soul Taker* (2001).

Tokyo Movie Shinsha (TMS)

This studio, among others, also opened its doors in the early 1960s and, although little known in the West, it is a major player on the anime scene in Tokyo. The late president Yutaka Fujioka, like Osamu Tezuka, began his operation as a cottage industry, with several artists working at home. He sold a black-and-white television series called *Big X* (actually conceived, but not animated, by Osamu Tezuka!) in 1964, in which a young boy is unintentionally irradiated by criminals who have a "growth gun"—a little cannon-like device that projects a beam of energized light—and the boy suddenly zooms to huge proportions, with muscles bulging enough to turn an American superhero green with envy! The boy becomes Big X, feared by criminals throughout the land!

From that modest beginning, TMS grew quickly in size and in skill. Switching to color after 1965, the studio soon produced a series called *Cobra!* in which their animation technique had become so sophisticated that it caught the eye of studio executives in California. TMS was called upon to produce television animation on a subcontract basis for a number of Hollywood studios, including Disney. Fujioka-San acquired rights to Winsor McCay's classic American comic strip, *Little Nemo in Slumberland*, with the idea of making it into a major movie; he saw the project as a way to propel TMS overnight into a studio with the stature of Disney itself. To supervise the project, he approached American producer Gary Kurtz, an avid animation and McCay fan who had produced Episodes 4 and 5 of *Star Wars* for George Lucas. (The production of *Little Nemo* became something of a legend in its own time, and the film, from which Kurtz later angrily resigned, would eventually leave TMS all but bankrupt. Needless to say, this turbulent episode could surely make a book unto itself.)

Around this time, in the spring of 1980, Hollywood's Filmation Studio received an order from CBS Television for a Saturday morning series based upon the famous character of Zorro. The CBS order came in May of 1980, too late for Filmation to meet CBS's scheduled September start. This writer, at Filmation's request for help, brought Mr. Fujioka to the Hollywood studio. Executives there were impressed with the quality of *Cobra* and a deal was struck for TMS to produce animation for the *Zorro* series in Tokyo. The resultant product was, of course, not anime; TMS, however, gained great experience in producing animation to international standards, and that experience was put to good use when TMS began work on the *Little Nemo* feature not just in Tokyo, but also in Hollywood.

Even as production was starting on *Little Nemo* in America, TMS Tokyo launched its color television series *Shin Tetsujin 28*, later to become *The*

NEW Adventures of Gigantor, described earlier. Indeed, all the finesse and skill that the studio had acquired in the months and years leading up to the beginning of shooting on *Shin Tetsujin 28* paid off: Production values were first-rate.

Also from TMS: (1) animated feature-length adventures of *Lupin the Third,* the charming gentleman burglar drawn as manga by artist Kazuhiko Kato (aka *Monkey Punch*) from the writings of French author Maurice LeBlanc; (2) the television series *Sonic X,* seen on Fox; (3) *Hamtaro,* and (4) the television version of *Lupin,* both of which have been seen on America's Cartoon Network.

Were the late Yutaka Fujioka alive today, TMS's former president would quite likely say that TMS's greatest triumph, its masterpiece, its crowning achievement, was the feature film *Little Nemo.* From a purely artistic point of view, Mr. Fujioka might have been right. After all, the story is an American classic and famed American animation director Bill Hurtz was placed in charge of production. Hurtz hired the best Hollywood animators he could find, made the animators comfortable in quarters located in the very heart of Hollywood, and spared no expense whatever (indeed, expenses were formidable) to make everything the best. The score for the completed production was performed by the London Symphony Orchestra. But when the picture was completed and it opened in the USA in 1992 amid great expectations, it lost money.

No major distributor would handle *Little Nemo.* The film was distributed on a scaled-down basis to less influential theater chains. It made the rounds quickly, and then disappeared from theater screens. By the start of the 21st century, *Little Nemo* was scarcely remembered in the Americas.

What *will* be remembered is that every anime series up to 1985 had been distributed by syndication; that is, sold to non-network, independent stations. But TMS's series *Galaxy High* was sold to a *network*—CBS—in 1985–86, smashing a precedent of distribution by syndication that had been in existence since *Astro Boy* landed on American shores in 1963.

And, in 1989, TMS's reputation for quality animation resulted in that studio's being awarded the contract to animate the adventures of *Peter Pan,* the series that launched the Fox Kids' Television Network!

When I congratulated Fujioka-san upon hearing that TMS had won the contract to animate *Peter Pan,* he thanked me, but said TMS would prefer to work on its own series—like *Galaxy High*—not just animate somebody else's property. "But you *accepted* the Fox assignment," I reminded him. "Yes," he replied; "TMS has a *right* pocket and a *left* pocket; the work for Fox will be done out of the *left* pocket."

Toei Doga

Much has been said, and written herein, about Toei Doga (Animation), the pioneering anime studio, Japan's first. After sending America one of its first postwar animated features, *Alakazam the Great* in 1961, Toei went on to produce several more animated features, in addition to those already named, to play in its own theaters in Japan: *Thumbelina, Fables from Hans Christian Andersen, Nobody's Boy, Samurai Express, Twelve Months, The Golden Bird,* and *The Great Adventures of Pelican Cuttakun,* to name but a few. With a steady diet of features, it is small wonder that Toei's Animation Department was considered as simply a special branch of the Feature Department. In general, those features were made for domestic, not foreign, consumption. They have had little exposure in the Americas, and have had no impact, to speak of, upon Western tastes for anime features.

With Toei's television series, however, it's a much different story. Toei Doga's chief, Chiaki Imada, bristled at the idea of "his" animation studio being considered as just an extension of Toei's Feature Department, or International Department, or any other department. Imada-San considered Toei's animation studio to be his turf — he wanted the freedom to run the studio as he saw fit. What he saw was Osamu Tezuka, once a collaborator with Toei Doga on its animated features, now selling America Tezuka's own television series. It was only a matter of time before Toei Doga joined the fray; Chiaki Imada would create *and sell* Doga's own anime. These included:

Force Five. This 1980 series is actually a collection of five different series produced under Mr. Imada — *Dangard Ace, Gaiking, Grandizer, Spacekeeters,* and *Starvengers.* A common story thread runs throughout every part of the series, that is, sooner or later a giant robot appears and becomes an integral part of the conflict. Giant robots were a favorite theme at Toei.

In *Dangard Ace,* created as *Wakusei Robo* in 1977 by Toei stalwart Leiji Matsumoto, Earth discovers a new planet called Promete. The planet is perfect for colonization, a haven for those seeking refuge from overcrowded planet Earth (a concept not unlike Tatsunoko's aborted *Tekkaman* series of 1975). Predictably, a ruthless space empire discovers Promete at the same time as the earthlings. A race is on, to colonize Promete first. *Dangard Ace* is a giant robot warship that fights off Earth's enemies!

In *Grandizer,* created as *UFO Robot Grandizer* by Go Nagai in 1975, and in *Starvengers,* created as *Getta-Robo G* by Go Nagai in 1977, giant robots are heroes who fight to defend Earth against space invaders who have come to attack us with their own giant robots.

Gaiking was created as *Ozora Maryu* in 1976; and *Spacekeeters,* as *SF Sayuki* in 1978 — the latter, again by the prolific Leiji Matsumoto.

(*Note:* In this period, Toei creators Leiji Matsumoto and Go Nagai were young men in the early stages of their careers, with Nagai being widely credited as the originator of the giant robot.)

As packaged in Los Angeles by independent producer Jim Terry, the emphasis in all five sections of *Force Five* is on giant robots. The concept of combining separate sections of seemingly unrelated, but similar, series would later be used by American Carl Macek in the milestone anime series *Robotech*.

Voltron: Defender of the Universe. This series is an assembly of two separate subseries animated by Toei: (1) a 52-episode group created circa 1981 as *Hyakuja-O Go-Lion*, and (2) a 56-episode group created circa 1982 as *Kiko Kantai Dairugger-XV.* Both subseries deal with a planet Earth of the future; integrating the two series was natural. One writer on the project was Jameson Brewer, who would later become the adapter of *Battle of the Planets.*

The premise of the first *Voltron* subseries: Earth is headquarters for a federation of planets, all craving peace but nonetheless prepared for intergalactic battle, if that should come. A team of five young explorers set out from Earth to Arus, a planet known to be devastated in spite of an incredible defense weapon consisting of five robot lions — lions that can merge into a single super-robot called Voltron. This super-robot, resembling a medieval knight with the stylized helmet of a lion, was believed to be invincible; but, in fact, it proved no match for the forces of a reptile king from a distant galaxy. (Oddly, Toei artists drew the reptile in the clothing of a colonial French courtier.)

The five young explorers discover that there's a princess on Aurus, Princess Allura, who had survived the attack by the reptile king. The earthmen vow to help the princess regain control of Arus. They do this by becoming instant pilots of the robot lions, and fighting battle after battle against the hordes of the reptile king!

Premise of the second subseries: Years have passed. The reptile king and his legions have been wiped out. Victorious, our five intrepid explorers have returned to Earth with the Voltron technology; now they use it to build a bigger, better Voltron — this one, composed of 15 (instead of five) smaller robots — from land, sea, and air. So armed, the 15 young explorers from Earth set out again — this time, with their supersized Voltron, seeking a planet suitable for mankind to inhabit. Too late, they discover that they are being followed on their quest — followed by a band of Drules whose planet is dying. (Drules don't find their own planets — like hyenas that live on spoils left behind by lions, Drules try to wrest away newfound planets from discoverers.) Drules are scavengers.

Surprise ending: In a style of ending rare for an anime series, Toei planners have Drule commander Hazar come to realize the folly, the futility of Drule ways. He sees that it is hopeless to fight the raw elements of new planets and, at the some time, wage battle against the human discoverers who found the new planets in the first place. Hazar explains his reasoning to the Drule emperor but, instead of being rewarded for his insight, Hazar is thrown into prison and accused of treason!

Later, he escapes. He joins a popular revolt against the emperor and the emperor's government, but, suddenly, the planet Drule begins to shake. It is going to self-destruct! Team Voltron arrives on the scene just in time to rescue the worthy citizens of Drule mere moments before that doomed planet explodes!

Only from Japan!

Teknoman, Force Five, Voltron — these series are reviewed here in considerable detail to illustrate how complex they, and other series in their genre, are, in content matter. These are tales of science fiction — edgy, intricate, apocalyptic — often peopled by heroes who demonstrate surprising character flaws, flaws normally associated with villains — all this, intended as *children's fare!* Nowhere in "kids' shows" made in the Americas or in Europe does one find such anti-heroic heroes or such mature sci-fi plots and subplots. Only from Japan!

Voltron proved to be heady but compelling stuff for what is purported to be a show for (Japanese) children. The series was brought to the United States and syndicated by World Events Productions. Of the two subseries, the second one — dubbed *Vehicle Team Voltron* — was the less popular; the first of the two subseries, called *Lion Force Voltron*, was more popular by far — so popular, in fact, that the distributor went back to Toei and commissioned the production of more episodes. By series' end, there were 125 completed *Voltron* shows "in the can." That is success by any standard.

Other Places, Other Faces

Besides those studios in Tokyo that blossomed in the wake of Osamu Tezuka's pioneering Mushi Production, and became major players in their own right, as spotlighted previously, a number of others arose whose names are little known in the Americas — even among many industry professionals — yet whose works nonetheless are famous.

Shogakukan is certainly not a household word in the West; nor, as a

Japanese name, does it have the zip of a *Toei*, a *Mushi*, or even a *TCJ*. But Shogakukan in Japan is huge. Shogakukan Production Co. is a major publisher that exploded on the anime scene in 1996 when it introduced a title called *Pokémon*.

Pokémon. Pokémon is actually a contraction of two English words — "pocket" and "monsters." The term "Pocket Monsters" itself conjures up a smile-inducing image of diminutive horrible creatures. One immediately wonders how horrible can these tiny monsters *be*? If they fit into a pocket, aren't they cute, adorable, and ideal little pets?

In Japan, the word "monster" connotes an imaginary creature, not necessarily a fearsome beast. A leprechaun can be a monster; an elf can be a monster. So the idea of a teeny-tiny creature that snuggles into one's pocket ("aw-w-w, isn't that *cute*?") can be charming and disarming.

Just as Hollywood's Hanna-Barbera Studio once made a cartoon series based upon a video game, *Pac Man,* so Shogakukan made an anime series of a children's video game designed by Satoshi Tajiri. In designing that game, Tajiri remembered his childhood and his fascination with unusual insects. (Recall that Tezuka, too, was fascinated by insects; and that, in the Orient, a cricket is believed to bring its owner good luck.) Tajiri's game featuring cute fantasy animals became a hit in Japan; publishing rights were snapped up by Shogakukan Production Co. for a series of comic books. The books, in turn, became so popular that Shogakukan decided to produce a *Pokémon* anime series that premiered in April 1997. That series was subsequently launched in the United States in September 1998 as a syndicated weekday entry; but less than six months later, it graduated to the Kids' WB Network and was seen coast-to-coast. (Such was the eagerness of Kids' WB to play the show that it agreed to let the show continue to play in syndication.)

Spectacular as its rise had been from Japanese video game to American network television sensation, that success would in turn be eclipsed by *Pokémon* becoming a theatrical superstar. *Pokémon: The First Movie* opened under the Warner Bros. banner in 1999, the "cute little characters" showed up on trading cards and on fast food kids' meals. Their images graced all sorts of merchandise. Industry insiders were agape at the phenomenon. There had never been anything like this in the Americas — and from *Japan,* no less!

Pokémon's popularity with the sought-after 7-to-14-year-old demographic — to borrow an industry term — seems to stem from a combination of (a) colorful, eye-catching character designs and (b) strong, easy-to-follow stories featuring a likable cast. Heading the cast is 10-year-old Ash Ketcham (that is probably the last Americanized name for a Japanese character). Travelling with Ash is the "electric mouse" Pikachu. Where these two go, children compete to capture and train one of the 150+ different Pokémon.

Likenesses of the Pokémon appear on trading cards; a really dedicated youngster seeks to acquire a full set of trading cards. Once he (or she) does so, that individual wins the coveted title of Master Pokémon Trainer. In this writer's neighborhood, that title was won not by a boy, not by a girl, but by the young father of a 9-year-old daughter. Between comic books, television series, and feature-length films, *Pokémon* — a video game — has been one of the greatest franchises of all time.

Yu-Gi-Oh! The title translates as "King of Games." It is the brainchild of cartoonist Kazuki Takahashi, begun in Japan's *Weekly Shonen Jump* manga magazine in 1996, when it became clear that Shogakukan's *Pokémon* was on-track to becoming a monster hit. A deal to create an anime series based on *Yu-Gi-Oh!* was made between Takahashi and Shogakukan's competitor, Toei Doga. The series was to be a 27-episode run, from April 4 to October 10, 1998 — enough time to give Toei the opportunity to see whether the trading-card craze created by *Pokémon* was ephemeral or durable. Indeed the craze continued for years; it was durable beyond most expectations, and so production of *Yu-Gi-Oh!* anime continued beyond 27 episodes — but not by Toei. Production shifted to a little-known group called Studio Gallop. Their television series *Yu-Gi-Oh! Duel Monsters,* began in April 2000.

The premise: At the dawn of civilization, 5,000 years ago, powerful Egyptian sorcerers held deadly serious contests called Shadow Games. There was a supernatural aspect to those games: the winner would hold world supremacy in his hands. As time went on, the games became more and more intense. Finally, the intensity of those games built to such feverish pitch that it actually threatened to destroy the world! At last, the most powerful of the good sorcerers, the one called Pharaoh, defeated his enemy, Anubis. To make certain no such earth-shattering game would ever be held again, the wise Pharaoh hid his secret magic and sealed it for eternity. Future generations of Egyptians would hail their monarch as the "Pharaoh" and the Lord of the Dead would be labeled "Anubis."

Eons later, at the dawn of the twenty-first century, a trading card–combat game suddenly emerges from the Far East and becomes a hot fad with the world's youth. In the game *Duel Monsters,* players compete with cards of magic, and with monsters bearing such mystic names as Summoned Skull, Blackland Fire Dragon, and Mystic Lamp. Each trader seeks to win a rival trader's "life points." Ominously, "Duel Monsters" is secretly a reincarnation of the ancient Shadow Games; sorcerers, master players of yore, are about to be reborn!

Now it so happens that there's a frail-looking boy named Yugi Moto, whose grandfather owns the most popular gaming shop in Tokyo. Grandpa has, in his private collection, a rare ancient Egyptian game, a pyramid-shaped object known as the Millennium Puzzle. No one has ever been able to solve that puzzle, not even Grandpa. One day, Grandpa gives the puzzle to Yugi — and the boy becomes obsessed with it. He works on the puzzle day and night — for years. He carries the puzzle with him to high school; classmates brand him a "nerd," until one day — miracle of miracles! — Yugi solves the puzzle. In so doing, he releases the soul of the Pharaoh. The Pharaoh, Yugi soon learns, is actually Yugi's psychic double; it has lived in the puzzle over the millennia!

So much for the premise. In the real world — Tokyo in the 1990s — the issue of Yugi's mystic alter ego was not revealed until after the anime series had been in production for about two years. In the original 27-episode Toei series, the alter ego was called Yam Yugi (Dark Yugi). Yugi's neighborhood was full of bullies who pushed Yugi around. Yugi had the courage to stand up to them but, because the boy was frail, he did not have the strength. In those instances, Dark Yugi took over the boy's body. It would challenge the bully to a game — a game that required skill and nerve rather than strength. Invariably, the bully would lose and, when that happened, a supernatural revenge would befall him!

By the end of the 1990s, the *Duel Monsters* card game had become an unexpected popular bonanza. *Yu-Gi-Oh!* videogames, comic books, and the anime series itself were hastily modified to conform to the card game *Duel Monsters.* New villains were introduced: Maximillion Pegasus, for one — a reincarnation of the sorcerer who invented Shadow Games 5,000 years ago. Seto Kaiba is introduced, a millionaire's spoiled teenage son who proclaims himself the world's next gaming champion (he cheats). To Yugi's credit, the still frail teenage boy understands that the cards have regained their ancient supernatural powers and that only he, Yugi Moto, can prevent their misuse and endangerment of the world. By anime episode #144, we learn that Dark Yugi is, in reality, the ancient Pharaoh!

This series, brought to the United States by a firm called 4Kids Entertainment, found a television home on Kids WB Network and it was distributed theatrically by Warner Bros. 4Kids was also the importer of *Pokémon.*

***Cardcaptors** (aka Cardcoptor Sakura). Cardcaptors* appeared on the anime scene in 1998, when a studio called Madhouse saw the success of *Sailor Moon* and *Pokémon* and decided that Madhouse should *go* for it too. They noted that famed cartoonist Mitsuteru Yokoyama, creator of *Tetsujin 28/ Gigantor,* had created a popular character called *Sally the Witch* with Toei Doga 30 years earlier; the lead character was a "magical girl" (not unlike *Sailor Moon*). *Yu-Gi-Oh* and *Pokémon* both featured the adventures of young boys; this seemed to be the right time to introduce a new "magical girl." Their instincts proved to be correct.

Madhouse went to an immensely popular team of four women cartoonists who called themselves CLAMP. They had created several of the most successful comic book series of the 1990s, series that had also made it to the television screen in the form of anime: *Rayearth* was one, *X* was another, and now they were working on a comic book serial called *Cardcaptor Sakura*. The Sakura of the title was 10-year-old, fourth grader Sakura Kinomoto, daughter of a distinguished college professor of archaeology.

Storyline: One day, Sakura opens a strange, aged book in her father's study. The book turns out to be a case for a deck of Tarot-like Clow Cards that suddenly come to life and escape! Luckily, the deck comes with a guardian — a mythical winged lion cub named Kero-chan; unluckily, Kero-chan was asleep on the job and, well, not to worry, the cub hands Sakura a magic wand that she can use to recapture the errant cards. Uh ... there is a caveat: each card is a personification of a part of nature — wind, rain, fire, light, shadow — and the cards need to be recaptured quickly, before they create havoc in the world!

At first, Sakura tells her secret to just one person — her best friend, Tomoyo Daidoji ("Madison Taylor" in the English version). Tomoyo is a "ditsy" little rich girl; her hobby is designing clothes, and she enjoys speaking in hip super-hero lingo: she hails Sakura as akin to "the defender of truth" and "the upholder of justice!" Tomoyo also designs a new "battle costume" for each new adventure upon which she embarks. (*Note:* In an obvious, tongue-in-cheek caper in the anime version, the author(s) employ Kero-chan to supply voice-over fashion commentary for the audience.) A rich girl in every respect, Tomoyo tags along on each adventure with Sakura, packing a video camcorder to tape all the action.

What began as a light-hearted romp, though, gradually grows heavier and heavier as Sakura starts encountering darker, more sinister, and more powerful cards. Then, in an unexpected development, a *new* cardcaptor enters the scene — a boy from Hong Kong, one Li Shao Lang! Li announces that, henceforth, *he* is in charge and is taking over what is clearly "a *man's* job!"

From that point Sakura, who is not content to step aside, or surrender someone's idea of "a man's job," joins forces with Li and, together, the two go forth to recapture the escaped cards and reckon with Clow, the ancient sorcerer who created those mystical cards.

(*Note:* The late introduction of a male lead, Li Shao Lang, to share plot honors with female lead Sakura Kinomoto, suggests that Western distributors and the ladies of CLAMP realized that the addition of a boy to play opposite the girl of the title would widen the series' appeal. The fact that the boy is Chinese, rather than Japanese, seems tacit recognition that CLAMP, in seeking mystical powers for their cards, tapped into the ancient legend of

The Five Chinese Brothers, in which each brother could control one of Nature's elements — wind, fire, water....

(Initially, this anime series was called *Cardcaptor Sakura*. The name was changed to *Cardcaptors* in this hemisphere when two North American distributors, Pioneer Entertainment USA [home video]) and Nelvana, itself a television animation studio in Toronto, Canada, acquired North American rights. Kids' WB Network aired the show in the United States.)

One can only wonder what the late artist Mitsuteru Yokoyama (*Sally the Witch)* must have thought about the difference in the role of young girls in anime circa 1966, and their role in anime today. (Might he have said in Japanese — he spoke no English — "The difference is day and night!"?)

Dragon Warrior. Within walking distance of Toei's offices in the Ginza, Tokyo, a studio called Nippon Animation spotted a video game called *Dragon Quest*, which appeared for the first time in 1986. The game was actually a combination of two Nintendo-created computer games, which were reportedly expensive to make and complicated to play. A backstory heralding the sword-and-sorcery angles of *Dragon Quest* appeared in a boy's magazine, where it proved so popular that Nippon Animation was tapped to create a 32-episode anime series based upon the game. That series was acquired and released in the United States under the name *Dragon Warrior* by Saban and a distributor called LBS. (The initials LB stand for Lexington Broadcasting, which was actually an offshoot of advertising agency Grey Advertising. Industry observers at the time (1989–90) speculated that Grey may have been borrowing a leaf from the book of Japan's giant Dentsu Advertising Agency in packaging anime for television, and then sponsoring those children's programs with commercials from its own clients.)

(*Note:* Saban is the packager that would acquire the live-action series *Power Rangers* from Toei International [not Toei Doga] and build it into a national sensation. The character of 16-year-old "Abel," the "Dragon Warrior," was designed by Akira Toriyama and looks as though he had stepped out of Toriyama's *Dragon Ball* series animated by — and available from — Toei Doga [not International]. Saban did not acquire *Dragon Ball*, Funimation did.)

Dragon Warrior, the series, was patterned after the video game from which it sprang: it's laid out in so-called Levels. Level One introduces the aforementioned "Abel," who sets out to find and destroy a huge winged monster called Baramos. Baramos, wielding a magic amulet called the Red Stone, threatens to expose mankind to the fury of the Great Dragon. The complication is that the Red Stone had been closely guarded for generations by Abel's childhood friend, 15-year-old Tiala. Each succeeding level introduces more characters and more plot turns because the series' backers had anticipated a long run. In fact, *Dragon Warrior* survived for only six months and then succumbed — the victim, apparently, of weak Sunday morning timeslots and ratings.

Thunderbirds 2086. An important film distributor in Japan is Tohokushinsha, whose founder, Bajiro Uemura, had forged an alliance with ITC Entertainment (Japan). Together, these two firms embarked upon a most singular project.

Initially, they had collaborated in 1966 with the team of Gerry and Sylvia Anderson to make *Thunderbirds* in a technique that was not anime, not "animation" in the conventional sense of the word (with animation cels), but rather a process that the Andersons called "Supermarionation." All the figures were marionettes, manipulated traditionally with strings, but the Andersons had enhanced the process by molding the puppets made of flexible plastic and adding electronic circuitry. That allowed the puppeteers, with electronic impulses, to make the puppets move their eyes, blink, raise their eyebrows — even move their lips well enough to give the semblance of lip-sync; hence, these were *super*marionettes.

The story action was set in the twenty-first century, depicting heroic missions of an international rescue team — based on a Pacific atoll — to save the lives, spectacularly, of many who would otherwise be doomed. Even more spectacularly, they foiled the foul schemes of interplanetary rascals and would-be invaders of Earth.

Twenty years after the original, Supermarionette series, *Thunderbirds 2086* emerged from the studios of Toei Doga — this time, in Toei's well-known style of conventional cel animation. Gone was the old team that looked as though all members belonged to the same family. In its place was a five-member "little United Nations" with red-haired Jesse Rigel, dark-haired Dylan Beda, African-American Jonathan Jordan Jr., blonde Kallan James, and silver-haired Gran Hanson, the senior member of the team.

Each member of this crew had his own personal shuttle vehicle. The main crafts — five of them — were reserved for heavy-duty search and rescue, with each one having its own special capability, such as a high-speed drill, or faster-than-sound speed, and so forth. And, whereas the original, twenty-year-old series relied heavily upon multipart stories, this new anime version made certain that each story was self-contained — no adventure was "To Be Continued." Twenty-four episodes were delivered by Toei Doga, all shown in the United States on pay cable network Showtime.

The *Pokémon* Phenomenon

The advent in 1998 of what is today considered the Pokémon *Phenomenon was so profound, so precedent-shattering, that Harvey Deneroff wrote several*

*articles about it for publication at the time. A summary of those articles fol-
lows.*

The huge and largely unexpected success in the United States of Shogakukan's *Pokémon* caught anime fans and industry observers almost by surprise.
If any Japanese animated film or television series were to break into the American mainstream at the end of the 1990s, most bets were on Hayao Miyazaki's
Princess Mononoke, which had broken all box office records in Japan and was
scheduled for distribution in the United States by Disney's Miramax division.
Yes, *Pokémon,* based on the popular Nintendo game, had been a big success
on Japanese television and had spawned a lucrative theatrical film; but, after
all, *Sailor Moon* had also been a big success in Japan, yet nevertheless had
failed to catch on with the American public. So, like other Japanese television shows brought into the American market, *Pokémon* was picked up for
distribution in syndication in 1998 by the Summit Media Group and was
ignored by both broadcast and cable networks. (At the time, the major American broadcast networks were just beginning to edge away from American-
or Canadian-made product.) Thus, when I wrote an article for the *Hollywood
Reporter*'s annual NAPTE (National Association of Television Program Executives) January 1999 issue, I mentioned the series almost as an afterthought,
ending with the words that Summit had picked up "the Japanese Nintendo-
based *Pokémon: The Series*" for the syndication market.

Unlike the case in a number of European countries, such as France and
Spain, Japanese animation historically had little real success on American television since the days of *Astro Boy* and *Speed Racer.* Until the emergence of
cable networks such as Nickelodeon and Cartoon Network, the major American networks basically controlled the animation airwaves and preferred doing
business with Hollywood studios, whose product they could closely supervise. The birth of new cable channels led to a fragmentation of the marketplace in the 1990s, which led to lower licensing fees and tighter profit margins
by both producers and broadcasters alike. This, in turn, led to a decline in
production by American studios and a search for lower-priced foreign productions to fill the gap. But even so, broadcast networks turned to European
sources and ignored Japan.

However, *Pokémon* was such a phenomenal success in syndication that
Kids WB, the struggling Warner Bros.–owned children's broadcast network,
made a deal to show the series while it was still playing in syndication! (Because
there were some 104 episodes already in the can and 52 more in production,
Summit Media was able to supply new shows to both markets.) *Pokémon* rapidly became the most popular children's show on American television and was
largely responsible for dramatically increasing the ratings of Kids WB, whose
ratings went to the head of the broadcast pack on both Saturday mornings

and weekday afternoons; as such, the network became competitive with Disney's formerly dominant One Saturday Morning programming block on ABC and the Nickelodeon cable channel. This then led Warner Bros. to take on the theatrical distribution of the then two-year-old *Pokémon: The First Movie* in the United States; in the process, *Pokémon* easily overshadowed the box office performance of Miyazaki's critically acclaimed *Princess Mononoke,* much to the chagrin of many anime fans who were not fans of the television series.

The show's success in turn spawned a huge merchandising bonanza that largely focused on trading cards, which American children (like those in other countries) took to carrying around to show and trade wherever they went. *Pokémon* websites on the newly popular Internet became wildly popular and children without home computers flocked to their local public libraries, which provided free Internet access.

But the strongest indication of the power of *Pokémon* was probably best demonstrated by the $22 million marketing campaign Burger King, the giant fast food chain, put on to advertise the toy and trading card giveaway tied to *Pokémon: The First Movie.* This represented the biggest such campaign in the company's history. While it perhaps paled in comparison to the $30 million McDonald's spent to promote its *Toy Story 2* toys, it is these sorts of figures that made the powers that be pay attention to the possibilities offered by Japanese animation and by movies based on successful television shows.

This generated speculation that American producers would now look to Japan to buy existing shows much cheaper than they could produce themselves, which is exactly what happened. And the rest is history.

CHAPTER 12

Boy Meets Giant Robot

Before robots were called "robots," they were called "automatons." A respected Czech writer, Josef Čapek, looked at the Czech word *robota* ("drudgery") and coined the word *robot,* a word that his brother Karel used in his famous 1920 play, *R.U.R. (Rossum's Universal Robots).* The theme of the play is that the robots, once invented (to perform menial, repetitive chores), decided that they were smarter than their creators, so they would simply eliminate their creators! (In 1920, that was a unique, startling idea.) Rossum's robots were the size of an average adult human male, no taller than you or I.

Thirty-one years later, 20th Century–Fox would make a feature film called *The Day the Earth Stood Still.* The film starred Michael Rennie as Klaatu, a man from outer space, come to Earth to warn mankind to stop brandishing nuclear weapons — or else! Accompanying Klaatu was the robot "Gort." (Recall the famous cry, "*Gort! Klaatu barada nikto!*") Gort was formidable and tall, but no giant.

The question then arises: Who, what, was the world's first giant robot? Chances are that it appeared in *The Mechanical Monsters* (1941), the second of the Max Fleischer *Superman* cartoons, which featured great flying robots that are used by its inventor to commit a series of robberies. Then there was France's Paul Grimault who introduced a truly giant robot in his 1953 animated feature *La Bergère et le ramoneur* (*The Shepherdess and the Chimney Sweep*), released in the United States as *The Curious Adventures of Mr. Wonderbird.* In both instances the robots were piloted by a man, not a young boy. And giant robots never became a craze in either the United States or France.

It must now be apparent, even to the casual reader, that Japan's manga and anime industries teem with ubiquitous young boys and equally ubiquitous giant robots. If young boys are not indigenous to Japan, giant robots certainly are. And nobody in Tokyo seems ready to explain how, or why, that phenomenon occurred.

This writer has seen learned treatises purporting to explain why the giant robot looms large in Japanese animation — and nowhere else. Some argue that the giant is a metaphor for a resurgent Japan, reawakening like a giant from the rubble of World War II. This writer opines that, actually, the giant robot arose logically in a series of steps: (1) Osamu Tezuka, charmed (as was this writer) by a little wooden puppet called Pinocchio, created a modern-day equivalent, a little boy robot called Tetsuan Atom, our Astro Boy; (2) Mitsuteru Yokoyama, seeing the phenomenal success of *Astro Boy* in America, decides that he, too, will design a profitable robot — but, if he makes the robot small, he will be accused of copycatting Tezuka, so he "runs the other way," he designs the giant Tetsujin 28, our Gigantor; (3) TMS creates a little boy who transforms into a mighty giant ("Big X"), and the race to gianthood is on! Conclusion: metaphors are fine; dollars and yen are seen as finer.

One can hear it said that the artist Go Nagai, in 1972, drew the first of the world's modern super-robots; he called his robot Mazinger. Mitsuteru Yokoyama points out, in an article that he called "Tetsujin-28 and I," that he drew *his* giant, Tetsujin 28, as early as — in his own (Japanese) words — "November of Showa 31 [that is 1956, in Western years]. The robot was 50 feet tall — as high as a 5-story building! — sometimes. At other times, it was 40 feet tall." *Why the difference?*

Continuing in Japanese, Yokoyama-San explained: "The comic books of those days always listed the vital statistics of the robot [probably referring to *Tetsuan Atom/Astro Boy*], including height, weight, and flying speed. I didn't really bother with that at the time. I thought that if I wanted to make Iron-man [Tetsujin 28/Gigantor] look bigger than usual — I would. And if I didn't want him to look too big, I made him smaller." (*Note:* I call that "artistic license," and let it go at that.)

But then Yokoyama-San added: "What I really wanted was to make him look expressionless, emotionless, and unbeatable."

(*Note:* Astro Boy's computer brain, invented five years before Gigantor's, enables Astro Boy to speak 60 different languages; Gigantor does not think or speak. Astro Boy packs an onboard machine gun; Gigantor "packs no heat"; Astro Boy flies by activating rockets in his feet; Gigantor flies when rockets on his back are activated. In Yokoyama's words, "I put two jets on the back of the robot to give it the feeling of speed.")

Osamu Tezuka's robot, Astro Boy, is diminutive, Pinocchio-sized, no taller than a 12-year-old boy. It is this writer's *theory* that Mitsuteru Yokoyama, seeking to be as different as possible from Tezuka and his small-boy robot, would — five years later — go the exact opposite way: he'd invent the world's *tallest* robot — and have the giant *controlled* by a 12-year-old boy.

"Expressionless ... emotionless ... unbeatable." Again, Mr. Yokoyama's words: "At the time, there was a popular professional wrestler called 'Riki-dosan.' I could have made 'Ironman 28' look like a professional wrestler." However, "I always liked the looks of armor from the Middle Ages. The armor worn by all the knights seemed refreshing.... I had to create a [robot] character who was on the side of Law and Order, Peace and Justice."

Benign by Design

Evidently, Yokoyama-San, seated at his drawing table, was thinking in terms of a pleasing countenance. He drew his robot not with a frightening look but, rather, with a wide-eyed look of innocence, and wearing a Trojan helmet with the mouth flap of medieval armor, *topped by a carrot-like needle nose* that this writer believes was intended to evoke a smile from young readers. The robot looks benign. Nonintimidating. *Friendly.* The same can be said of Yokoyama's *other* giant mecha: Giant Robot, for example, wears the headdress of an ancient pharaoh and has a human face that looks suitably concerned, but nonthreatening.

Before the decade of the 1950s had come to an end, readers of manga in Japan could look to two robots — one small, one large — to fight for the ideals of law and order, peace and justice. Astro Boy, the small, Pinocchio-like robot, differs from that innocent wooden puppet of old (who could not tell right from wrong) in that Astro Boy *always knows right from wrong.* Gigantor, on the other hand, is a machine that has no values of any kind — but his young master *does.*

Battle Bots

When the Wright Brothers invented the airplane in 1903, they thought of their aircraft as: (1) proof that a vehicle heavier than air could fly, and (2) a demonstration that man could someday use the aircraft to travel from point A to point B. Before long, a military mind calculated that an aircraft could be used to fly over enemy territory and drop bombs; in other words, the airplane could be a weapon.

When Osamu Tezuka conceived his Tetsuan Atom in the 1950s, he envisioned it as a little fighter for justice. Mitsuteru Yokoyama's Tetsujin 28, conceived shortly after the "birth" of Tetsuan Atom, was initially conceived to be a giant-sized weapon, but, soon thereafter, it was converted to the peaceful pursuit of law, order, truth, and justice.

The role of the robot in society changed in 1972, however, when Go

Nagai, aided and abetted by Toei Animation, brought forth Nagai's *Mazinger Z* in an animated television series. The show went on the air in December and became an instant hit. By the time the series ended in 1974, 92 half-hour episodes had aired, two Cinemascope featurettes had played in (Toei) theaters, and a television series sequel of 52 episodes had been launched. With the arrival of the year 1975, the super-robot was firmly established. *Mazinger Z* had spawned a new generation of robots that were not only huge — *they could be used as weapons!*

The "Boy" Angle

Tetsujin 28 (Gigantor), an early giant, used only his brute strength in battle; his young master, our Jimmy Sparks, "choreographed" the robot's moves against an enemy by standing nearby, manipulating the joystick on a convenient, hand-held remote control box.

Mazinger Z was controlled by teenager Koji Kabuto, who, unlike Jimmy Sparks, did not watch the battle from a vantage point nearby; rather, he flew a small hovercraft-like vehicle right into the robot's head, tucked it neatly into a berth and, from that point, the boy became the robot's *brain*. Like a pilot aboard a jet fighter, Koji could direct Mazinger Z to throw a rocket-propelled punch, zap a laser beam from an emblem on the robot's massive chest, and more.

Jimmy Sparks (*Gigantor*), Koji Kabuto (*Mazinger Z*), Amuro Ray and Char Aznable (*Gundam*), Shinji Ikari (*Neon Genesis Evangelion*) — these are all boys who control the world's giant robots. Jimmy Sparks controls Gigantor from without, the rest control their giants from within. None of the robots control themselves, they do not think, they do not have artificial intelligence. That would change, somewhat, in the mid–1970s.

At Last — A Giant Robot with a Brain!
(Not Just Another Pretty Faceplate)

Yes, Pinocchio, the little wooden puppet, could think — but he was on the cusp of becoming a real boy. Yes, little Astro Boy could think — but, after all, he was invented to replace a human, a grieving father's dead son. Even the Scarecrow, in the Land of Oz, finally got a brain! Why, then, (one well may ask) didn't anyone in the world have the foresight to create a giant robot with a brain?

Actually, someone did. Early in 1976, Yoshitake Suzuki created a giant robot capable of thinking thoughts — albeit *primitive* thoughts — from a rudimentary mind. The robot's name was "Brave Raideen" and the story of how Raideen (Japanese for thunderbolt), tracing his roots back several millennia, even came to *be,* is a story unto itself.

According to Suzuki-San, Earth was invaded even before the time of the pharaohs by a Devil Empire. Those prehistoric invaders had the ability to conjure up armies of beasts made of stone. All seemed lost when, suddenly, from out of the sea, rose an island crowned with a towering Colossus-like statue of Egyptian design! That statue turned out to be Raideen, built by engineers of ancient Mu to be the island's invincible protector. Mu receded back into the sea long ago, but not before Raideen had fended off the Devil Empire and been programmed to rise again if that enemy should ever return.

The Devil Empire has not returned, but other enemies — more deadly than even the Devil Empire — are upon us. Raideen has re-arisen. Brave Raideen was given a brain of sorts — the best those ancient engineers could devise in the days before transistors, capacitors, and microcircuitry. Still, Raideen had enough self-awareness to know that his elementary mind lacked the computing power needed to survive in the twentieth century; he would need a human pilot to guide him through the intricacies of modern-day life.

There was a catch: the ancient engineers of Mu had programmed Raideen's mind to accept guidance only from a human who is brave and pure of heart. The call was Raideen's. So, whom did the robot select? He picked a high school soccer champ/motorcyclist named Akira Habiki. Akira was, in a sense, teleported into Raideen's control center — located where the heart is found in the human body — and there the teenager was telepathically coached in the art of mastering Raideen's controls.

From this, it would seem that the human pilot would be the driving force in the relationship of human-to-robot. In fact, the opposite was true. Brave Raideen continued to call the shots; Akira deferred to Brave Raideen. (In the American version, just the opposite: the Akira character, renamed Richard Carson, pilots the robot as though it were a tank or a jet plane.)

So, to the names of boys who skipper giant robots from within or without, including Jimmy Sparks, Koji Kabuto, Amuro Ray, Shinji Ikari, Char Aznable, and others, we now add the name of Akira Habiki. (If all those stalwart teenage boys had somehow met, and formed the world's most exclusive fraternity — the Giant Robot Young Pilot's Club — what wonderful tales they could have swapped!)

(*Note: Brave Raideen*, which became the most popular of all super-robots in Japan, was filmed by Tohokushinsha Film Co., which also gave us the *Thunderbirds* series.)

Go Getta Giant

What may sound to some like a strange suggestion, indeed, is actually the name of a specialized robot designed by Go Nagai. The word *getta* means *combined*. Nagai devised a *segmented* robot, comprised of modular units that fit together, Rubik cube-style, into a wide variety of shapes, for example, three of Nagai's designated jet fighter planes could link together *in flight* to form a single, giant getta humanoid. The (Go) getta giant could then be used either defensively or offensively and, yes, the three jet fighter segments were piloted by three teenage boys — Ryu, Hayato, and Masahi.

The getta concept of individual units combining into a new shape was an animator's delight. Units could be made to combine into a straight line, a circle, a pretzel, or whatever shape grabbed the animator's fancy. (Try achieving that effect in live-action!) Toei Animation artists who were animating the series called *Getta Robo* (in the United States, *The Starvengers*) conceived so many playful ideas that the concept soon "played itself out" and the super-robot returned to the familiar single-unit type.

There are those in the industry who argue that *Brave Raideen* went *Getta Robo* one better in that Raideen could transform not just into a humanoid shape, but also into a jet fighter called the Godbird.

Consensus in the industry, however, is that, beginning with giant robot Tetsujin 28/Gigantor, the most important single concept to be introduced is that of the *human pilot.* Recall that Rossum's Universal Robots (*R.U.R.*) as early as 1920 threatened to destroy mankind — machines gone berserk, technology spun out of control. That same issue is echoed in the series *Patlabor,* but on a giant scale: Will unchecked technology outpace man's ability to control it? Therefore, that threat, that danger is mitigated in anime by having a human being, a boy, in command of the robot; the human gives the orders, the robot obeys — not the other way around. Moral: if all this futuristic technology can be controlled (even) by children, why should adults fear progress?

Again, the words of Gigantor's creator, Mitsuteru Yokoyama, in his article "Tetsujin 28 and I": "The idea I had was that a number of Frankenstein-like monsters would destroy the city, and a boy — a mere boy — would melt them and destroy them."

CHAPTER 13

Religious, Not Litigious

Temples and shrines abound in Japan. Buddhism, Shinto, and Christianity are all well established. There is, furthermore, a unique aspect of Japanese belief in that virtually everyone seems to embrace the notion that all things natural are endowed with a spirit. I can recall, on that first trip to Japan, hearing about "the spirit of a spider"—in a human being! Anyone who has seen Hayao Miyazaki's Academy Award–winning feature film *Spirited Away* has seen that animator's concept of an astonishing variety of spirits, including a river spirit, a spirit with no face—even a *stink spirit!* Small wonder, then, that the Japanese ancestor-revering society would have its own notion about the finality of death.

The idea of having no face is a key one, too—or losing face. The face seems to be tied in, somehow, to the soul. He who loses face loses all. And, once a person loses face, he loses credibility permanently; there seems to be no going back. A person who goes into bankruptcy loses face; a businessman who declares bankruptcy is a pariah. Even if that businessman should recover, get back on his feet, he is marked for life, and finds that the road back leads only to a dead end. Litigation is to be avoided. To lose a case must surely be akin to losing face. No one wants to lose face, or see his neighbor lose face.

A question I am frequently asked is, "Did Tezuka Studio ever sue Disney, with its *The Lion King* for (alleged) infringement of *Kimba the White Lion?*" My answer is: No, the Japanese are known as a society that eschews litigation. Besides, the Tokyo-based studio took the position that Tezuka, who was a great respecter of Disney's work, would have been flattered if the Disney studio had indeed been inspired by Tezuka's work.

Despite a distaste for litigation, Tezuka Productions did file suit against Fumio Suzuki, the agent who once represented Tezuka in negotiations with NBC Enterprises. Suit was filed when Tezuka Productions learned, belatedly, that Suzuki had managed to acquire the English versions of *Astro Boy* and *Kimba* from bankrupt Mushi Production!

One wonders "how could that have happened? How could any party other than Tezuka own Tezuka's pictures? What's going on here?" The chronology is this:

1. NBC Enterprises informs Mushi Production in 1975 that NBC's license for *Astro Boy* has terminated and therefore NBC is returning all film elements — English prints, negatives, and soundtracks — to Mushi; Mushi would need to pay some shipping expenses.

2. The caretaker for Mushi, an attorney named Ikea (spelling is phonetic) replies that Mushi, since 1973, is bankrupt so, therefore, cannot pay any costs associated with the return of materials. Fuji Television Network, the broadcaster of those shows in Japan, says, essentially, we can't accept the materials, either; we suggest that you simply destroy all the elements and issue a Certificate of Destruction. NBC, seeing no other option, does destroy all materials, and issues a Certificate of Destruction to Mushi Production, together with all paperwork required to show that all right, title, and interest in the series is hereby reverting to Mushi.

3. Fumio Suzuki speaks with the caretaker of Mushi, and he pays a negotiated amount for rights to the black-and-white *Astro Boy* series, plus rights to *Kimba the White Lion,* including any surviving film materials. (Materials for *Astro Boy* had been destroyed, but prints and negatives for *Kimba* were still intact in the United States.) Suzuki then makes a deal (described earlier in these pages) with Todd Ferson, president of Century Systems, a Des Moines, Iowa, computer firm, to store and distribute the *Kimba* series, plus whatever was available for *Astro Boy.*

4. Long after Osamu Tezuka's death, Tezuka Productions learns, to its surprise, that Mushi Production has made a deal with Fumio Suzuki for all shows returned from NBC Enterprises. The news comes as a shock! The Tezuka interests ask for an explanation: how could Mushi transfer rights to Suzuki? Mushi's position is, in effect, that we have every right to do so; after all, everything returned from NBC is an asset of Mushi Production, even in bankruptcy. The creditors of Mushi have a right to get their investment back, so a deal was struck with Mr. Suzuki and "our" negatives and prints were sold to his company. Perfectly legal.

5. *Perfectly legal?* The Tezuka people didn't think so. Their position: The *films* (16mm negatives and prints) may have been an asset of Mushi Production, but the *images* on those films are characters created and owned by Tezuka. Those images are the exclusive intellectual property of Tezuka, and Mushi had no right to sell those images.

6. The Tezuka people file a claim in court. When the claim is heard, the judge announces that, indeed, both sides have some legitimacy in their claims; he orders both sides to get together and work it out between them-

selves. Several meetings are held, but no agreement is reached. Finally, the judge takes a position: the *images* created by Osamu Tezuka are national icons and, indeed, are famous throughout the world; they are a unique body of work. Therefore (after several years), the judge rules in Tezuka's favor; Suzuki may not traffic in the disputed films.

Suzuki-San, meanwhile, *had* trafficked in the disputed films. Believing that he had the right to do so, he had applied for copyright renewals, as the claimant, in the U.S. Copyright Office. He had given distribution rights to Todd Ferson and an associate, Shawne Kleckner, in a firm named the Right Stuf International, Inc. to distribute the programs on videocassettes for home use. Suzuki had also authorized a firm known as Landmark, builders of theme parks, to manufacture a *colorized* version of an old black-and-white *Astro Boy* program. So, clearly, Suzuki did have a substantial investment in properties that he believed he had bought. In all likelihood, the Tezuka people eventually reached some settlement with Suzuki's company and the litigation was finally over — in Japan!

7. Litigation in the United States is held later, in Los Angeles. This writer is called upon to appear as an expert witness, giving historical insight into the events of 1963–66, the "NBC years" of both *Astro Boy* and *Kimba*. Again the Tezuka side prevailed, settlements were made, and the litigation was finally over.

8. Happy Endings: (a):The Right Stuf International remained the distributor of *Astro Boy* and *Kimba* home videos in North America. (b) Rights to distribute those two series in homevideo formats in Australia and New Zealand are won by a Melbourne-based firm called Madman Entertainment. They prove themselves to be film wizards. They go back to Tokyo, make copies of *Astro Boy* and *Kimba* programs from the original materials, synchronize those with the best copy of the English tracks, and release spanking new DVD editions at the end of the year 2005. The programs look as good as ever! Those copies are available in North America from the Right Stuf International.

"Old Mushi Production," as we have seen, is gone. But in its place has come "New Mushi," a studio formed by a nucleus of key employees of the old, original Mushi Production. Relationships between "New Mushi" and present-day Tezuka Productions are cordial. As the North American saying goes, "All's well that ends well."

CHAPTER 14

Speaking of Dying...

The earliest comic strips (American manga, if you will) I can remember are *Tillie the Toiler, Gasoline Alley* (with a boy named Skeezix), *Dick Tracy, Li'l Abner,* and *Blondie.* Blondie and Dagwood had two children; I remember the two children growing older, but not Blondie and Dagwood; they always stayed the same. Come to think of it, all the other characters stayed the same, too. They never aged. *None of the comic strip characters ever died.*

That is not the way things happen in manga. Japanese characters have life cycles. After they reach a given stage, manga characters die. The Japanese see that as normal. It would be abnormal for those characters *not* to die — true for manga, true for anime.

Case in point: Osamu Tezuka created *Tetsuan Atom (Mighty Atom),* our *Astro Boy.* Astro Boy, let it never be forgotten, is a robot. For all his real, boyish ways, the character is nevertheless a robot. Conventional wisdom would tell any North, Central, or South American that robots, especially comic strip robots, do not, *cannot* die. And that is what I thought as I wrote the English adaptation for that first *Astro Boy* film, the pilot, Show #1: *Birth of Astro Boy.* Certainly I could accept the notion that a robot would be "born," but — once invented, once born — it *stays* born. Doesn't it?

For 52 episodes, the voice cast and I "laid down" tracks for adventures in which Astro Boy — thank goodness! — saved the day for them, for you, and for me. And, when those 52 adventures were in the can, we went to work on 52 more. That made 104 English adventures in all, but we knew that Tezuka's Mushi Production, before calling it a wrap, would complete 193 episodes in Japanese, as they were required to do under their contact with the Fuji Television Network.

I never knew what happened at the end of episode 193. I *assumed* that, by that stage, the Mushi writers would simply have run out of ideas, and put the series to bed. After all, that's the American way: *Seinfeld* ended, the

Bob Newhart Show ended, *Everybody Loves Raymond* ended, *Friends* ended, *Murphy Brown*— ad infinitum.

Not until Tezuka produced a shorter, color remake of the old, black-and-white *Astro Boy* series in 1980 did I realize that Astro Boy, the loveable little boy robot, was *not* destined to go on forever — he was scheduled to *die at the end!*

I could not believe it. Astro Boy *die?* (Did Pinocchio die? No, he graduated to real boyhood! Did Snow White or Cinderella die? No, they lived happily ever after! Then, what on earth was Tezuka thinking, in wiping out Astro Boy?)

Tezuka's grand scheme of things at the end was to have Astro Boy meet, and come to cherish, a lovely girl robot. But the girl robot is, in reality, a powerful and deadly superbomb! She is set to go off— at any moment! Once she detonates, it's the end of the world! To save the world, Astro Boy takes hold of the "girl," flies with her into the sun, and there she explodes! Earth is saved, but the girl robot, and the loveable little boy robot — Astro Boy — are destroyed.

Case in point: Tezuka again, in *Jungle Emperor Leo,* our *Kimba the White Lion,* runs true to form. Note that in "Outline for Jungle Emperor," printed elsewhere in these pages (see Chapter 4, "Whole Story"), Tezuka writes, very explicitly:

> A group of scientists one day try to explore Mt. Moon looking for the moonlight stone, which is composed of super-energy and which once caused continental slides. Mt. Moon has a bad air current; prehistoric animals, such as dinosaurs and woolly mammoths live there, making scientific expeditions impossible.
>
> But, inasmuch as Leo/Kimba was familiar with Ofukurosan, a mammoth living on Mt. Moon, he cooperated with the expedition....
>
> Suddenly a snowstorm swoops down upon Mt. Moon, 5,000 feet above sea level. The party carrying the expedition records starts descending the mountain. But on the way, one person falls down ... and then, another. Finally, the last man is going to break down. "Bring the expedition records to the world." ... Leo killed himself and gives his own body to save the last man in the expedition from hunger. Leo did not die, but lived on in [ideal].

What could be clearer? Tezuka says, specifically, that Kimba kills himself at the end, to provide his body as food, as sustenance for the last man still alive in the expedition (who, by the way, is the character called Mr. Pompous in our *Astro Boy* series. Australians and New Zealanders call him "Daddy Walrus.")

Tezuka Productions in 1997–98 produced a feature-length animated film, *Jungulu Taitei Leo,* based faithfully on Tezuka's "Plan of Jungle Emperor." The little white lion cub sacrifices himself at the end. Other Westerners sitting with me in the audience at the world premiere in Tokyo were surprised and dismayed at the finale. An agent from Canada left the theater with a glum look and predicted — accurately — that the film's prospects in the Western Hemisphere would be dim.

At NBC Enterprises in New York, we had thirty years earlier adapted 52 half-hour episodes for television. In our final episode, Production 52, we leave Kimba alive, and well, and living in the jungle. Nobody dies.

Another case in point: TMS Studio, in its 1980 color series *Shin Tetsu-jin 28*, our *The NEW Adventures of Gigantor*, devotes several episodes to the adventures/*mis*adventures of a giant robot called Black Ox. (In our English adaptation we renamed the character Blue Ox, simply because TMS artists had painted the character blue, instead of black.) I found the character interesting, in that its fictional creator had died before completing work upon the Ox's brain. The Ox therefore had the mental capacity of a four-year-old child; "he" got into the kind of trouble that a four-year-old boy would, and therefore — even as he wreaked monumental damage — had an endearing quality about him.

Near the end of the television series, the Ox perceives that a bomb, created by a master villain, is set to go off. The bomb is no conventional bomb; it's a *super*bomb! It can destroy the planet! Blue Ox, intelligent enough to understand the peril, breaks free of Earth's superhot magma — where he has been trapped — seizes the bomb and flies with it high into the sky! There it explodes — harmlessly! Earth is saved — saved by the endearing, selfless Ox! The robot, though, is blown to bits! We are as sad to see him go as we were to see the cataclysmic demise of Astro Boy!

Case in point: *Sailor Moon*. For 64 half-hour television episodes, Sailor Moon and her fellow sailor scouts — Sailor Mercury, Sailor Venus, Sailor Mars, Sailor Jupiter — elude their deadly enemy, Queen Beryl, queen of the negaverse! At the end of the story arc covered, though (at the end of the initial series), the girls' luck finally runs out and they *die*! *Sailor Moon* fans fear naught, however; they know that the girls are all somehow miraculously *restored* — just in time to start the Next Exciting Sailor Moon Series!

Characters that do not live forever, characters that die — here we find yet another notch in the tally of differences between cartoons of the West and anime of the East.

CHAPTER 15

Tezuka on Tezuka,
Yokoyama on Yokoyama

Let a writer in New York or Los Angeles sell a television series called *Buddies,* and he'll be back next week with a pitch for his new series to be called *Pals.* Let a cartoonist in Tokyo have a hit with his anime series *Iron-Fisted Robot,* and he'll soon be back with a proposed new series to be called *Golden Robot.* That, in essence, is what happened to Osamu Tezuka when he stunned Tokyo with his surprise hit *Tetsuan Atom (Astro Boy).*

Toei Animation's Chiaki Imada promptly asked Tezuka to "give us (Toei) another *Tetsuan Atom,* give us another *Astro Boy!*" Recall that Osamu Tezuka was no stranger to Toei Animation; he had worked there with studio chief Chiaki Imada on more than one feature-length film. Now, Imada-San was approaching Tezuka with the proposition that Tezuka create a variation of *Tetsuan Atom* as a television series for Toei. (Television was new territory for Imada in the 1960s; all of Toei Animation's output till then had consisted of features for Toei-owned theaters.)

Tezuka obliged. He came back to Imada-San with a project called *Jet Mars.* The concept was that two robotologists — one, a peace-loving man and, the other, a militaristic type — create a little robot that looks like Astro Boy's kid brother. The peace-loving man wants to name the robot "Jet"; the militaristic man wants to name it "Mars: god of war." They compromise and name the robot "Jet Mars."

Tezuka being Tezuka, and following the tale of *Pinocchio* that he loved so well, knew that the little robot needed a conscience. In *Pinocchio,* the little wooden puppet had a cricket for a conscience. Astro Boy was given Doctor Ochanomizu (our Doctor Elefun) to guide him along the pathways of life. For Jet Mars, Tezuka created a little (14 years old in appearance) girl robot to act as Jet's older sister — an advisor and confidante — in effect, a conscience.

Jet Mars was designed to fly with the aid of rockets in his feet, à la Astro

Boy, and with horsepower greater than Astro Boy's. In addition, perhaps to separate him more from Astro Boy, whom he strongly resembled, he wore a little cape around his shoulders that, in flight, flared outward into a small delta wing.

Toei Doga (Animation) did produce a *Jet Mars* anime series, Toei's publishing arm did turn out a series of manga, but the character never really "flew" in Japan, never really became "another *Astro Boy.*"

Nonetheless, *l'affaire Jet Mars* is a perfect example, a classic case, of Tezuka on Tezuka — an artist's attempt to replicate, perhaps even surpass, an earlier success.

Early fans of Tezuka's *Kimba the White Lion* must have been surprised, as I was, to see characters from *Astro Boy* turning up in *Kimba.* One particularly oily, smarmy-looking character whom Tezuka called *Hamegg* appeared as a circus master in the very first episode of *Astro Boy.* I renamed the character "Cacciatori" (as in chicken cacciatore, roast chicken in a tomato sauce). That character appeared in *Kimba* episode #1 as an unscrupulous hunter who traps, then shoots, Kimba's noble father. For reasons best known to Tezuka, the artist *kept* the name of Hamegg for that character in the new series. Inasmuch as the character now showed up as a villainous hunter, I named him "Viper Snakely."

The character called Mr. Pompous in *Astro Boy* (Higeoyagi, in *Tetsuan Atom*) returns in *Kimba,* too; he is, in fact, the very character who would have perished atop Mount Moon had it not been for Kimba's act of self-sacrifice.

I regard this kind of carryover, from an older series to a younger one, as another fine example of Tezuka on Tezuka.

Mitsuteru Yokoyama recycled ideas from his older series to his newer ones, too — in spades! The artist, born in Kobe (western Japan) in 1934, writes in Japanese in his article "Tetsujin 28 and I": "By the time I was 20, I had started in the cartoon business. Small publishing companies gave me assignments. The fourth assignment I started was called *Tetsujin 28* [*Ironman 28,* later to become our *Gigantor*]." Yokoyama-San began work on *Tetsujin 28* in 1956, five years after Osamu Tezuka had introduced *Tetsuan Atom.* Under no circumstances would Yokoyama-San devise a small boy-size robot like Tezuka's Tetsuan Atom. The two artists were not friends; if anything, they were rivals. As mentioned earlier, Yokoyama-San would "go the other way"; he would create a robot that was a giant.

There were additional factors, as well, that led to the creation of a giant robot: "One day," Yokoyama writes, "I saw a movie called *Frankenstein.* With no expression on his face, the [tall] emotionless monster would kill people. The emotionless face of that monster was something I could not forget." That monster and Yokoyama's robot both have expressionless faces; extrapolating the size of the robot to that of a five-story-high giant was not much of a stretch.

The concept of a giant robot controlled by a young boy quickly struck the nation's fancy. Yokoyama-San had struck pay dirt! In fairly rapid succession, the artist developed *Giant Robo* (described earlier in these pages) and *Giant Robot.* (The latter, developed as a live-action series *for Toei* was released in the United States as *Johnny Sokko and His Flying Robot.*) These successive series, both extrapolations of Yokoyama's original *Tetsujin 28* series, were clearly prime examples of Yokoyama on Yokoyama.

Of interest, however, is that Tetsujin 28 and Giant Robot are both robots with no capacity to think. They are simply machines, as automobiles are machines, with no capability to drive themselves. Both robots are manipulated by young boys stationed outside the machine, or *mecha.* But, with *Giant Robot,* artist Yokoyama injects a new twist: the robot, uniquely attired in the headdress of an Egyptian pharaoh, appears only when summoned by a young boy; once the robot has restored law and order and is, in effect, dismissed by the young boy, the robot disappears — not to return until again so summoned.

Does this mean that the robot has some independence, some thought process of its own? And does the headdress of an ancient pharaoh suggest that this robot is (like Brave Raideen, who appeared years later) the handiwork of Egyptian engineers of antiquity? Nowhere do these queries appear to be answered. One can only assume that Yokoyama-San, who acknowledges that he was intrigued by helmets worn by ancient Roman warriors, was intrigued as well by the headdress worn by ancient Egyptian royalty.

Would Mitsuteru Yokoyama, had he not died in 2004, have created more variations of his giant robot? In his own words, "Sometimes I think ... what kind of robot would I have created if I had been a child now?"

What's So Funny about Names?

Both Osamu Tezuka and Mitsuteru Yokoyama had keen senses of humor. The latter's humor was most visible in his portrayal of characters, particularly villains, that he would draw with quirky features (as with Captain Spider, designed as a caricature of a European-style dictator), and with camera angles such as a despot's words being spoken from a point of view inside the despot's mouth. No obvious attempt was made to give his characters patently outrageous names; Captain Spider did not *resemble* a spider, but a spider was the emblem emblazoned on Captain Spider's national flag.

Osamu Tezuka did enjoy the use of outrageous names for some of his characters. This is a trait that he and I both shared, and I believe that was one of the bases for the friendship that developed between the artist and this writer. Mention has been made here of Tezuka's fondness for the character that he called Hamegg. The name is obviously a combination of the English words for a breakfast favorite, ham and eggs. Tezuka found that notion amusing, even with the knowledge that most of his (manga) readers spoke no English.

Seeing that character appear in the very first episode of *Astro Boy,* I named him Cacciatori, which I would have done whether Tezuka had named him Hamegg or not. Both names refer to food, and both the artist and I found humor in using the word for a foodstuff as the name for a character intended by the author to "get laughs."

With the same intent, I named Astro Boy's detractors, stationed at police headquarters, Chief McLaw and Detective Gumshoe. The names are meant to amuse by their very outrageously obvious meanings.

What's in a name? Maybe, humor.

CHAPTER 16

Samurai on Cels

In Toei Doga's animated feature, *Puss in Boots,* the production team use mice in much the same way that Disney animators used mice in *Cinderella*—for comic relief. The mice are cute; they invariably "take on the big guys," biting off more than they can chew, but, at the end of the day, after a lot of close scrapes, the mice get the job done and land on their feet. They're heroes!

In *Puss in Boots,* one mouse assures Puss that he — the mouse — can easily handle the villainous ogre. The mouse, in the English version, says, "Don't worry. Just leave that ogre ... to *me!*" On the word "*me,*" the mouse swirls his sword in front of his face and flourishes it, with the point of the blade pointing skyward. That is bravado.

I also knew, in writing the dialogue, that the mouse's militaristic gesture was the move of a samurai warrior. (That gesture is, for Japanese audiences, where the humor lay. They understand the culture of the samurai, and so applaud the mouse.)

In my meeting with a team of young writers working with Osamu Tezuka at Mushi Production, a meeting described earlier, one fellow understood that my comments about certain gestures seen in an *Astro Boy* episode pertained to samurai tradition. He then reenacted the gestures and explained: just as the cowboy symbolizes the spirit of the old American West, the samurai symbolizes the spirit of old Japan. The samurai was a member of Japan's elite class — a warrior with unwavering loyalty to his (feudal) lord. Unlike the American cowboy who is perceived as an independent spirit and "his own man," the samurai's way adhered closely to a code that was a blend of Buddhism, Confucianism, and Shinto —*bushido,* in short — and that meant the samurai was expected to be stoic, unattached to the material world —*or life itself*—and if that meant self-sacrifice, so be it.

(*Note:* I could not know it at the time of that meeting with Mushi's writers, but realized later that the samurai concept of self-sacrifice would explain

Astro Boy's flying into the sun to save mankind from extinction, and Kimba's sacrificing himself to save an expedition from extinction atop Mt. Moon.)

The way of the samurai, I came to understand, is more than merely being a soldier, or even a mercenary, fighting to protect his lord or patron on a feudal fiefdom. It is an all-encompassing Code of Honor.

It is understandable, in light of this code, whose influence survives in Japan to this day, that the young Mushi writer would take a pessimistic view of the American gunfighter of the Old West, who would kill, not to defend his lord's life or domain, but for personal gain or a petty grudge or even just for the fun of it!

Westerners who visit Japan today see neon lights everywhere, Big Macs and Whoppers, rich U.S.-branded ice cream and denim jeans, and assume that they are seeing a Far Eastern form of Western democracy. But look at the anime that unspools like a fast-running stream from studios all around Tokyo. The *bushido* ethic, the way of the samurai, is still alive and well and thriving in Japan. Individual desire is subordinated to the greater good. Men and boys are still expected to think like "warriors," to carry on in spite of hardship or adversity.

In the anime series *Sailor Moon,* Luna, one of two cats who have fled the moon along with Usagi (the heroine, our Serena) scolds her young mistress, at one point, for not behaving like "a warrior." That scene remains vivid in my memory to this day. Serena, a girl, along with Sailor Mercury, Sailor Venus, Sailor Mars, Sailor Jupiter — five girls — expected to be "warriors"? How strange, I thought. How different from the image of girls in Western culture! On the other hand, these five girls, all 14 years old, all in high school, all thinking about boys, are *themselves* fulfilling the roles of boys when they unite to battle the evil queen of the negaverse!

Going into battle mode, Serena — the young girl just returned from a pajama party — calls out "Moon ... Prism ... Power!"; and, with that, she begins her magical transformation into the persona of Sailor Moon, girl *warrior!* At the end of the magical transformation, she crosses her arms, one over the other, upright fashion, one hand pointing to the sky. Clearly, the gesture is that of the samurai preparing for battle. The gesture, in fact, is virtually the same as that of the brave little mouse in *Puss in Boots* preparing to take on the ogre.

The Japanese are a homogeneous society. They are not a "melting pot," as is the United States, nor a mixture of cultures like Canada, where the inhabitants of the province of Quebec speak French, while those in the rest of the country speak English. They are not like Latinos, widely sharing both European and native Indian heritage. There is a uniformity among the Japanese and, to this day, the nation cherishes its samurai past.

CHAPTER 17

Mars: Gateway to Anime?

Mars? Anime? What's the connection? one well may ask. How can Mars be a gateway to anything — except, maybe, our outlying planets?

There is indeed a pathway from the planet Mars to the advent of anime in the Americas, strange as that may seem. Work on the pathway began in 1957.

By the spring of 1957, this writer had already adapted several European-animated short subjects for U.S. television. These short subjects consisted mainly of two-reelers (18 minutes long) and three-reelers (28 minutes long), all made to play in European theaters, where such short subjects are standard fare.

In the spring of 1957, my then-employer — William Cayton — acquired rights to a Russian-made 28-minute featurette with the Russian title *Pavel Klushantsev*, and with an intriguing story line: An astronaut (the Russians used the term *cosmonaut*) sets off on a trip to the Moon; on the way, his ship becomes disabled, so a rescue mission sets out to save him. The cosmonaut's young son stows away aboard the rescue ship. Near the end of the third reel, the young stowaway's father is discovered, safely waiting on the Moon, to be rescued. Rescue comes just in time, the disabled ship is once more made space worthy, the two ships return triumphantly to Earth, and, presumably, the animated stars of the film, reunited, live happily ever after.

"Nice story," we thought, "too bad the film isn't longer, so that the young stowaway, who's discovered in reel two, can get the opportunity to see some spatial phenomena and learn about them on the way."

As fate would have it, there *was* a way to lengthen the picture — in fact, *two* ways! The first way was to acquire rights to another featurette, which was reportedly made by Karel Zeman, the famed Czech puppet filmmaker. (His 1958 live-action/animated feature *A Deadly Invention* delighted both critics and audiences alike when it was shown in the United States as *The Fabulous World of Jules Verne*.) Additionally, Zeman was said to have made a film called

Univers (*Universe*) that showed, with stunning photography, the planets that make up our solar system. (Eastern Europeans used the word "Kosmos.")

The second way was to acquire rights to an old black-and-white, short German film called *Weltraumschiff 1 Startet* (*Spaceship 1 Launches*). That featurette starred popular German actors of the day (that was of no value to us), but also had marvelous shots of a (model) teardrop-shaped spaceship blasting off, circling the Moon, and returning to Earth. *Perfect!* The design of the animated Russian ship matched the design of the German-made model ship; I'd be able to intercut the two with no one really noticing any slight differences.

What a lucky break! All three pictures — Russian, Czech, German — could be blended into a single, expanded story, with the cosmonaut, now an astronaut, heading for planet Mars — instead of the moon — and running into trouble along the way!

I selected scenes of the ship from the black-and-white German film, arranged for them to be tinted blue (to blend with the other two pictures, both of which were shot in color), made a preliminary rough cut of the proposed new 60-minute picture, and left with my wife and two children for summer vacation on Cape Cod, Massachusetts.

What timing! A day or two after our arrival on Cape Cod in the summer of 1957, the Russians boosted their satellite *Sputnik* into orbit — the first man-made object ever to be put into space — and my boss, William "Bill" Cayton, was on the phone, saying I needed to rush right back to New York, finish the picture in a hurry so that we could express copies of it to all those television stations hungry to have it at once!

I did indeed rush back to New York, finished the rough cut, and showed it to Dr. Franklyn M. Branley of New York City's Hayden Planetarium. My question to him was: given that the Russians have now broken the space barrier, how long would it be before man sets foot on Mars? Dr. Branley thought for a moment and then said, "Well, given that the Russians have boosted an object that heavy into space, I'd say man has a good chance of reaching Mars by the year 1978." (*Note:* NASA's Pioneer Venus spacecraft, loaded with instruments, was targeted to enter Venus' day side on December 9, 1978!)

The date of 1978 that was at the time twenty years into the future then became the fictional date for the ensuing drama that we called *The Space Explorers*. (The film is now a cult classic, as can be seen by such fan sites as www.thespaceexplorers.com.) The astronaut who seeks to become the first man to set foot on Mars in the film is Commander Neil Perry; his ship is the *Polaris I*; and it is his 10-year-old son Jim Perry who stows away aboard the rescue ship *Polaris II* after his father's space ship gets into trouble near the orbit of Mars. Once Jimmy is discovered, the voyage to Mars provides a perfect opportunity for the boy to see the planets close up, and learn all about space.

When this feature-length film was completed in 1958, we cut it into six-minute episodes and sold it as a miniseries to television stations coast-to-coast. The series was an instant success — so much so, that we immediately went to work on a sequel, *The New Adventures of the Space Explorers*.

Timing Is Everything

While we were recording dialogue for the sequel, a fellow named Norm Prescott was working in a studio directly across the hall. During a break, he peeked into our studio, saw the *Space Explorers* characters on the screen, and approached me. "Are you the one who did *The Space Explorers*?" he asked. I nodded affirmatively. Prescott then surprised me by saying that this meeting was fortuitous; he had seen *The Space Explorers* running in Boston, where he lived, and wondered if I'd be interested in joining him in making a feature-length animated cartoon to be called — he urged me not to laugh — *Pinocchio in Outer Space*. I laughed.

Pinocchio in Outer Space? I thought the idea ridiculous. The very concept sounded shlocky — like a "B" or "C" film made on a shoestring, and playing on the bottom half of a double bill in theaters headlining something like *Abbot and Costello Meet Beauty and the Beast on the Moon*! I promptly, almost contemptuously, dismissed the idea and went back to recording *The New Adventures of the Space Explorers*.

But a few weeks later, riding the train back to my home in the suburbs, I began thinking, "Wait a second ... the classic tale of *Pinocchio,* written by Carlo Collodi in 1880, has Pinocchio going to an island where bad boys are turned into donkeys. *What if* ... (if one is a writer, one always asks oneself *what if* ...), what if Pinocchio goes *not* to an island where boys turn into donkeys but, instead, goes to *Mars!* Instead of Jimmy Perry going to the orbit of Mars, Pinocchio goes to Mars and *lands* there! And maybe he finds life on Mars! And ... what if..."

The idea took root and began to possess me. I wrote a five-page synopsis. I showed it to Norm Prescott. He liked it. Prescott knew of a mid-size animation studio in Brussels, Belgium. He presented my synopsis to Raymond Leblanc, owner of the Brussels studio. Leblanc, too, liked the idea (after all, Pinocchio is a European character) and offered not only to provide animation services, but also to co-finance the picture!

We were off and running! While I was at it, I thought, *why not portray*

Mars legitimately?—with a close look at the "canals" ... and polar ice caps ... battered by mega-sand storms ... and, yes, even possessing water.

Just as I had done with *The Space Explorers,* I did with *Pinocchio in Outer Space,* I sat down with Dr. Franklyn M. Branley of the Hayden Planetarium and reviewed script points. He was delighted by the idea of giving a fictional story some solid authenticity. "Mars is farther from the sun than we are," he reminded me, "so the sky would be darker. The sand is reddish-brown. As for water, well, there *could* be water there — we don't know yet — but if there *is* water on Mars, it's probably underground." (Forty years later, NASA would confirm that.) The finished film shows water underground on Mars.

Martin Caiden, author of books about aviation and coauthor of *Destination Mars,* suggested, "If there *were* Martians, they'd probably have huge chests to breathe Martian air low in oxygen." I wrote a scene in which Pinocchio, on Mars, encounters a suit of armor built with room for a huge humanesque chest. (The scene was deleted when we found we were running long and overbudget.) And, yes, a horrific sandstorm nearly buries Pinocchio's spacecraft.

Pinocchio in Outer Space, the 72-minute animated feature, was begun in 1960, completed in 1964, and distributed throughout the Americas by Universal Pictures in 1965. In 1966, the film received a standing ovation as an official entry in the prestigious La Biennale di Venezia XVII Mostra Internazionale Film per Ragazzi in Venice, Italy (aka the 17th annual Venice Film Festival).

The Space Explorers and *Pinocchio in Outer Space* were both known to Jim Dodd at NBC Enterprises in New York. *The Space Explorers* and *The New Adventures of the Space Explorers* (which was finished in 1960) racked up impressive sales in syndication. So, in 1963, when Jim Dodd and company were presented with the Japanese television series that became *Astro Boy,* buzz about *Pinocchio in Outer Space* was already making the rounds about town.

(Recall that, when making the English-language version of the very first *Astro Boy* episode, this writer recommended that the NBC sales team make a sample reel consisting not only of *The Birth of Astro Boy,* but also *Expedition to Mars.* Osamu Tezuka had already recognized the "tweak" value of a landing on Mars; he made that particular adventure the third in his series of 193 episodes. Tezuka's appreciation of Mars, and my appreciation of that red planet, is one of the things that brought us together, right from the start. Our tastes were remarkably similar.)

So it is that this writer has long considered the red planet Mars as a gate on the pathway leading to anime in the Americas today.

Big World, Little Adam

Using the same technique as that which had worked so well in *The Space Explorers,* I launched a new series of 104, six-minute cartoons made from existent material gleaned from several sources — especially, the U.S. Department of Defense and various contractors engaged in America's race for space. The series is called *The Big World of Little Adam,* a kids' eye view of outer space as it actually exists. The technical advisor was again Dr. Franklyn M. Branley of the Hayden Planetarium. *The Big World of Little Adam,* launched in 1963, at the same time that shows as disparate as *Astro Boy* and *Sesame Street* were also launching. The series was commended by the National Education Association for nonviolent excellence.

CHAPTER 18

Homogeneous? Yes. Bisexual?

Crossing the Pacific, heading to Japan for the first time on that eventful 1964 trip, I naturally had certain preconceived notions of what I would find in Tokyo. Of one thing I was certain: in Japan, the man is king. The women serve the men. That was the first notion that was challenged, once I arrived.

"This is 1964," I was reminded by my hosts at dinner. "Things are different now ... not like before." Dinner was served in a festive room that seemed more like a nightclub than a restaurant. In "olden days," Kaoru Anami, head of production for Mushi Studio, was saying, "that was true. Now, since the war (i.e., World War II), things changed. Women are wanting more rights. They don't stay home so much any more." Fumio Suzuki, agent/liaison for Mushi in relations with NBC, agreed. Suzuki's wife, in fact, owned a beauty parlor and was away from home during the day, six days a week, Monday through Saturday. Suzuki's young son, Masayuki, was fed and tended by Suzuki's mother.

My wife, Eileen, was amused by this rather frank dinner talk. She nodded agreement with our hosts and explained that, in America, women talk constantly about "women's lib"; women want to get out of the kitchen and have their own career, she explained — "not just live in the shadow of the man."

Next day, at lunch, while Mrs. L shopped, Suzuki and I were joined by two other men — Tatsuo Takai, composer of the score for *Astro Boy,* and Sam Okudaira, procurement agent for Toei Co. This time, the conversation actually startled me. The topic, introduced by Tatsuo Takai, came around to homosexuality.

Homosexuality in Japan? Japan, where the man is still king? Sam Okudaira nodded and agreed that it was true: homosexuality was becoming very popular, he said, especially with girls; they are amused to see young boys going with other young boys. In fact, stories with underlying bisexual themes were becoming commonplace in girls' (manga) comic stories, Okudaira said.

145

Japanese pornography has long been known in Asia and the West. The advent of home video in the mid–1970s is said to have been instigated and promoted, in fact, by the pornography industry, acknowledged to be huge in Japan. In the 1960s, before Sony's invention of Betamax, the first home video cassette format, filmic pornography was available as 8mm home movies. Knowing this, I had difficulty nonetheless in accepting the notion of bisexuality in Japan. The notion seemed incongruous.

A few years later, in 1967, Osamu Tezuka sent NBC Enterprises the first episode of Mushi Production's newest series, *Ribon no Kishi* (*Princess Knight*), described earlier in these pages. Recall that the heroine was a girl, a princess, but was born to a king and queen who needed a male heir that could ascend to the throne, so they raised their daughter as a boy. Viewing an early episode in NBC's screening room, I did see traces of Greek mythology, traditional European pageantry, and, yes, a trace of bisexuality; but the subject was treated with such subtlety, such discretion, that I was sure we could overcome any Western objections with a carefully worded adaptation.

No matter, NBC was having none of it. They were taking no chances. Given the climate of the times, the constant threat posed against such anime content by Action for Children's Television and the Federal Communications Commission, NBC's decision was understandable.

Not until the arrival in North America of *Sailor Moon* in 1995 did "deviant" sexual content in anime again become an issue. Two of the series' characters, agents of wicked Queen Beryl, appeared on the scene. The two were lovers: one, with striking white hair — we called him Malachite — fondles and cuddles a diminutive blonde with long tresses; our name for this character was Zoysite.

From the first scene in which this pair appear, I was puzzled by Zoysite's unusually deep voice. What odd casting, I thought; why would any Japanese director cast an actress with such a deep, virile voice to recite Zoysite's ultrafeminine lines? Then, later, from the Japanese dialogue I realized that Zoysite was not a woman, at all — Zoysite was a man! *Holy smoke,* I said aloud — she's a *guy!* Homosexuality comes to children's anime!

And these scenes were actually broadcast in Japan, exactly as I was seeing them on the viewer — uncut — in California! (No wonder this television series was so popular with young Japanese girls! What Sam Okudaira had said, thirty years earlier, was absolutely right.)

The American studio DIC Entertainment had imported the series. DIC's solution to the male lovers situation in *Sailor Moon* was to do the only thing DIC could do, under the circumstances, namely, identify Zoysite as a woman and completely skirt the issue of homosexuality. No other solution would have satisfied a U.S. broadcaster's department of Standards and Practices. To heighten the problem, DIC had been attaching a brief, made-in-house Pro-Social Message at the end of each *Sailor Moon* episode; how, then, could DIC have presented an ongoing homosexual love affair, which would have indicated DIC's apparent approval of behavior considered deviant in the Western world?

A phalanx of fans did write to protest DIC's decision. Those fans were familiar with the Japanese and Chinese homevideo versions of the series, so they knew that the Zoysite character was a man. When those fans, though, understood DIC's dilemma — make the change or forget about broadcasting the offending sequences on the air — the fans grew quiet.

It is for sociologists to explain why young Japanese girls are titillated at the prospect of young Japanese boys engaging in homosexual and bisexual affairs. (Perhaps it's for the same reason that men are excited by women engaging in similar behavior with other women.) But the phenomenon is real, it is being exploited, and — as cash register receipts attest — it is profitable.

Curious Yuki

The son of a Toei Company rep stationed in New York City several years ago had a son, Kenji (not the boy's real name), who was then 14 years old. My own son was then 12. At lunch one day, the rep and I were discussing various issues that confront teenagers. Sex seemed to be the biggest single issue.

Erotic manga (comics) are very big in Japan, the rep was saying. You know who reads erotic manga? The rep answered his own question: not adult men with unhappy home lives, he said. Most of the readers are junior high school kids and high school boys like Kenji. They're curious about sex. They have no experience with women.

And the women? (The rep had a daughter two years older than Kenji.) They peek at magazines that their brothers buy, or their boyfriends, or husbands. Women in Japan don't like to be seen buying erotic manga for themselves. But manga for ladies, especially for girls, show it as romance. It's softer.

Kenji was a boy living abroad. The Toei rep spoke with special interest about teenage boys living abroad. At that age in Japan, he said, most boys and girls have very little to do with the opposite sex. But they are curious.

They think love between boys in another country is okay. Those boys are far away, so they're not threatening. (I would call that vicarious experience.)

Of special interest to this writer is the fact that erotica is no longer confined to manga; it is entering the mainstream through anime, and, little by little, it is gaining acceptance.

CHAPTER 19

Giants among Giants

Osamu Tezuka

One cannot discuss giants of anime without paying homage first to Osamu Tezuka, *Manga no Kamisama,* the god of anime, the giant of all giants in the pantheon of Japanese greats. Much has been written about Tezuka-San in these pages, citing his seminal role in launching the anime industry in Japan in the mid–1960s. From the vantage point of the twenty-first century, we add that a museum dedicated to his memory, the Osamu Tezuka Manga Museum, has opened in his home town of Takarazuka, near Osaka, some four hours (by bullet train) from Tokyo. The museum houses a permanent exhibit of his works (he drew 150,000 pages of comics in his lifetime), an entrance hall that re-creates the fairy tale-like World of Princess Knight, an area dedicated to Leo/Kimba the White Lion, and even an animation classroom fashioned as the robot factory in which Astro Boy was built.

Hundreds of Tezuka's drawings were collected into an exhibit that opened in the National Gallery of Victoria in Melbourne, Australia, in 2006 and then in the Asian Museum in San Francisco in June, 2007.

No other Japanese artist/animator has been so honored or so cherished. When Osamu Tezuka died in February 1989, the newspaper *Asahi* wrote: "...One explanation for the popularity of comics in Japan ... is that Japan had Osamu Tezuka, whereas other nations did not. Without Dr. Tezuka, the postwar explosion in comics in Japan would have been inconceivable."

Chiaki Imada

Chiaki Imada, former head of Toei Animation and undeniably a producer ranking high among giant figures in the history of anime, would eventually prove to have a downside as well. In mid–1980, Filmation Studio in

Hollywood determined that a series of 12 animated feature-length fairy tales for release in theaters worldwide would be a worthy project. A project of that scope, however, requires substantial financing — far more than Filmation itself was equipped to manage. The studio asked if I could help bring such a project to fruition — ideally, with the help of a studio in Tokyo. (Filmation executives knew of my acquisition of ten short animated fairy tales from Toei and my strong ties to that studio's International Department.) I put the Filmation project to Toei's Chiaki Imada one night on one of his rare visits to Los Angeles and, with the Filmation executives in attendance, asked Imada-San if he would consider embarking upon a project of co-producing twelve animated feature-length fairy tales. The concept certainly seemed to make sense; Imada was already at work on a program to produce animated feature films for delivery to Toei Studios for exhibition in Toei's own theaters in Japan. To the surprise of all, the producer from Toei, when we suggested partnering with Filmation on *Aladdin and His Wonderful Lamp,* quickly and enthusiastically said "Yes!"

The very next morning, Filmation began work on Aladdin character designs and script ideas for the screenplay (these were to be some of the elements for which Filmation was to be responsible).

Less than a month later, I would learn, while lunching with Toei's local rep, that, in fact, Imada had already begun work on developing characters and script for a feature version of *Aladdin* that Toei was making *on its own* — without the participation of Filmation or any other studio!

When I complained of this to friends at Toei's International Department, with whose help years earlier I had acquired the ten short fairy tales from Toei Animation, International's Mr. Homma shook his head and said, simply, "That's unfortunate. Mr. Imada has done that a number of times in the past."

As a result, when Filmation needed help in meeting CBS-TV deadlines for Filmation's *Zorro* series early in 1980, no one considered Toei. I brought in Tokyo Movie Shinsha (TMS) studio, instead, to subcontract much of the animation work laid out by Filmation. Fortunately, TMS performed honorably and well. *Zorro* premiered on CBS in the fall of 1980 to the satisfaction of all parties concerned.

Comics Are *Manga,* Animation Is *Anime*

Osamu Tezuka always considered himself an artist, not an animator. What he drew was manga, not anime. And, as used in this book, *anime* has referred primarily to Japanese animation as it is seen in animated television program *series* for children. This leads us to Chiaki Imada, the giant who built Toei Animation. Certainly Toei Doga feature-length animated films — *Puss in Boots, Treasure Island, Little Norse Prince,* among others — qualify as anime too, and deserve their moment in the sun. Indeed, in the earliest days of Toei Doga, that studio produced only animated features to be exhibited in Toei-owned theaters. It was when Osamu Tezuka stunned the animation community in Tokyo with Mushi Productions' television sale to Japan and America of *Tetsuan Atom* that Chiaki Imada decided that Toei, too, should be in the business of producing anime series for television.

Imada hired the likes of Leiji Matsumoto and Go Nagai to create television series concepts that Toei Doga could sell initially to Japanese television networks, then to the West. The gambit paid off. Toei Doga, with its ongoing slate of fully animated feature films for theaters, plus skeins of lesser animated series for television, grew from a modest supplier of features for Toei's Feature Division into a mighty powerhouse that emerged as a stand-alone fiefdom of Chiaki Imada.

So, Imada-San, though an aggressive producer — and not a creative genius in the mold of Osamu Tezuka or Hiyao Miyazaki — must rank in the league of anime's giants among giants.

Hayao Miyazaki

Hayao Miyazaki, widely regarded as the new "Walt Disney of Japan" after the death of pioneer Osamu Tezuka, is generally hailed as the towering giant on the Tokyo animation scene today, well into the twenty-first century. Miyazaki began his career after graduating from Tokyo's Gakushuin University with a degree in political science and economics in 1963 — just as Tezuka was launching the famed *Tetsuan Atom/Astro Boy* series for television; in fact, Miyazaki credits Tezuka as one of his very earliest influences.

Without missing a beat, Miyazaki went right from the university into a staff job at Toei Animation, working for Chiaki Imada in Imada's newly formed television cartoon production unit (not Toei's theatrical division). Working there as an in-betweener (not as a lead animator — just drawing the action *in-between* an assistant animator's positions). Miyazaki met fellow animator Isao Takahata and the two soon became close friends. They worked together mainly on television series, learning their craft and acquiring skills, especially the skills of creating special effects (such as rain and mist), from seasoned, feature-caliber animators.

Chiaki Imada was impressed from the start with the two young animators. He realized that the two had gained enough experience working on tele-

vision series, such as *Secret Little Akko,* and had accumulated enough senior-
ity by 1968 for Takahata to be named director — and Miyazaki, scene designer — of the studio's upcoming theatrical feature *Little Norse Prince* (for
which this writer created the English adaptation). Oddly, Toei's International
Department displayed little enthusiasm for that picture, though I thought the
characterizations and storyline were compelling; further, as if in defiance of
Toei's International Department, *Little Norse Prince* became Toei's most popular and critically acclaimed film at the time, both domestically and interna-
tionally.

We have seen, in earlier pages, how the bright young talent Leiji Matsumoto became attached to Toei's television division and developed one successful anime series after another (*Star Blazers, Space Pirate Captain Harlock,*
among others). That did not happen with Hayao Miyazaki or Isao Takahata.
Instead, they took a step backward: They left Toei — regarded as a huge mistake at the time — and went to work at smaller studios, notably TMS, that
specialized in television animation. Miyazaki's explanation for having made
a move that puzzled many: He was gaining more control over his projects.

It was at TMS that he made *The Castle of Cagliostro* (1979), the feature
that brought Miyazaki major public attention. He was given carte blanche to
write the story, redesign the character of Lupin III — Master Thief, originally
drawn by Kazuhiko Kato (popularly known as Monkey Punch) — and direct.
The picture was a smash in Japan and at several international festivals.

In that same year — 1979 — Tokuma Publishing Co., Ltd., a major publisher in Japan, published one of Miyazaki's science-fiction tales as a manga
serial. Miyazaki himself wrote and drew the first installments. The tale was
Nausicaa of the Valley of the Winds. Popular response was so strong that Tokuma
financed a feature film version of it; the 1984 feature, in turn, became Japan's
most successful animated feature to that time, eclipsing even *Little Norse
Prince.* Miyazaki's reputation was made!

Tokuma, correctly sensing that they had hitched their wagon to a rising
star, actually built a studio, Studio Ghibli, for Miyazaki and collaborator Isao
Takahata. The energetic young pair quickly hit their stride. Beginning in
1985, they delivered an astonishing average of a feature a year! No other studio in the world, including Disney, was matching that rate. For comparison,
Walt Disney's *Snow White, Pinocchio,* and *Bambi* each took four years to
make. Yet, Hayao Miyazaki and Isao Takahata, working alternately, delivered
Laputa: Castle in the Sky in 1986, *My Neighbor Totoro* and *Grave of the Fireflies*
in 1988 (both released initially on what must be considered the greatest first-
run double bill in film history), *Kiki's Delivery Service* in 1989, *Only Yesterday* in 1991, *Porco Rosso* in 1992, *Pom Poko* in 1994, *Princess Mononoke* in 1997,
Spirited Away in 2001, *Howl's Moving Castle* in 2005, and the studio shows

no sign of letting up the blistering pace! Not only were these films enthusi-astically received by critics, but starting with *My Neighbor Totoro,* they became increasingly huge financial hits, with the last few breaking several Japanese and international box office records. Truly, Hayao Miyazaki, supported by his collaborator Iasao Takahata, is a giant among giants.

Katsuhiro Otomo

Thirteen years younger than Hayao Miyazaki — Miyazaki was born in 1941 and Otomo in 1954 — and not so prolific as Miyazaki, Katsuhiro Otomo is nonetheless a giant figure on the Tokyo anime scene. He caught Osamu Tezuka's eye early, when Tezuka was laying the groundwork for the feature film version of his *Metropolis* manga. Tezuka gave Otomo much key work to do in drawing the storyboard, knowing that Otomo had become an outstand-ing storyboard artist before reaching the age of 20.

While still a very young man, and finding whatever work he could — even as crew — the artist was impressed with what are now regarded as the Vietnam "rebel movies." He could understand the James Dean role in *Rebel without a Cause.* Otomo then contributed one of the nine segments for *Robot Carnival* and one of the three in *Neo-Tokyo* (both pictures dated to 1987), then went directly into production of the acknowledged masterpiece that would catapult him to international fame, *Akira* (1988). Thus, at age 34, Kat-suhiro Otomo found himself in the same league as Hayao Miyazaki and, con-sequently, could write his own ticket as a character designer, author, director, and producer.

Akira is a story of rebellious youth in Neo-Tokyo, a tale which takes place well into the twenty-first century after World War III. That tale, based upon Otomo's manga, tells of Tetsuo, a drag-racing biker (Otomo's James Dean or *Easy Rider*'s Peter Fonda?) who's selected by the army in the belief that the boy's unusual mentality might be just the thing to revive its long-dormant Akira Project. What is ultimately revived, however, is Tetsuo's reawakened sense of power — power that quickly grows out of control. (The Akira Pro-ject had created a Frankenstein monster!) Tetsuo's festering resentment over a lifetime of second-rate existence leads to Tetsuo's lashing out with destruc-tive force! Animated in minute detail, detail that would become an Otomo hallmark, *Akira* racked up surprisingly high box office grosses in the United States and became a worldwide success.

In 2004, Otomo released his second full-length anime feature *Steamboy.* This epic, too, is a tale of unbridled power; but it's the kind of superpower that comes to industrial-age Victorian England in the era of steam. The race for power is *on*—not just for great power or maximum power but for *super-power*, the power that comes only from steam that is heated and compressed beyond the limits of nature. Only one device in the world is capable of forcing steam into an unnaturally compressed and explosive state—and that device is the one invented by Steamboy's grandfather. Every industrialist in the world wants to get his hands on that device, including the boy's own father.

Greed is the order of the day! Predictably, the device falls into "the wrong hands," is used to superheat steam beyond the device's capacity to control it, and the result is a cataclysmic explosion. Building after building explodes! Window after window shatters under the hurricane force of exploding steam! Computer-driven effects show the city of Manchester, England, being rent asunder by violent blasts of uncontrolled power! This is Katsuhiro Otomo at his minutely detailed best.

These, then, are the greats:

Osamu Tezuka, artist

Chiaki Imada, producer

Hayao Miyazaki, artist

Katsuhiro Otomo, artist

In this writer's opinion, they are giants among the giants of anime at the beginning of the twenty-first century. Who knows what others are waiting in the wings?

CHAPTER 20

Other Giant Robots
I Have Known

Once Osamu Tezuka showed Tokyo that there's gold in robots, the robot gold rush was on. Mitsuteru Yokoyama was not alone in the perception that a giant robot, such as Tetsujin-28, would strike the public fancy; other studios large and small quickly produced their own versions. Toei alone came up with five robotic giants, starring in their own series.

Golion. This was a 26-episode series from Toei Animation. The story line, set several hundred years in the future, was that another world war had broken out on Earth, hydrogen bombs had exploded everywhere, the human race was virtually annihilated, and the planet was desolate. Seizing what he saw as an opportunity, the Great Emperor Bazal of the Galra Empire (also known as Bazal, the Emperor of Vice, ruler of space) packed any survivors into a spaceship, brought them to him, picked out the healthiest men, then tried to convert them into half-beast fighting robots! But five young men — Akira, Takashi, Tsuyoshi, Isamu, and Hiroshi — escape and, riding on the backs of five lion-shaped giant robots, they march toward the Great Emperor Bazal.

Daikengo, Guardian of Space. This 26-episode tale concerns Ryger, a prince of the star Emperious in the Alliance Galaxy. Ryger has an older brother, the crown prince, who dies sadly in a battle with the invading Magerans. The Magerans have sweeping plans: They intend to conquer not only the star Emperious, but also the entire Alliance Galaxy! (How the Magerans would actually *rule* the entire galaxy is not made clear.) With the crown prince gone, Ryger is named to succeed his father, the king. But Ryger prefers to fight evil, rather than sit on the royal throne; so he passes the throne to his younger brother while he, Ryger, rides the giant robot Daikengo into battle!

Sun Vulcan, 26 live-action episodes. Cashing in on the craze for giant robots, and anticipating the advent of what would become their Power

154

Rangers, Toei Studio (not the animation division) designed a character named Ryusuke Owashi. His secret identity was Vul Eagle. Then came young Kinya Samejima, secretly Vul Shark. And Asao Hyo, secretly Vul Panther. All three were members of Vulcan, the Sun Combat Unit organized to fight against Black Magma, a mechanized empire commanded by Generalissimo Hell Satan, whose very name told his enemies that the generalissimo was up to no good. When challenged, the three young heroes rode into battle in a bomber called the Cosmo Vulcan and a tank called the Bull Vulcan. Finally, when those two formidable war machines were inadequate by themselves, they *combined*, "Getta Robot"–style, into an even stronger machine, the Sun Vulcan robot!

Denjiman. Another Toei live-action series with overtones of anime, a series so successful it stretched to 51 episodes. The enemy here is the Vader [*sic*] tribe, an aggregation of living organisms that come from another *dimension*. These technologically advanced creatures with bodies like Earth's protozoa can transform into plants, animals, and parasites that feed on human beings. Mankind's only salvation is Denjiman, the Electro Combat Unit formed of five young fighters selected from all over the world. Their only protection against the invaders is their specially made body armor — and Icie, an electro dog.

And, finally, from Toei — the studio that gave us *Giant Robot* from Mitsuteru Yokoyama, creator of the giant robot "Ironman 28":

Iron Robot 17! This was another live-action adventure series, 35 episodes, so similar in concept to Mr. Yokoyama's Tetsujin 28, that it is difficult to imagine him not taking umbrage. Here, too, we find a young boy, Saburo, as the hero; he slips in a snow bank while mountain climbing and discovers, embedded in the snow, a newly invented electronic brain recently stolen from the laboratory where it was built. The Brain is "alive"; it is using its own army of giant robots to protect itself from man and to help it take over the world! One of those robots working for the Brain is Iron Robot 17! But clever Saburo co-opts the robot and together — Saburo and Iron Robot 17 — they foil the foul schemes of the Brain.

(*Note:* Mitsuteru Yokoyama had licensed Toei Co., Ltd. to produce a live-action series based upon his concept of Giant Robot — a series called, in English, *Johnny Sokko and His Flying Robot*; he had, additionally, licensed Toei Animation to produce his series *Sally the Witch*. But he licensed his most famous series, *Tetsujin 28* (Gigantor), to Dentsu Advertising Agency, which produced the series not at Toei, but at TCJ [Television Corporation of Japan]. TCJ, in turn, later unleashed its own giant robot, *Diapollon*.)

Tetsujin 28 FX. These 49 episodes, described earlier as the latest, and transforming, incarnation of Mitsuteru Yokoyama's boy-driven giant robot. But the boy driver this time is not the Japanese 12-year-old called Shotaro

Kaneda. Nor is he that boy's English persona, Jimmy Sparks. Instead, production studio TMS took a fresh look at the boy, and realized that — thirty years after he first appeared — that young man, in the year 1993 a.d., was 42 years old! He had his own 12-year-old boy — a fine lad who was every bit as brave and adventuresome as Jimmy had been when he was his son's age! So the series was, in effect, *Tetsujin 28-FX* (thirty years) *After*.

(*Note:* Mr. Yokoyama, in his origin story for Tetsujin 28, explained that the robot's inventors had built 27 prototypes of the robot — all failures — before finally reaching successful #28. But the public had never seen the 27 failed models. That changed when TMS studio produced its series, *The NEW Adventures of Gigantor*. TMS introduced Tetsujin model #8. The character was likeable, ingratiating, not much taller than a 12-year-old boy — rather like *Star Wars'* meant-to-be-cute little robot R2D2.)

A Japanese firm called Popy has manufactured a line of jumbo-size (two feet tall) polyethylene robots with names like Sky Zero, Red Baron, Hajime Jaguar, Lenzari — names for giant robots all but unknown in the West. All are indigenous to Japan. One cannot help but wonder why the giant-robot phenomenon grew and flourished in Japan far more than anywhere else on Earth.

CHAPTER 21

OVA + VHS + DVD =
Home Video

Astro Boy, Gigantor, 8th Man, Kimba, Marine Boy, Speed Racer— all those historic, first-wave anime series had been made for, and released to, television in the decade of the 1960s. No other market for them existed at the time.

All that changed in 1975. Sony Japan announced that it had perfected a revolutionary new technology. They called it Betamax. The new invention allowed viewers like you and me to sit at home and watch television and not necessarily watch any program then being aired; we could watch content *pre-recorded!* We could sit in our living room or office, and see a replay of a program that had aired yesterday, or a year ago, or that had been animated a week earlier in Japan and rushed to us in the mail.

In my office in Times Square one morning, I received a parcel from Fumio Suzuki (former agent for Tezuka's then-shuttered Mushi Production)— a parcel containing three, maybe four, Betamax cassettes. The label on the cassettes gave the date in 1975 when the cassettes had been made, it identified the programs recorded thereon, and asked that I please notify the sender, Suzuki, of my early reaction to the programs. I'd gladly have done so, but *who could play the cassettes?* I had no Betamax player in my office and knew of none in the building, so I walked to NBC Studios a few blocks away. By then, the men of Enterprises (Rittenberg, Schmidt, Dodd, Liebenguth) were gone, so I went directly to a broadcast control room, pulled up a chair, and watched a monitor while an engineer graciously ran the cassettes — at double speed. I was impressed with the new technology, but not with the programs on the cassette — and told Suzuki so — by telex, the high-speed communication technology at the time.

Betamax soon gave way to VHS (unfortunate, because Betamax had better resolution and stored more information in less space) and more and more anime began to appear on VHS cassettes. Some anime was even being created expressly for videocassette. By 1978, a fan named Carl Gafford coined the word "Japanimation"; and English subtitled cassettes, often made by fans of Japanimation (a term no longer in vogue), were becoming commonplace.

OVA means Original Video Animation. That's a term created by Japanese producers, not Westerners. When the acronym first arose, it referred to anime made for distribution to the home video market, regardless of whether a television sale was (eventually) involved, or not (see *Escaflowne* and *Vampire Hunter D* below). Because the OVA market is not subject to standards set by the television industry, OVAs are often lurid, violent, pornographic — or all of the above!

The first OVA is generally considered to be 1983's science-fiction drama *Dallos*. (*Note:* How many pornographic films, made expressly for the home video market were made before 1980 is a figure that will probably never be known.) When I first heard the title *Dirty Pair* in the mid–1980s, I thought that was a mini–OVA series made for the "adult" market. As for an episode of *Dirty Pair* being hailed later as "the first *DP video* dubbed into English," I thought, "Hmm, the adult market for anime in the Americas must be bigger than I thought!" I could not imagine any broadcaster in Asia or in the West going on the air with a title like the *Dirty Pair*. (Actually, the *DP* stories proved to be more violent and humorous than sexy.)

VHS and DVD are the distribution system(s) for home video. Early in the twenty-first century, twenty years after the appearance of the first OVA, so many titles were available for home video, in VHS and/or DVD format, that a separate book could be written to list and describe them all. A relative few, however, are so singular, so distinctive, so enduring, that they are clearly of more than routine interest and are mentioned here, in brief:

Ambassador Magma. Osamu Tezuka's concept of a golden human rocket created to defend Earth. Magma's arch enemy is Goa, a foe that Magma had defeated earlier, but who now returns to try again to capture the planet.

Appleseed. Masamune Shirow's vision of a world devastated after World War III. The remnants of scattered governments create a worldwide force of Biodroids — half-human, half-robot, to enforce law and order. This does not sit well with much of the world's remaining population. (Who wants to take orders from a Biodroid?)

A feature-length version was made in 2004. Its most notable feature seemed to be the process in which the film was shot: a unique process of shading gave the characters a feeling of roundness, of depth, creating an illusion of 3-D without the expense of actually shooting in a digital, 3-D method.

Barefoot Gen. Keiji Nakazawa's recollection of how he, as a child, and his family struggled to survive incredible hardships in World War II–devastated Hiroshima.

Bubblegum Crisis. Suzuki Toshimichi's tale of Mega-Tokyo in the year 2032. This time, the city is rising from the ashes caused not by war, but from an earthquake. A small band of Knight Sabers declare war on an evil organization that has arisen from the rubble—the Genom Corporation and its dreaded android "Boomers" Corporation.

Casshan, Robot Hunter. Tatsunoko Studio's dark vision of civilization cringing from enslavement by an army of sinister robots. Young and old alike look to a mysterious avenger known only as "Casshan" (The Robot Hunter) to defeat their ruthless enemy.

Dirty Pair. Created as a series by Haruka Takachiho. The aptly named "Lovely Angels," Kei and Yuri, find themselves, in one adventure, trapped in a wooded wonderland on the planet Ukbar. A routine investigation by the two special agents, the Dirty Pair, uncovers a plot by two evil masterminds to seize control of everything in sight. Each episode in the series is self-contained.

The Vision of Escaflowne. A 26-episode video series that found its way to America's Fox Kids Network. Hitomi is a high school girl who suddenly finds herself sucked into another world, Gaea. There she meets Van, a boy her age. Together, she and Van join forces—she, with her psychic vision and he, with his giant robot dragon Escaflowne, to defeat the destructive evil empire, Zaibach.

Evangelion. Studio Gainax series about Shinji Ikari, a 14-year-old boy brought to Nerv, a military-laboratory operation dedicated to fighting "angels," which are giant robots—all one of a kind—but with a single purpose, namely, to destroy mankind. Shinji is to pilot an Evangelion (shortened to "Eva") a super-huge robot that must "synch" with a 14-year-old pilot. Problem: Evas occasionally malfunction and go on rampages of their own!

Giant Robo. Another giant robot piloted by a boy, this one from the artist Mitsuteru Yokoyama, who gave us *Tetsujin28/Gigantor*. This boy/pilot's name is Daisaku; he serves the Experts of Justice in their desperate effort to protect Dr. Shizuma, inventor of the Shizuma Drive, the world's greatest source of power! A criminal organization seeking to seize the Shizuma Drive is "Big Fire"—and, needless to say, they'll stop at nothing to seize it.

Lensman (1984). A 107-minute sci-fi tale of a dying Lensman who entrusts young Kimball Kinnison with a mystery Lens that contains information essential for the destruction of the evil Boskone Horde. Lensmen are heroes who have learned how to tap into the mystic powers of the cosmos. Civilization is counting on them!

Neo-Tokyo (1987). Actually a 50-minute collection of three short films by three famous anime directors: (1) "Labyrinth" is Rin Taro's "Through the Looking Glass" vision of what happens when young Sachi and her cat fall through a mirror into an alleyway behind their house and, while following a sinister clown, hear invisible children playing in the darkness as trolley cars filled with skeletons rumble by; (2) "Running Man": Yoshiaki Kawajiri's twenty-first century cyberpunk action thriller of a death-race driver who, after ten years of being literally plugged into his car and finishing first, finds that his nerves are shot; (3) In "The Order to Stop Construction," Katsuhiro Otomo shows what happens when a young bureaucrat, the sole human being at a construction site deep in the Amazon jungle, tries to order his robots to stop working.

Patlabor. Mamoru Oshii's dark vision of a future in which mankind, to ease the burden of hard labor upon human workers, invents giant robots to do the "heavy lifting" of construction. These robots are "Patrol Labors"— "Patlabors"— and, as machines with no more intelligence than enormous gantries, they work well when in the hands of trained operators. But when cyberpunk hackers begin programming the robots, the giant *mecha* run amok and create widespread havoc!

Robot Carnival (1987). Nine leading Japanese animators, including Katsuhiro Otomo, contributed their own short segments to this 100-minute video, which is all about robots. (Nine robots, nine flavors.)

Silent Mobius (1991). Modern-day "nice" witches combine their own special powers with scientists and police to combat predators able to travel with ease from one dimension to another. Written by Kia Asamiya.

Tokyo Babylon (1992). It's up to Subaru Sumeragi, the most gifted, most powerful medium in Japan, to divine and piece together all the clues to a series of killings. Adapted from CLAMP's popular manga.

Vampire Hunter D (1985). Adapted from a novel by Hideyuki Kikuchi, this OVA proved so popular in Japan that it was picked up in America in 1993 by the Science-Fiction Channel. The story is one of a young girl kidnapped and carried far off by a powerful vampire. But a chase by police turns up evidence that the girl may, in fact, have willingly eloped with the handsome vampire.

It's a Bird! It's a Plane! It's ULTRAMAN!

One well may ask: Ultraman? Is Ultraman anime?

He's Japanese. He looks like a robot — a big robot, at that. And his adventures have appeared in animation. (Like Superman, who came from the planet Krypton and now poses as Clark Kent, mild-mannered reporter, Ultraman came to Earth from Nebula M78 and now poses as Hayata, member of a special task force known as the Science Patrol). When Earth is invaded by alien creatures from space, or threatened by a giant prehistoric monster — and all Earth defenses fail — Hayata transforms into the giant superhero Ultraman, and, from that moment on, the enemies of Earth are doomed!

Yet, it's true that Ultraman is at heart an artifact of live action; he was intended, from the get-go, to be a creation of live action. The question then arises: why include him in any other category?

This writer has always believed that improbable images, images that are the unique work product of an artist's mind and hands and that are captured on film one frame at a time, constitute animation: Willis O'Brien's King Kong, pounding his chest atop the Empire State building in the 1933 film classic, is animation. The monster Godzilla tramping through the (actual) streets of Tokyo is animation. Gerry and Sylvia Anderson's Supermarionette (puppet) Thunderbirds are rendered in animation.

Eiji Tsuburaya, the special-effects wizard who created Godzilla, knew in the 1970s that he wanted to produce an *Ultraman* series for television in Japan. But, to do so, he needed an optical device called a beam-splitter, that is, equipment that allows a filmmaker to integrate an (animated) image into a live-action shot. No beam-splitter meeting Tsuburaya's needs and, perhaps, purse, was available in Japan.

Now it so happened that Eiji Tsuburaya knew a representative in Japan named Sam Okudaira. And it so happened that Okudaira is the representative who came to me a year earlier to acquire my cartoon feature *Pinocchio in Outer Space* for distribution in Japan by Toei Animation. And — another coincidence — I knew that an Oxberry Model 1200 beam-splitter was sitting, unused, in the special-effects shop of Howard A. Anderson on the Paramount lot in Hollywood. That beam-slitter had seen yeoman duty in creating special effects shots for the *Star Trek* series; now it was sitting unused because the series had wrapped, and Howard Anderson wanted to replace that early beam-splitter with a newer, improved model.

Happy ending: Howard Anderson's early beam-splitter went to Tokyo, was installed for Mr. Tsuburaya and has, since then, delivered many a special-effects shot showing Ultraman in action — action impossible for live actors to achieve without a beam-splitter. This writer, since enabling Eiji Tsuburaya to obtain his essential beam-splitter (a device that itself sounds as though it is a component of a science-fiction tale), has felt a special affinity for Hayata and Ultraman. It is a pleasure to report that they are alive, well, and living among other giant icons in Tokyo.

CHAPTER 22

Fandom of the Anime

The Japanese had a word for it — an English word: *maniacs*. That was the word they used in the 1960s when describing intense fans. Now the word they use is Japanese: *otaku*. The term is meant to be indulgent but not flattering.

Fan clubs are certainly nothing new in the Americas. Stars of the silent movie screen in the United States, stars like John Gilbert, Mary Pickford, and Douglas Fairbanks, found themselves being adored by starstruck fans early in the twentieth century. The advent of talking pictures in 1927, spearheaded by Warner Bros.'s *The Jazz Singer* starring Al Jolson, only seemed to swell the ranks of fans who organized into clubs. But these clubs lionized, and continue to lionize, living actors — not animated drawings.

My first encounter with a fan of anime occurred in 1966, when a young girl — I assumed she must have been a "tweeny," a girl between the ages of 9 and 12, wrote an adoring note to Billie Lou Watt, then being heard on television as the voice of Jimmy Sparks, the animated 12-year-old boy who controls the giant robot Gigantor. The girl evidently thought that Billie Lou Watt was a *boy*; after all, Billy is a boy's name and Lou, short for Louis, is a boy's name, so, surely, Billie Lou Watt must be a boy. In fact, the late Billie Lou Watt was a woman, a mother, in her 40s. (Billie Lou kindly responded to the girl, was careful not to deceive or mislead her, and the two eventually became pen pals.)

Soon thereafter, a number of fan letters began to arrive, some from adults, and some from fans thousands of miles away. I began to wonder if Mickey Mouse, Donald Duck, or Popeye were receiving fan mail.

Not long after the *Kimba* series had run its first course and largely disappeared from the airwaves, a delegation of three young men from Los Angeles, all fans of *Kimba* and headed by one Robin Leydon who had befriended Osamu Tezuka, came to my Times Square office to ask me, please help put *Kimba* back on the air! (Repeat: Three young men, all apparently in their

20s, were asking me to please bring *Kimba* back to the airwaves. Certainly, I thought, this was unprecedented; and, if these three men — one an animator working on new scenes for *Battle of the Planets*—were campaigning for a return of *Kimba,* how many other adults across the country were thinking the same thing?)

The fact is that Japanese-animated adventure series, 30 minutes in length and with edgy stories and characters, were developing fan bases while most American-made cartoon series were not.

(*Note:* As context, Stan Lee at Marvel Comics and Julius Schwartz at DC Comics in the mid–1960s revived the costumed superheroes of the 1930s and '40s in comic books. Hollywood's Filmation Studio in the late 1960s animated the adventures of Superman, recording the voices in New York at the same studio and with the same actors who were performing in anime series. All this undoubtedly helped animated television fandom get started.)

Finally, one writer, based in Los Angeles and working at the time as a librarian for an aircraft manufacturer, became so enamored with Japanese anime that he and a few like-minded friends organized what they called the Cartoon/Fantasy Organization (C/FO). The year was 1977, the writer was Fred Patten, and C/FO was probably the first organized fan club for anime in the United States. Another writer, Jerry Beck, then living in New York City, headed an East Coast branch of C/FO.

Impressively, the Tokyo anime community took note of this organization, and came to realize that Japanese works were having a significant impact on the culture of the West. No less luminaries than Osamu Tezuka and Kazuhiko Kato (already famous under his nom-de-plume, Monkey Punch), appeared in person to address crowded C/FO meetings in Los Angeles. Not just on the East and West Coasts of the United States, but also in such interior cities as Philadelphia and Chicago, fan clubs sprang up under the guidance of young men like Bill Thomas III (Philadelphia) and Doug Rice (Chicago) who understood that Japanese cartoons, with their science-fiction themes, were not just for children.

Even European comic properties, such as Tintin (Belgium's popular 18-year-old investigative reporter), Asterix (France's diminutive Celtic warrior), Lucky Luke (Belgian version of a U.S. frontier cowboy hero), Bernard Prince, and other popular heroes of the 1960s — all of which had strong story values (indeed, this writer adapted a *Lucky Luke* animated feature in which impersonator Rich Little performed all the voices of Luke, plus the four Dalton Brothers in a comically convoluted robbery scheme!) — failed to match anime's compelling treatments of mature subjects, such as love, sex, jealousy, death, coming of age, and complex, adult science-fiction adventures, to name but a few. Anime was as bold as it was unique.

From the anime clubs that were springing up all over the United States, even on college campuses, came the next logical outgrowth, the anime convention. Perhaps inspired by popular Star Trek conventions, anime conventions began to coalesce. Notable among these is an event called Comic-Con that began in 1969 in San Diego, California. Though geared for American comics and their creators, the convention soon began attracting top Japanese artists and their works. In 1979, Monkey Punch, creator of the *Lupin III* strip, visited Comic-Con and, the following year, Osamu Tezuka arrived with a print of his theatrical feature *Phoenix 2772*. Go Nagai, of giant-robot fame, attended too, as did representatives of Tokyo Movie Shinsha with a demonstration of 3D television. Japanese comic books could be seen everywhere in the dealers' room. If it had not been apparent before, it certainly was obvious now: Anime and, yes, manga had arrived in the Americas — Big Time.

In 2001 this writer was invited to Toronto to participate in that city's huge Anime North convention. Ostensibly, the occasion would provide a forum for Mr. Takahashi of the Consulate General of Japan to present Fred Ladd with an inscribed cut-glass trophy saluting the American for having introduced anime to North America. In fact, what impressed "the American honoree" most was the line of attendees waiting to be admitted to the convention hall! The line, formed of thousands of enthusiastic young fans, stretched out from the hall's box offices to the end of the block — easily, a four- or five-minute walk to the corner — then, around the corner, midway to the next parallel street! Here were throngs of fans, waiting to be admitted to a convention, all about anime! (Half the girls, it seemed, were dressed as Sailor Moon, in costumes so elaborate they rivaled any made by the costume departments of major Hollywood studios!) The sheer size of those lines demonstrated forcibly what a major and adult phenomenon anime had become in the Americas.

The following year, Mr. Takayuki Matsutani, president of Tezuka Productions, Tokyo, was the convention's honoree and, I am told, the convention's attendance was even higher than it had been in the previous year — a new record! Indeed, attendance kept increasing year by year.

As guest of honor at AWA 9, Anime Weekend Atlanta, Year 9 (2003), I saw attendees take over an entire major hotel in an event where attendance topped even the record numbers in Toronto. And this was not New York, Chicago, or Los Angeles — it was Atlanta, Georgia, a midsize city in America's old South.

By the year 2007, any list of major anime conventions ("cons," to devotees and *otaku*) had to include Anime Weekend Atlanta (September), Katsucon in Washington, D.C. (February), Sakura Con in Seattle (April), Anime Central in Chicago/Rosemont (May), Anime North in Toronto (Memorial

Yu Takahashi, consul general of Japan in Toronto, presents glass obelisk to Fred Ladd, held aloft by Anime North organizer Tamara MacDonald at Memorial Day 2001 convention. Inscription in glass reads, in part, "Presented to FRED LADD In deepest gratitude for his valuable role in bringing the art of Japanese animation to international audiences." The woman seated on right is Fred's wife Eileen. Photo courtesy of Ian Stuart and Anime North.

Day), Fanime Con in San Jose, California (Memorial Day, USA), Project A-kon in Dallas (June), Anime Mid-Atlantic in Richmond (June), Otakon in Baltimore (July), and Nan Desu Kon in Denver (September). OhioCon and Anime Los Angeles are on a list of somewhat smaller fan conventions, a list growing longer, year by year.

By far the largest of anime fan conventions is Anime Expo. In 2006, this convention was housed in the huge Convention Center in Anaheim, California, where, on opening day — July 1, a Saturday — crowds reportedly topped 40,000 attendees! In 2007, the convention headed for the sprawling Convention Center, in Long Beach, California, where thousands of fans waited for hours just to be admitted. Every year the event grows larger. Only anime, those singular and incredibly popular animated programs from Japan, can lay claim to this kind of popularity.

Anime Is Big Business

A study by the Japan External Trade Organization (JETRO) in Los Angeles reported that, in 2004, Japanese anime sales in the United States alone, including anime character products, surpassed ¥520 billion — that is, US$4.51 *billion* dollars and, if not for piracy run rampart, figures for 2006 would have been even more stellar. Globally, according to an estimate by the Stanford Japan Center, the anime industry is expected to grow into a market worth more than 10 trillion yen, that is, US$86.88 billion.

Beyond any doubt, anime is alive and well and flourishing in the Americas. Not only is it big business by any sense of the word, anime and its brethren — manga, cosplay, toys, films, and even music — have changed the pop culture of the Americas profoundly.

Anime Fandom: An Interview with Fred Ladd

Fred Ladd chose not to elaborate about his involvement with anime fandom, but acceded to Harvey Deneroff's request for an interview about the subject. That interview was conducted via email December 5–8, 2006, and is reprinted here in its entirety.

When did you become aware of how fans were responding to the various anime projects you were working on, starting with *Astro Boy?* Did early American anime fans seem different in any particular way?

The first fans of which I became aware were those few young people who wrote to NBC in 1964 to say that they, the fans, are glued to their television sets whenever *Astro Boy* comes on. However, the first fan mail I ever saw was the near-love letter written by a teen, or pre-teen, girl to actress Billie Lou Watt, in the mistaken belief that Billie Lou was a boy (instead of a mother), who voiced the role of Jimmy Sparks, the 12-year-old boy who controls the robot Gigantor. The girl was thrilled with the exploits of Jimmy. I recall, thinking at the time, that (with the possible exception of Hanna-Barbera's *Jonny Quest* [1964]), there was no comparable American cartoon character that would capture the young fan's fancy.

Later, particularly with the arrival of *Speed Racer,* I began to notice that fan mail was coming not just from young kids, but (mainly) from young males closer to 20 than to 12.

When did you become aware of what Fred Patten was doing with the Cartoon/Fantasy Organization (C/FO)? When did you meet with him and other anime club members? Were you invited to speak to any of them in their formative years? What was your initial reaction to all this?

I arrived at Filmation Studios in Los Angeles in mid–May 1980, ostensibly to help the studio set up and program a cable channel that was to be called the Fat Albert Channel. The studio did not have a library sufficient to sustain an ongoing schedule ("critical mass") for a channel that would operate on a daily basis and was looking to me to acquire and adapt anime series for that purpose. The very morning in which I "moved into" my desk, the phone rang. The caller was someone who identified himself as Wendall Washer, an artist whose office on the second floor was directly over mine. I was astounded! "How did you know I was here?" I asked.

He answered that "everybody" knew I was there; word had spread that I had moved into the studio. Later that day, I met him. Through Washer, I met with Robin Leydon, the super-fan of *Kimba* (the same chap who had visited me in New York to petition me to please bring back *Kimba*). Shortly thereafter, I was introduced to Fred Patten, a fan-cum-author and librarian, who had been instrumental in forming the Cartoon/Fantasy Organization (C/FO).

Mere days after that, I found myself addressing a C/FO meeting — perhaps 60 or 70 young fans, mostly males in their twenties — and was not a little surprised to find the organizers projecting rare film prints (rather than grainy videocassettes) of *Astro Boy, Gigantor,* and *Kimba*— programs which I had produced in New York! (Their having prints of *Astro Boy* proved fortuitous ten years later, long after NBC had destroyed all available prints; copies of the English soundtracks on those C/FO prints were eventually used to create the Australian restoration of the series in 2005.) And Fred Patten, one of the organizers of the C/FO, would later become a respected writer-authority on the status of anime in America.

What was your sense of how fast these groups started to spread?

I learned that fans of anime were grouping into clubs all throughout the state of California — from San Diego to San Francisco. That was a revelation; until that time, I had no realization of how such clubs were proliferating. And the *passion* of those fans seemed to know no bounds. More than once, as a visitor to a club meeting, I found myself in a Q and A session, being asked questions about matters in which the fans were more knowledgeable than I — they remembered details in my scripts that I, myself, had forgotten!

What was the first anime convention of which you became aware?

Shortly after relocating to Los Angeles in 1980 and encountering Robin Leydon, he informed me of a fan convention to be held in late July: Comic-Con, to take place on the lower level of the U.S. Grant Hotel in San Diego. I understood that earlier editions had been held in the El Cortez Hotel. Apparently that event, intended initially to celebrate comic books and their creators (in Japan that would be manga) had outgrown the El Cortez and now, swollen with the ranks of new manga and anime dealers, an enlarged Comic-Con was relocating to the U.S. Grant.

This phenomenon surely was unique. This was not merely a copycat of a Star Trek convention, not just a big fan club of a long-gone television series; Comic-Con was a forum for recognizing American artists and publishers of comic books and, increasingly, the genres of Japanese manga and anime. This was new. This was exciting. I had never seen anything like it. This had to be the genesis, the granddaddy of anime/manga fan conventions. Today, anime "cons" are ubiquitous, they've mushroomed throughout the Americas.

What was the first purely anime/manga event you attended?

In 1993, Takayuki Matsutani and I were honored guests at an anime "con" held in the convention center of the San Jose (California) Red Lion Inn. Mr. Matsutani attended as president of Tezuka Productions, I attended as president of the Greatest Tales Company; highlight of the event was the celebration of Astro Boy's thirtieth birthday. The convention's organizers had thoughtfully prepared a giant birthday cake bearing thirty candles. I sang the *Astro Boy* theme song in English, Mr. Matsutani sang in it Japanese; attendees were astonished to learn that the English lyrics were written before the Japanese lyrics, and the Japanese lyrics were patterned after the English (dubbing, in reverse)!

Also in attendance were Billie Lou Watt, the English voice of Astro Boy; Ray Owens, voice of Doctor Elefun; Carl Macek and Jerry Beck, heads of Streamline Pictures (they had distributed the feature *Akira*); and Todd Ferson and Shawne Kleckner, heads of The Right Stuf International, distributors of *Astro Boy* videocassettes.

What was your impression of those early conventions?

The aforementioned 1993 event in San Jose impressed me mightily as the maturing of the anime fan convention. Organizers had flown Mr. Matsutani from Tokyo and Watt and Owens from New York City. They had booked a major convention center for a weekend, booked entire floors of the Red Lion Inn. Thousands of fans could do more than merely visit the dealers' room; they could see anime videos on television sets in their rooms, and they could attend panel discussions about a wide variety of anime-related subjects. This event was clearly a major undertaking. The only comic books on view were Japanese *manga*; the only animation on view was *anime*. This con, dubbed "Anime America," was more than a side attraction of a show dedicated primarily to American icons; this con was all about *Japanese anime and manga*. That concept was new and daring. It was bold, risky, and one that would require substantial underwriting. Nonetheless, the show's organizers pulled it off. As a result, the anime fan convention would never be a one-room event again.

CHAPTER 23

Anime Today: Where It Is, Where It's Heading

Not surprisingly, many of the most popular anime series of the late 1990s persisted and carried over into the early years of the new century. Titles like *Pokémon, Digimon, Dragon Ball Z, Yu-Gi-Oh, Gundam, Sonic,* and others of the era could still be found in daily program listings.

But after the year 2000 new names and new editions of famous older series began to appear. The most surprising new edition, to this viewer, was the reappearance of the very first anime series ever.

Astro Boy, the pioneering manga-turned-anime that started the anime tsunami in 1963 (even though that animation was rendered in black and white and action was severely limited), first reemerged in color in 1980—but to a lukewarm reception in Japan and the United States; then it reemerged *again* as a new series in 2003. The latest reincarnation was superbly animated—computers had smoothed-out the action. The color was bright and vivid, anticipation for the new series was running high, and then, in September, the series premiered nationally in North America on the Kids WB Network. The show, to borrow a theatrical expression, laid an egg. Gone was the plucky little robot boy who fought a never-ending battle against an endless array of quirky crooks; in its place was a diminutive advocate of robots' rights, pleading for robots and humans to respect each other, to live together in harmony and peace. (Think *Kimba*; mutual respect among species, all creatures living together in harmony and peace — these were Osamu Tezuka's favorite themes.)

Ratings of the new series dropped from the very beginning. By the end of the third week, it was clear to all at the network that the new *Astro Boy* series had to go. And go, it did. It went to Cartoon Network, a Time-Warner cable affiliate of Kids WB's broadcast network. There, to no one's surprise, the series again performed poorly. The cable network dropped the series, sent it back to Kids WB. WB, in turn, tried once again to slot the series, but, by then, advertisers had soured on the show, they were demanding refunds, and *Astro Boy,* the 2003 edition, was taken off the air — permanently.

Several fan letters were received in this writer's office through the remainder of 2003, asking why I had shifted the emphasis of the new series away from the fun and action of the original (1963) series to the talkative, more philosophical approach of the new series. The answer was simple: I had nothing to do with the new series. The English adaptation was created entirely by Sony Pictures Entertainment (USA) Inc., who had worked hand-in-glove with Tezuka Productions creating the series in Tokyo.

Even so, the question arises: would a more fun-filled adaptation — at least, in the English dialogue — have made the series more palatable for Western tastes? Maybe not. Mickey Mouse, the perky little rodent who had built an empire for Walt Disney, had lost much of his luster long before the twenty-first century. The Disney Studios' roster of short subjects made for theatrical release looked less and less to Mickey for fun, and more and more to the irascible Donald Duck. (Could Astro Boy, similarly, be a character whose time has come [do you mean "gone"]?)

Going into the twenty-first century, anime fans looked less and less toward the traditional style of older series coming from Japan, and more and more toward new series perceived to be more *edgy.* Some of them include the following:

Naruto. Naruto is such a series. The manga was first published in 1999, on the very cusp of the new century. Its main character is Naruto Uzumaki, a boisterous, restless adolescent ninja constantly searching for approval and recognition as the strongest and bravest ninja (the *hokage*) in his village — the antithesis *of* Astro Boy! *Naruto,* heavy on martial arts, was picked up for animation by Studio Pierrot and Aniplex; it appeared on Animax satellite television in the fall of 2002 and, midway through the first decade of the new century, was still being seen in the West on Cartoon Network's Toonami television channel.

Dragon Ball Z. The durable, ongoing *Dragon Ball Z,* described earlier, is another popular anime series based, like *Naruto,* on martial arts. Its hero, loosely styled after Goku, the Monkey King of Chinese legend, seeks ways to fend off attacks on Earth by aliens from outer space.

(*Note:* With heightened emphasis on martial arts, and growing popularity of *cosplay* [costume playing], fans have been attending conventions dressed in costumes that more and more feature weaponry. Lloyd Carter, principal in AWA [Anime Weekend Atlanta], reports that guards at the doors now check cosplayers to be sure that anything resembling a weapon is fake, and not the real thing.)

Eureka 7. This series follows the adventures of a boy who joins a band of rebels fighting a tyrannical, outlaw state. The boy, "Renton," is a skate-boarder, as are others in the band; they use a stream of energy to hover or fly through the air. However, giant enemy robots are out there (just when we thought we'd seen the last of the giant robots) and they skateboard, too. Luckily, Renton has a special connection with giant robot Eureka 7, thanks to a key given to Renton by his older brother. This prize-winning anime series captured several best-of-kind awards at the Tokyo Anime Fair, 2006.

Bleach. High school student Ichigo Kurosaki has the ability to see ghosts! So can a girl "soul reaper" named Rukia Kuchiki, who is surprised by Ichigo's ability to see her. One day, while struggling to capture an evil spirit known as a "hollow," Rukia is injured. She transfers her powers to Ichigo, the two join forces, and together they go forth to search for hollows. Tite Kubo is the author of *Bleach,* the manga. Since its debut in 2001, the property has been adapted into an anime series, two OVAs, an anime film, a rock musical, and several video games. Clearly, this series is a child of the new century.

Fullmetal Alchemist. Alchemists, in olden days, were those who sought to turn lead into gold. In this modern Japanese adaptation, two young brothers seek to bring their dead mother back to life, though that would violate a sacred rule of alchemy. In the process, the older brother loses his arm and a leg (replaced by bionic, metallic limbs); the younger brother tragically loses his entire body. To save the soul, the soul is locked into an empty suit of armor. This done, the brothers set out on a quest to reunite body with soul (in effect, playing God), but, instead, they discover secret governmental military plots. (Appropriately, this series was animated by Studio Bones; it is peculiarly Japanese in concept, yet enjoys great popularity in North America.)

Inu Yasha. The words mean "dog spirit" (note that, in Japan, even spiders are believed to have a spirit). This anime series features a middle school girl who travels backward through time with an eclectic assortment of highly unconventional friends, including a half-dog demon, a demon slayer, and an unprincipled monk, seeking to do good and right wrongs in feudal Japan. The manga from which this series springs was published by Shogakukan, who gave us *Pokémon,* and animated by Sunrise, famous for its many series of *Gundam,* including the recent *Gundam Seed.*

Gunsword. A strange man suddenly appears in town, carrying a sword that can summon a giant robot to do battle — battle against a man with a claw, a man who has kidnapped or slain several characters on the planet. The planet, we soon discover, is actually a prison planet with ties to Earth.

Oban Star-Racers. An unusual Japanese-French co-production created, written, and produced by Savin Yeatman-Eiffel, who grew up in the heyday of anime series like *Captain Harlock* and *Speed Racer. Oban* tells the story of Eva 15, daughter of race manager Don Wei. The girl, under the alias "Molly," joins her father's famous star-racer team of the greatest pilots in the universe. Every 10,000 years, the greatest pilots face-off in a race shrouded in mystery: the Great Race to Oban! The outcome can transform the balance of power in the galaxy! Filmed in combination 2D/3D animation process. Broadcast in the United States on Toon Disney.

Trigun. This sci-fi, space western follows two improbable sleuths, Meryl and Milly Thompson, employees of an insurance society, as they attempt to track down a gunfighter called Vash, the Stampede, a human typhoon. Chaos and damage seem to follow Vash wherever he goes! The ladies' assignment: eliminate, or at least minimize, the harm created by Vash. Turns out, though, that — surprise! — Vash is a gunfighter who is more clumsy than (intentionally) destructive, an inept but crack marksman who only wants, in his words, "love and peace." He uses his weapons only to save lives wherever he can. The destruction, as the lady sleuths discover, is caused not by Vash, but by a *real* villain!

Zatch Bell. An unusual teaming between Toei Doga and Shogakukan (ShoPro) produces this tale of 14-year-old Kiyo, who one day acquires a gift, *Mamodo,* a being named Zatch, from another world. Mamodos, possessing elemental powers, are controlled by a spellbook; their lives depend on it. Kiyo soon learns that Zatch is just one of many Mamodos on Earth, all competing with each other for supremacy, and all in danger of falling into the wrong hands. Kiyo and Zatch bond, they learn about life here on Earth, and they find that each strengthens the other in their friendship.

To be sure, other anime series flow from relatively new studios budding in Tokyo, studios formed to feed the insatiable appetites of cable and satellite television — series with titles like *.hack* (dot hack, wherein virtually all the world's future computers use one operating system), *Initial D* (street racing), *Kirby* (he's pink, fights monsters sent by an evil king), *Megaman* (boy with AI program fights evil), *Medabots* (boy with robot battles other robots), *One Piece* (sailor and pirate crew find great treasure), *Ultimate Muscle* (space wrestlers come to Earth to wrestle for supreme domination), and a series with the improbable name of *Bo Bobo* inspired, perhaps, by Samson of the Bible's Samson and Delilah: one man possesses an incredible ability to hear voices of *hair!* He uses that ability to fend off minions of the Margarita Empire who are stealing hair to empower their emperor!

Anime: Where It's Heading

Predicting the future of anime series in the 1970s was a no-brainer. The artist Go Nagai had reinvented the giant robot (named *Mazinger)* in 1972 with

Toei Doga, setting off a virtual explosion of copycat giant robots in that studio; Toei Doga was the dominant animation studio in Japan at the time, and the remainder of that decade was easily dominated by the genre of the giant robot.

Predicting the future of anime series midway through the first decade of the twenty-first century is less certain. No clear genre had surfaced. Martial arts remained popular and, increasingly, girls—rather than boys — were becoming the protagonists. Mitsuteru Yokoyama had, forty years earlier, persuaded Toei to gamble on a girl-themed series called *Sally the Witch,* and it did well enough in Japan to merit a follow-up sequel, but *Sally* never became a huge international hit. She remained virtually unknown in the West.

Sailor Moon changed all that in 1995, when the manga — and the Toei-animated series about a group of very capable girls — burst upon the scene in Japan, Europe, and the West. *Sailor Moon,* aka *Usagi and Serena,* became an overnight sensation not only in entertainment media, but also in merchandising, where those closely associated with the property reaped instant and impressive wealth.

Teenage boys continued to dominate anime for the remainder of the twentieth century and, as we have seen, a few hardy giant robots controlled by boys persisted. But now, famed artist Hayao Miyazaki was featuring girl protagonists in his animated features —*Kiki's Delivery Service, My Neighbor Totoro, Princess Mononoke, Spirited Away, Howl's Moving Castle* —and all these girl-driven adventures have met with record-breaking success.

Bleach, Inu Yasha, Oban Star-Racers, Trigun

These precedent-setting anime series have bloomed just since the arrival of the twenty-first century. All are driven by female characters in the lead. It is no coincidence that the Japan Cultural Center (JACCC) in Little Tokyo, Los Angeles — an accurate barometer of trends in Japan — mounted a major exhibit in the summer of 2007, an exhibit that celebrated the roles of girls — and *only* girls — in anime and manga in modern-day Japan.

Japanese and Korean Meet at the Egyptian

The date of March 31, 2007, will surely go down in cultural history as the red-letter day on which Japanese anime and Korean animation met face-to-face in the United States, for the first time, at the Egyptian Theater in Hollywood, California.

The Egyptian Theater is a splendid movie palace, erected circa 1922 by the late master showman Sid Grauman, builder of famous Grauman's Chinese Theater. In association with the American Cinematheque, the Japan Foundation (Los Angeles) and the Korean Cultural Center (Los Angeles) presented an "Exclusive Premiere" of two feature-length animated cartoons. The Japanese entry is called *The Girl Who Leapt Through Time*; the Korean production bears the title *Aachi and Ssipak*. Both films bear a year 2006 copyright. This writer sat in the Egyptian theater with an invited audience and left that night with the impression that the two films just screened were accurate harbingers of what's to come from the Japanese-Korean corner of the world.

What makes *Aachi and Ssipak* so noteworthy is that it seems to have broken a long-held international view of Korean animation as being long on technical skill but short on creativity. Throughout the 1980s and 1990s, Seoul was seen by Western producers, such as Gracie Films and Film Roman, as a hub where television series like *The Simpsons* and *King of the Hill* could be animated inexpensively. Few locally conceived and financed Korean projects, though, caught on with audiences overseas. Now it was becoming suddenly apparent that director Bum-jin Joe and the creative team behind *Aachi and Ssipak* were raising hopes in Seoul for a possible Korean animation renaissance.

Such a renaissance, if indeed one should actually arise, would come none too soon. Prices for animation contracted with Seoul studios had been rising for years. Western producers, at the beginning of the new century, were already outsourcing their animation work to lower-cost studios in India, China, the Philippines, and elsewhere. Now, suddenly, on the heels of *Aachi and Ssipak,* comes word reported in *Variety* (September 3, 2007), the entertainment industry's reputable newspaper, that the Weinstein Co., successful U.S. distributor of the cartoon feature *Hoodwinked!* and in association with the management firm the Gotham Group and Chungcheongnam-do Province in Korea will team to co-produce and co-finance a slate of from six to ten animated features, all — like *Hoodwinked!* — to be shot in 3-D and budgeted at about $40 million each.

Furthermore, led by the Media Center in Chungcheongnam-do, production work on the films will reportedly be done by a consortium of thirty local animation and computer graphics companies, starting in October 2007, with the children's book favorite *A Cricket in Times Square* (previously made as a television special by Chuck Jones). As announced in *Variety,* preproduction and screenplay development are to be carried out in the United States and actual production will be rendered in Korea.

Emerging early as a pivotal year for Korean animation on the world stage, 2007 would prove to be a winner in terms of animation conceived for the domestic market as well. Feature animation, traditionally disappointing in the

Land of Morning Calm, would earn Sunwoo Entertainment's *Yobi, the Five-Tailed Fox* a surprisingly high $3.3 million upon its release in January.

As is the case in China, though, Korea's most rewarding segment of the animation industry in 2007 would prove to be children's television programming in 3-D. Outstanding examples of this include Iconix Entertainment's *Pororo, the Little Penguin,* a hit at home and abroad, and Ocon's *Dibo, the Gift Dragon,* scheduled for showing in Central and South America (through Disney's Playhouse Channel). *Eon Kid,* another successful children's series at home, was heading for U.S. release in 2007 on America's Kids WB Network.

And again following China's lead, various governmental agencies in Korea are beginning to join the trek toward nurturing the growth of the native animation industry, particularly with 3D animation. In addition to the Chungcheongnam-do deal with the Weinstein Company, the city of Seoul, famous so far for its numerous animation studios that provide animation services for American producers, is building a fund of nearly $30 million to support the growing native animation industry.

How Many Tezukas Work in Seoul?

Surely, Osamu Tezuka was unique — as unique in Japan as Walt Disney was in the United States. And, in terms of greatness, Tezuka became as revered in Japan as Disney had become in America. Indeed, Tezuka had been universally hailed as "the Walt Disney of Japan."

Early in the twenty-first century, no one will say with certainty that a new Osamu Tezuka has risen in Korea. Or that a new Walt Disney is warming up in a bullpen in Pusan. But the director Bum-Jin Joe (*Aachi and Ssipak*) is definitely regarded as a young (42, in 2007) man to watch.

Aaron Lim is one of the most recognized younger animators in Korea. Lim studied at San Francisco's Academy of Art University, was inspired by the 3-D animated feature *Toy Story,* switched his major to animation, and returned to Korea to make the feature *Mug Travel,* starring a polar bear, a penguin, and a baby. The feature opened in Seoul in March 2007 and proved immensely popular immediately. Look for lots more from Lim. Lee Sung-gang, Korea's best-known animator, exceeded all expectations when his *Yobi, the Five-Tailed Cat* opened in January.

The Girl Who Leapt Through Time, a sweet tale of a young girl coming of age, directed by Mamoru Hosoda, not only features a female character in the lead, it shows the influence of Hayao Miyazaki (Studio Ghibli) in styling and narrative: A young girl's wistful flight to the future and her encounter therewith a winsome teenage boy reminds one of Miyazaki's young heroine who is "spirited away" to a strange place where she meets a boy who is, and must remain, an unobtainable part of another world. Production values in this film from Tokikake Film Partners are first-rate and, in the opinion of this viewer, a match for any coming from Japan in the new century's first decade.

Aachi and Ssipak, a "controversial sci-fi comedy" described by its Korean director, Bum-Jin Joe, as far-out "edgy," shows us a bleak world of the future, a world in which Earth's natural resources have been exhausted, and now the major supply of energy comes from human solid waste. Gangs of bikers ruthlessly prowl the streets, preying upon small, blue, blob-like mutants who have arisen under Earth's harsh condition. Prized are those humans who are prolific producers of solid waste, who spend hour after hour in the bathroom, delivering raw material; in fact, the government has installed computer chips in every anus to measure output while government controls the population by distributing addictive, popsicle-like "juicy bars." Aachi & Ssipak are a Mutt and Jeff–like team, neither American nor Japanese in appearance, conniving to survive in hard times. Bum-Jin Joe, directing for Seoul-based Studio 2.0, explains that the film, scheduled to be in production for two years, and demonstrating superb special effects and videogame-like sequences, was planned for completion in two years; the production repeatedly ran out of money, though, and actually took eight years to complete — surely a record of sorts.

The Laws of Eternity, which premiered in Los Angeles in mid–May 2007, is a breathtakingly beautiful animated feature, as remarkable for its stunning visual effects as it is unusual. The film was produced (by Ryoho Okawa of *Cowboy Bebop* and *Animatrix* fame) in the Tokyo studio of Toei Doga, yet was made not as a conventional Toei picture but in association with a Buddhist organization called IRH-USA (Institute for Research in Human Happiness). And it is aimed directly at teenage audiences — not at children nor adults.

The tale follows four teenage students on vacation from school, visiting a museum in New York, where they see Thomas Edison's invention, the phonograph. They also see another of his inventions — the spirit phone — intended to permit living persons to call upon spirits in the world beyond. Outside the museum, a mysterious old woman surprises the four by declaring that she "has a message for [them] ... from the spirit world." That message inspires the leading boy, Ryuta, to actually build a spirit phone soon after his return to school. Before long, Ryuta and his girlfriend Yuko are ascending to the spirit world. There they encounter a tall, commanding human figure hailed as God Eagle. Guided by that mysterious figure, Ryuta and Yuko fly through a multidimensional spirit world, transversing (1) the Fourth Dimension, *Time,* (2) the Fifth Dimension, *Spirituality/Goodness,* (3) the Sixth Dimension, *Knowl-*

edge of Truth, (4) the Seventh Dimension, *Altruism,* (5) the rarified Eighth Dimension, *Compassion,* and (6) the all but unobtainable Ninth Dimension, *Universe,* wherein dwell the great guiding spirits of humanity, notably, Jesus Christ and Buddha.

Remarkably, brilliantly lit spacescapes aglow with vibrant colors make these sequences dazzling to behold. The film is literally a feast for the eyes. Toei Animation has come a long way from its modest origins in the late 1950s.

Such is the status of anime and near-anime early in the twenty-first century. Gone is the unchallenged dominance of North America in the realm of quality, world-class animation. On the rise in the Orient is formidable Toei Doga and, close on its heels, Korea. Can China, with vast infusions of a prosperous and committed government's money, be far behind?

Afterthoughts That Linger Long (... and Will Not Go Away)

Events described earlier herein have been entered on a timeline basis — that is, first things are described first and last things last. Still, along the way, a number of events have occurred that have little to do with dates or timelines; they simply remain indelibly etched in this writer's memory. They linger. Here now, in no particular order, are some of the more prominent, more memorable of those events, and the personalities who made them.

Tezuka, Tezuka

Japanese businessmen rarely, if ever, take foreign associates home to "meet the wife." That simply is not done. Instead, the businessman will take his guest(s) to a restaurant, a club, a bar where the businessman may boast that he keeps several bottles of his own liquor. Though I had once been invited to visit the home of agent Fumio Suzuki, he has been married twice and I have never met either wife. Osamu Tezuka, in his Mushi Production days, took Eileen and me to a famous restaurant (Chinzanso) in Tokyo, but I had never met Mrs. Tezuka.

That is to say, I never met her until the summer of 1998, nine years after her husband died. She and I both happened to be (a) in the Takadanobaba office of Tezuka Productions, and (b) when we were both at the world premiere of the studio's animated feature *Jungle Emperor Leo.* Mrs. Tezuka reminded me that her husband regularly referred to Mr. Ladd as "the Godfather of Astro Boy" and she knew that her husband and I both loved the character Pinocchio. I thanked the lady for her kind memories and reminded her that I always considered Osamu Tezuka to be a great visionary; he could accurately foresee a day when men would come to resent the robot as a device that would replace the man at work. (More than once in his anime, Tezuka would have one of his human characters shout: "I'm not taking orders from any robot!")

With Mrs. Tezuka, I was careful not to refer to Osamu Tezuka's love for erotica. He did, however, collaborate with Toei Animation on that studio's feature film *1001 Arabian Nights.* I screened that picture, alone, in the projection room of distributor Nippon Herald and was astonished by the degree of erotica shown vividly on the big screen. The year was 1969, American animator Ralph Bakshi had created *Fritz the Cat,* America's first X-rated cartoon, and now here was this Japanese film, showing sex more explicitly than had ever been shown in a live-action film projected in American theaters!

When I mentioned this incident later to Osamu Tezuka, he smiled but offered no explanation. Pornographic films had been a staple in Japan for generations; they were commonplace. What Tezuka had done, in his estimation, was to bring explicit sex gracefully, naturally, *artfully* to the big screen. That had never been done before in Japan. Clearly, the artist was pleased with his achievement.

Before *anime (animation),* there was *manga (comics),* and before manga, there were woodblock prints. The art of making woodblock prints —*ukio-e*— existed in Japan for hundreds of years, long before anyone began drawing stories in the form of manga. The last great master of *ukio-e* is considered to be Taiso Yoshitoshi, an artist whose career spanned two eras, from 1839 to 1892. During his lifetime, Yoshitoshi saw Japan reach out once more to the outside world, from which it had withdrawn 200 years earlier. A notable woodblock print of Yoshitoshi's is one called, in English, "Mount Yoshino Moon at Midnight." The print portrays a bleak, desolate landscape under a moon visible only as a faint ring of light girdling a blacked-out moon. The work is believed to have been rendered in 1886. It is the belief of this writer that Osamu Tezuka knew of that masterwork, knew it well, and was in fact so influenced by it that he incorporated it in his manga masterwork, *Jugulu Taitei Leo,* then in his anime version of that tale (our *Kimba the White Lion*). Recall that Kimba accompanies an expedition to the perilous upper reaches of "Mount Moon." There the expedition, after surviving foul vapors and a number of pitfalls, is trapped in a blinding snowstorm. Atop that mysterious mountain, most members of the expedition — even Kimba himself— perish.

Ukio-e, old woodcut prints mentioned above, literally means "pictures of a floating world." The pictures, in those pre-photography days, typically concentrated on objects of nature: Japan's beloved Mount Fuji, artistic land-scapes, still lifes, floral arrangements, and the like. What Osamu Tezuka did was to inject a feeling of motion into a still-life subject: He would draw a picture of Mount Fuji, Mount Moon, or Astro Boy, for example, then draw the same subject *a little closer*, then draw another picture of the same subject *even closer*—as though the successive drawings were being seen through the lens of a movie camera slowly moving in for a close-up. (That way, the artist was instilling a feeling of *motion* to a still subject. That is how he created action in his manga, and, then, in his anime.)

Remarkably, Tezuka kept drawing his famous manga in huge numbers even while his studio, Mushi Production, was churning out features and ani-mated series, one after another, at breakneck speed! In 1967 alone, Tezuka began drawing what he considered his great work, *The Phoenix,* targeting it at a more adult audience (*gekiga*). That manga, in turn, would then serve as inspiration for Tezuka's animated feature of the same name. (Later, Tezuka personally screened the movie for an enthusiastic audience at San Diego's 1980 Comic-Con convention.)

In 1968, even in the face of increasing economic adversity — Mushi Pro-duction was by then on the verge of collapse — Tezuka was envisioning the creation of *Black Jack, Buddha,* and *Ludwig B* in manga form. Those prop-erties, rendered later and little known in the Americas, have been quite pop-ular in the Far East.

That same year, 1968, Osamu Tezuka formed a new company that he called Tezuka Production (later, under American advice, amended to Tezuka Production*s*). The first anime to come from that studio was a 1970 television series all but unknown in the West, *Marvelous Melmo,* whose title character was a police woman. Melmo can go from adult woman to a child by chew-ing candy — metamorphosis pills — shaped like gumdrops: red ones transform her into an adult, blue ones reverse the effect. Melmo was granted those mys-terious pills when her mother died in an automobile accident (shades of Doc-tor Tenma's son, Tobio, who died in a similar accident in *Tetsuan Atom*); Melmo's mother, in heaven, implores the gods to grant Melmo the power to look after herself and her kid brother. Magic pills are the gods' solution.

NBC Enterprises, even if it were still in acquisition mode in the 1970s, would surely have rejected this series. NBC executives fretted about *Princess Knight*'s perceived "sex switch" a few years earlier; in *Melmo* they would likely be leery of the star's swallowing what appear to be pills.

Other outstanding manga, in addition to those previously mentioned, that came from the pen of Osamu Tezuka:

Bomba! Early tale of Otokotani, a young boy who, suffering from dementia, conjures into existence a demonic horse called "Bomba" that kills all those who belittle Otokoani, including the boy's parents.

Crime and Punishment. Dostoevsky's epic work as seen in 1953 through the eyes of Osamu Tezuka. Just as Tezuka had re-versioned Robert Louis Stevenson's novel *Treasure Island* by turning its human creatures into animal stereotypes (Jim Hawkins is portrayed as a rabbit, Squire Trelawney is portrayed as a pig), so Tezuka re-versions *Crime and Punishment* by having the repentant character of Raskolnikov portrayed as a Japanese version of a Russian doll.

Marvelous Melmo was the first series to be produced in the new (1970) Tezuka Productions studio. Melmo is a young police woman who can morph into a child and back, simply by chewing colored candy. Courtesy of Tezuka Productions. © Tezuka Productions.

Eulogy for Kirihito. Dr. Kirihito Osanai, a talented young researcher (modeled, perhaps, after Tezuka himself, when the artist was still a young medical student) studies a rare congenital disease called "monmo." The disease turns human beings into canine mutations. Sadly, Kirihito contracts the debilitating disease himself and understands that he can no longer remain in Japan. He leaves everything behind and embarks upon a nomadic existence that takes him everywhere from Taiwan to Syria. Ultimately, the character is transformed from victim to savior.

(*Note:* Transformation and metamorphosis became Tezuka's pet theme. He was intrigued by the notion of having characters evolve from one state into another — not unlike the gentle Dr. Jekyll who, after drinking a powerful concoction of his own making, morphed into the evil Mr. Hyde.)

Human Metamorphosis.

another manga that dwells on the theme of transformation featured earlier, as in *Marvelous Melmo*. In *Human Metamorphosis*, a beautiful, but deceitful, actress, Tomura, subtly evolves from being a famous actress to being a famous designer; then, she becomes a famous novelist. At each step along the way, Tomura discards those around her who can no longer be of use to her in her newest phase.

Buddha. This manga seems to conclude that the enlightenment sought so desperately by Buddha for so many years is, in fact, the realization that one must continually seek enlightenment. The *Ludwig B* of the manga title is Ludwig van Beethoven, and this work is Osamu Tezuka's ornate portrait of a troubled genius, a great composer aware that he is slowly going deaf.

Black Jack. A brooding manga that, some wags say, could reflect the dark thoughts of Tezuka's evil twin, if Tezuka had a twin (he did not) and that twin had gone on from medical school to become a doctor. Black Jack is a disbarred surgeon who, typically, caters to the rich and famous; they summon him when they have an incurable disease or condition with which no one else can help. Then Black Jack operates on the inoperable, cures the incurable, and presents his patients with a staggering bill. Black Jack is not "your friendly neighborhood doctor" and this series is not one that parents would encourage their children to read. Yet, Black Jack proved to be unexpectedly popular and was serialized for over five years!

Also from Tezuka: A manga called *MW,* based upon actual events stemming from a nerve gas developed by the United States for possible use in Vietnam but stored on an island off the coast of Okinawa. In Tezuka's twist on this bit of reality, the gas begins leaking and kills everyone on the island except two delinquent children — Michio and Iwao — who escape extinction and vow to live to tell the tale.

Note: (This spinning of a fictional tale based upon a real-life incident was a favorite technique of Tezuka's — one that he used again in an early *Astro Boy* episode: Shortly after American astronaut John Glenn completed his initial orbit of Earth, Glenn reported seeing what looked like fireflies in space. Tezuka seized upon that report and animated an adventure in which space fireflies not only existed — they were in fact toxic "mist men" come to Earth to do us harm.)

Much space has been devoted in these pages to Osamu Tezuka because he was, in a very real sense, the "Walt Disney of Japan." Just as Disney built a studio of his own to animate his own characters, so Tezuka built his own studio — Mushi Production — to animate his own famed characters.

Tezuka's early contemporaries — Mitsuteru Yokoyama, Kazumasa Hirai, and Jiro Kuwata, among them — did not build animation studios; instead, they licensed their characters to a producer (in this case, Dentsu) and the producer, in turn, commissioned an animation studio (in this case, TCJ) to render the animation itself for Yokoyama's *Tetsujin 28* and Hirai-Kuwata's *8th Man*. Ironically, just as Mushi Production eventually failed, so too did TCJ! Mushi gave way to Tezuka Productions; TCJ reemerged later as Eiken Production.

Tatsunoko Production

Tatsunoko Production, creators of the three *Gatchaman* Series — later variously adapted in English as (1) *Battle of the Planets*, (2) *G-Force*, and (3) *Saban's Eagle Riders* — in the late 1990s, attempted yet another story arc to add to the previous three. This time, however, the plan was to *redesign the characters:* the five young action heroes would in essence retain their identities, but they would be made to look much younger. Tatsunoko executive Koki Narushima showed me the new character designs. The five young heroes all looked as though they were perhaps 13 or 14 years old — too young, I thought, to "carry their own weight," too young to pilot a sophisticated ship like their upgraded "Phoenix" (no relation to the Tezuka character), too young to do serious battle with the arch-villains of planet Earth. Midway through the first decade of the twenty-first century, no Western buyer with check in hand had come forward with a purchase agreement for Tatsunoko's proposed new series.

Lip Synchronization (Sync)

When visitors to Los Angeles from Tokyo Movie Shinsha, the animation studio behind our *New Adventures of Gigantor* came to the recording studio where we were creating the English version of their *Shin Tetsujin-28*, they were astounded at the precision of the lip sync. The animated characters, they said, seemed to be speaking with better lip synchronization in English than they had in the original Japanese version. One studio head observed: "The [English] words 'hang better in the mouth' ... looks like that guy is really talking English."

Years later, a resident of Tokyo, now living in Los Angeles, would say that imperfect lip sync doesn't bother him at all; he listens for the *meaning* of the words, and does not care whether the voice appears to be coming out of a particular character's mouth, or not. (An old saying goes "Y'pays your money, y'takes your choice.")

The importance, or unimportance, of fine lip sync was driven home for this writer in the mid–1970s when Belgium was celebrating 150 years of nationhood under its monarchy. Belgian television had filmed a program called *Cages,* an off-beat tale of a bored, middle-class, middle-age housewife who unexpectedly meets a released prisoner and becomes intrigued by him. I had written and directed the English version, which was then shown nationally in the United States on public television. One critic in San Francisco wrote, astonishingly, after seeing the program that he was puzzled as to why the film was shot in English. *Shot in English?*

Suddenly it became clear that the English dubbing must have been precise enough so that not even a professional critic could spot the difference. The moral, if there is one, must be that the dubber's job is a thankless one; the kindest thing that can be said of a dubbed film is that the film does not *look* dubbed.

The Land of Oz

The Land of Oz, that mythical place conjured by American author L. Frank Baum, also resonates in Japan. The Tokyo-based Toho Co. produced an animated version of Baum's tale *The Wonderful Wizard of Oz* circa 1980; this writer became creative director of the English-language version.

Because the English version was to be produced in Canada, with Canadian writers, Canadian directors, and Canadian actors replacing the Japanese voices, it was deemed mandatory that I go to Toronto to supervise the recording sessions.

Actor Lorne Greene, widely believed to be an American movie star, was in fact Canadian. Greene was cast to re-voice the role of the wizard. Young actress Aileen Quinn, praised for her singing and acting the lead role in the 1982 film version of the musical *Annie,* was permitted by Canadian authorities to re-voice the part of Dorothy, the girl who is swept away by a tornado to the Land of Oz.

Meeting Lorne Greene for the first time, I went to introduce myself and shake his hand. "Hello, Lorne," I said. He smiled, extended his hand, and said, "Hello." The force of his voice startled me. I had not expected it. That was easily the most powerful voice I had ever heard. Studio engineers modulate that power when they record it, but hearing it firsthand — unmodulated, unsuppressed — was an awesome experience. Both Greene and Aileen Quinn, with their musical timing, proved to be natural dubbers; they had no problem lip-syncing English dialogue to replace the Japanese lines.

Musical timing and a sense of rhythm are the keys. Invariably, those performers with musical talent prove, in the recording studio, to be the most adept at replacing foreign-language dialogue.

Journey Back to Oz

Journey Back to Oz, written by this writer as an animated sequel twenty years before Toho would animate the classic tale described above, was initially offered to Mushi Production to animate. The late Mushi Production studio chief, Kaoru Anami, looked at the complicated storyboard (manga-style illustration of the story), realized that the tale was long (at 90+ minutes) and difficult to animate, and pronounced it "suicide!" Toei Animation, too, showed no enthusiasm for the project, even without seeing any story-board.

At that time (1963), Belvision Studio in Brussels was deep into the animation of the feature *Pinocchio in Outer Space* and simply lacked the capacity to take on another long feature film. Eventually, my partner, Norman Prescott, and I signed Zagreb Film, in Yugoslavia, to animate at least the film's six-minute prologue, a sequence that explains how and why Dorothy returned to the Land of Oz.

This film is based upon L. Frank Baum's own sequel to his highly successful original Oz novel, and is all about the Land of Oz — without Dorothy. The young protagonist in Baum's sequel is not Dorothy but a lad named Tip. The boy, however, turns out not to be a boy at all — "he" is a girl under a witch's spell! The sex switch did not work well dramatically for me (Shades of Osamu Tezuka's *Princess Knight*, wherein the young lead character who seems to be a "boy" is, in reality, a princess!) Dramatically, *Journey Back to Oz* would seem to work better as a sequel if Dorothy did somehow return to Oz, reunite with her old friends and some new ones, and pick up the adventure where the old, original one leaves off. And that is how the story was finally written.

Norman Prescott, a one-time radio disc jockey in Boston, Massachusetts, had a friend in the music business, the late Mortimer (Mort) Palitz. Mort, who was close to the successful song-writing team of Sammy Cahn and Jimmy van Heusen, knew that they were "between assignments" (scheduled to begin work soon on the upcoming Broadway show *The Night They Raided Minsky's*) and persuaded the team to fill-in between assignments by composing a score for *Journey Back to Oz*. Cahn and van Heusen had written a string of hits for Frank Sinatra — hits like "Love and Marriage," "Call Me Irresponsible," and "The Tender Trap"; before long, an interested Sinatra insisted that Reprise Records, which he owned, put out the soundtrack album that would stem from the animated feature.

In addition, Frank Sinatra — to "load" the album with famous singers — persuaded his "pal," Hollywood star Peter Lawford, to voice the role of the Scarecrow in the film. Soon thereafter, in short order, comedian Danny Thomas was set to voice the role of the Tinman, television comedian Milton Berle was on board as the voice of the Cowardly Lion, Broadway singing star Ethel Merman agreed to voice the role of Mombi, the wicked witch, and a (then) 15-year-old Liza Minnelli, daughter of Judy Garland (Dorothy in the most celebrated film version of *The Wizard of Oz*) was set to voice the role of Dorothy in *Journey Back to Oz*.

Bringing all those stars into a sound studio at the same time was an impossibility; the stars had to be scheduled separately, one at a time. Liza Minnelli was recorded first, in a studio in Manhattan (even at age 15, Liza sounded and sang like her famous mother!). She proved to be the ideal voice for the role of Dorothy.

Actor Peter Lawford, next to be recorded in the same studio, posed a special problem. Although he had sung exceedingly well in Hollywood musicals, he had difficulty in mastering the melody for the Scarecrow's song, "B-R-A-N-E Spells Brain." That one-minute tune took Lawford over an hour to record. Then he spoke his dialogue and we knew we were in trouble: faced with delivering the line "Why, she can't do that!" Lawford, with his upper-class British dialect, kept saying "Why, she *cawnt* do that!" (A Kansas scarecrow with a consistent British dialect?) Later, Peter Lawford's lines were replaced by film star Mickey Rooney.

Danny Thomas as the Tinman and television star Herschel Bernardi as the Carousel Horse were recorded, separately, in Los Angeles.

Milton Berle's song, "N-E-R-V-E Spells Nerve," and his dialogue for the role of The Cowardly Lion, were recorded in Las Vegas.

In a casting switch, veteran Hollywood actress Margaret Hamilton — the wicked, green-faced witch in the 1939 MGM film *The Wizard of Oz* and Dorothy's nemesis in that film — voiced the role of kindly Aunt Em in our animated sequel.

Most of the recording sessions went smoothly, which, given the professionalism of the seasoned stars cast in their respective roles, came as no surprise. A major surprise did come, however, when the time came to record Ethel Merman as Mombi, a wicked witch unrelated to any other in Oz. Miss Merman, a friend of Jimmy van Heusen (she kept calling him by his real name, Chester Babcock), was a Broadway star of the first magnitude. She was known as one who made all her characters her own, who brooked no interference even from top Broadway directors. With no small degree of apprehension, then, I took her through a rehearsal of her part, hesitant to offer any suggestions that might be perceived as contradictory. But, surprise! On the contrary, the lady was *hungry* for direction! She had never acted in an animated film before, felt unsure of herself in a new medium, wanted to be great, and wanted to be aware of any nuance that might help her deliver a memorable performance, so she gladly listened to any suggestion that she felt would "make it" — especially from a witch's point of view. Working with the fabled Ethel Merman was a delight!

Once all the character lines were recorded, they were edited in sequence and animated — except for the six-minute prologue made in Zagreb — by Filmation Studio in California. *Journey Back to Oz* was completed in 1974. It had no splashy theatrical opening, but it did enjoy a brief run in theaters, then was shown nationally in the United States on ABC network television.

Lyricist Sammy Cahn, who wrote the words for twelve songs heard in *Journey,* had actually written thirteen lyrics. However, "What Does a Wogglebug Do?" was cut from the film when L. Frank Baum's character of the Wogglebug was cut from the script. (Dorothy, returning to Oz and replacing the boy Tip, made Tip's Wogglebug friend extraneous.) Shortly thereafter, Cahn and Jimmy van Heusen sold dancer Gene Kelly a song called "What Does a Wogglebird Do?" for a Kelly television special. (Twenty years later, Cahn would write English lyrics for three Japanese songs composed and sung in Tokyo for Toho's animated version of *The Wizard of Oz.* Aileen Quinn, as Dorothy, performed the English versions in Toronto.)

Journey Back to Oz, restored to its full brilliance, was released on DVD in North America in 2006.

Coincidentally, some of the same recording techniques employed in *Journey Back to Oz* were put to use in the adaptation of Osamu Tezuka's *Kimba the White Lion* television series. Tezuka, clearly influenced by American musicals, indicated spots in the continuity in which some of the animals actually sang and danced. These "song spots" posed special problems for us in the recording studio. First, the Japanese lyrics had to be translated and adapted to fit the Japanese melodies — no small task in itself. Then, since none in the voice cast were professional singers, we had to plan and rehearse ways in which the cast could, in effect, *talk* the lyrics in musical fashion. That these techniques, none ideal, worked at all is a tribute to the actors who wrote and voiced the English lines.

An earlier chapter describes Tezuka's surprise at hearing lyrics — English lyrics — added to the *Astro Boy* theme song, where none were ever contemplated in Japan. Delighted at what he heard, Tezuka ordered that Japanese lyrics be written immediately and added to the Japanese programs, replacing the orchestral version used in the first five programs. That was done, but the first five Japanese-language programs were already "in the can." The Japanese version of the theme song is heard for the first time in program #6; the first five programs remain unchanged, without lyrics of any kind, to this day.

The Japanese version of *Jungulu Taitei Leo* similarly opens with no theme song; instead, a sweeping symphonic score underlines all the action from Program Beginning to Program End. NBC Enterprises commissioned songsmiths

Bill Giant, Bernie Baum, and Florence Kaye to write the theme song heard in every *Kimba* episode. However, neither the song's lyrics nor its melody are heard in the Japanese version of the series.

Late in the 1990s, Tezuka Productions' head man, Takayuki Matsutani, stunned this writer by declaring that the studio was giving serious thought to dropping the name "Kimba." *Drop the name "Kimba"?* (Surely, Mr. Matsutani was not being serious!)

Indeed, the speaker was being serious. After all, he explained, Tezuka-San himself had chosen the name *Leo,* the little lion was known as Leo in Japan and many other parts of the world, and now the studio was beginning to think that the cub should have the same name all over the world.

I pleaded with Mr. Matsutani not to change the character's name; "millions of children," I argued, "had grown up with the name *Kimba;* they would not understand nor welcome a change of name." Beside, even Mickey Mouse is not known as Mickey Mouse all over the world; in Latin America, he is known as "Miguelito." Well into the twenty-first century, *Kimba the White Lion* is still known as *Kimba the White Lion.*

Round-Eyed Robot Boy Comes Full Circle

Much has been written in these pages about how *Tetsuan Atom,* Osamu Tezuka's popular manga of the 1950s, became the star of the animated television series of that name and, in 1963 — as *Astro Boy* — the world's first anime series.

We have seen how NBC Enterprises, the importer and distributor of that *Astro Boy* series, successfully licensed an unprecedented 104 episodes to independent television stations in North America and around the world. They did this until 1975, when their own license from Japan expired and they were obligated to return the series to its creator in Tokyo. We saw how Mushi Production, the studio that produced the series, had gone bankrupt and was in no position to accept the thousands of film prints, negatives, and soundtracks due to be returned from the United States.

We also saw how, tragically, those materials were destroyed en masse, and a simple certificate of destruction issued to attest to the wholesale destruction of that vast body of work.

From 1975 until 1989, that classic *Astro Boy* series was but a memory in the minds of those who knew (and loved) the series for what it was. In 1989, Todd Ferson, a young computer dealer in Des Moines, Iowa, decided that he did not want to be remembered as a successful seller and servicer of computers; rather, he wanted to be known as the man who brought back that wonderful black-and-white *Astro Boy* series that he and his friends had loved when he was a child. Ferson called collectors wherever he could find them, borrowed any *Astro Boy* print they would lend him, and eventually amassed copies of some 65 episodes that he, and young friend Shawne Kleckner, would release as VHS cassettes under their Right Stuf label.

These were prints that have the English soundtracks that Australian distributor Madman Entertainment would combine with new images from Japan for the restored version of the series released on DVD near the end of 2005.

Full Circle

Any animated series made in 1963 was produced either for theatrical release (as evidence MGM's *Tom and Jerry* and Warner Bros.'s *Bugs Bunny*) or for television (*Clutch Cargo, The Big World of Little Adam, Crusader Rabbit*). Osamu Tezuka's *Tetsuan Atom,* though made as a series of half-hours (rather than as 6-minute episodes typical of American studios at the time), was contemplated only for television; home video would not come into being until a dozen years later, when Sony introduced its revolutionary Betamax technology, a new process for playing a videocassette on a device that displayed recorded images on a television screen. Yet, for over thirty years —1975 to 2007 — the classic *Astro Boy* series could be viewed only by playing a videocassette; nowhere was the series to be seen, as originally intended, on free, national, or regional television.

That would change in mid–2007. On July 1, 2007, America's Cartoon Network began running scheduled performances of Osamu Tezuka's original 1963 series, *Astro Boy.*

The series, as restored, was broadcast weekly at 2:00 A.M. on the channel's Adult Swim service, aimed squarely at young adults — not children — but, rather, to parents who fondly remembered the series from their childhood and who now wanted *their* children to see and enjoy the series as they, the parents, had seen and enjoyed the series a generation earlier.

So it was that, after more than thirty years of relative obscurity, Tezuka's and Ladd's original, classic *Astro Boy* series was back on television, where, some say, it "belonged." The little boy robot with the big, round eyes had come full circle. *Astro Boy* was home.

CHAPTER 24

What Hath Tezuka Wrought?

In this book, we have attempted to relate, accurately and in firsthand detail, the true story of how anime was born, how it found its audience in Japan, and how it came to the Americas and, subsequently, to the rest of the Western world.

In brief review: *Tetsuan Atom,* the first Japanese-animated television series, found its way to Manhattan in 1963, planted its flag on U.S. soil, and became *Astro Boy,* the first anime to come to the Americas.

The genre quickly took root, flourished, and blossomed "overnight" with *Tetsujin28/Gigantor, 8th Man,* and *Jungulu Taitei Leo/Kimba.* From there it spread: *Marine Boy* and *Speed Racer* emerged as major American cultural icons at the end of the decade of the 1960s.

The 1970s saw the genre decline and grow moribund as Japanese television series grew more and more violent in content — content that was acceptable in Japan's culture but unacceptable for children's television on the other (eastern) side of the Pacific.

Then, in the decade of the 1980s, a revitalization of anime as America's threshold for violence in children's television was lowered.

With the 1990s came a virtual explosion of anime, as television series like TMS's *NEW Adventures of Gigantor,* Toei's *Sailor Moon,* and ShoPro's *Pokémon* swept across North America.

Sailor Moon ended the epoch in which children's programs animated in Japan were acquired and Westernized in every respect. Already, in *Sailor Moon,* the Japanese title of the series was retained, and pictured storefronts were permitted to retain their Japanese names — with Japanese writing (*kanji*) and all, though dialogue was based on Western slang.

Early in the twenty-first century, anime series such as *Dragonball Z, Yu-gi-oh,* and *Naruto* remain the rage in the Americas. Series uniformly retain their original Japanese titles. Even merchandise such as T-shirts feature character names spelled in kanji! Teenagers routinely prefer anime to American-made cartoons. Indeed, anime has grown into a multibillion dollar industry in the Americas, alone!

And to think that it all started with a modest, unassuming doctor-turned-artist, the late Osamu Tezuka. As part of his legacy, he wrote: "What I try to [say] through my works is simple: Love all creatures. Love everything that has life." Inspired by the puppet Pinocchio, Osamu Tezuka created one of the world's greatest, most enduring cultural icons: *Tetsuan Atom*: America's — and now the world's — beloved *Astro Boy*.

Editor's Note: In 2007, a new, animated feature-length *Astro Boy* film was launched — but not at Tezuka Productions, as one might expect; nor at Mushi Production, Tokyo. In fact, the animation studio is not located in Japan at all. It is based in Hong Kong and Los Angeles! It's called IMAGI STUDIOS.

IMAGI had previously rendered CG (computer graphics) animation services on DreamWorks' television series *Father of the Pride* and had produced the successful theatrical feature *TMNT*; now the studio was poised to film Japan's iconic *Astro Boy* as a CG-animated motion picture with veteran director David Bowers at the helm. In addition, IMAGI was simultaneously working on a feature-length film version of Tatsunoko Production's signature series, *Gatchaman*.

All this would surely have impressed Osamu Tezuka. Never had he seen his little boy robot, Tetsuan Atom, star in a theatrical feature — one in which all characters appear three-dimensional rather than flat. Nor could the artist have failed to admire an animation studio capable of working on two animated features —*simultaneously*!

Of a certainty, Osamu Tezuka would have marveled at the sight of artists in Hong Kong comparing production notes and making corrections *by teleconference* with a creative team thousands of miles away in Los Angeles! Such 21st century techniques were undreamt of in Tezuka's day.

Nicolas Cage and Donald Sutherland play leading voice roles in the English version of the *Astro Boy* film, set for theatrical release by Summit Entertainment in October 2009.

APPENDIX 1

Milestones on the Anime Highway

Odd as it may seem, Japanese anime did not originate in Japan, but in the United States and France.

In America, J. Stuart Blackton, an artist, humorist, and pioneer filmmaker, was intrigued by the possibilities of exposing one frame of film at a time. He flirted with this technique in 1900 in his *Enchanted Drawing,* which used very primitive frame-by-frame techniques to make some of his drawings he had just drawn on camera "come to life." In 1906, he made *Humorous Phases of Funny Faces,* another short film that's generally regarded as the first fully animated film. In it, some simply-drawn human figures seem to come alive.

Then, in 1908, French artist Émile Cohl one-upped Blackton with *Fantasmagorie,* which was the first animated cartoon that fully explored the artistic possibilities that animation offered. It was probably this film that inspired legendary American comic strip artist Winsor McCay to bring his popular *Little Nemo in Slumberland* strip to life as *Little Nemo* in 1911. One day, he amazed an audience when he drew an amiable dinosaur he called *Gertie* that, suddenly and whimsically, "comes to life" and seems to take a pumpkin from McCay's hand.

Then, in Japan, an artist named Oten Shimokawa, using pen and ink, began drawing shapes directly onto film and his first film, *Imokawa Muzuko the Concierge,* premiered in January 1917. Shimokawa's contemporary, Seitaro Kitayama, who had begun experimenting with animation in 1913, went considerably further: he animated a film called *Momotaro* (The Peach Boy) that was shown in the West in 1918. Yet, while animation in the West flourished in the hands of France's Cohl, Sweden's Victor Bergdahl, and America's John Randolph Bray, Max Fleischer, and Walt Disney, animation in Japan lay virtually dormant for almost half a century.

(*Note:* In 2005, a strip of animation said to date back to 1907 reportedly was discovered in Japan — animation said to last only three seconds and probably not publicly shown. Prints of Shimokawa's and Kitayama's earliest animation were reported destroyed in the great earthquake and fire that leveled Tokyo in 1923.)

- 1962. Japan's first animated TV series, *Manga Calendar,* began a two-year run.
- Hard on the heels of *Manga Calendar,* Osamu Tezuka's anime series *Tetsuan Atom* (soon to become *Astro Boy*) created a sensation when it debuted in Japan on New Year's Day, 1963.
- Later that same year, Television Corporation of Japan (TCJ) and Tokyo Movie Shinsha (TMS) opened their doors for business.
- From TCJ in 1964 came our *Gigantor, 8th Man,* and *Prince Planet* series; TMS gave us *Big X,* a series that, though rather primitive in animation technique, nevertheless established TMS as a major player in the blossoming new industry.
- In 1965, Japan's first color series went on the air in Tokyo as *Jungulu Taitei Leo*; the series debuted in the United States soon after as *Kimba the White Lion.*
- That same year, Tatsunoko Production, founded in 1962 as a manga studio, sold its black-and-white series *Space Ace* to television.
- 1967. *Speed Racer* appeared on U.S. television and smashed all previous records for anime popularity.
- 1972. Go Nagai's giant robot, *Mazinger Z,* was born and launched a new wave of popularity for the genre. The series came to the United States as *TranZor Z.*
- 1979. Tatsunoko's *Gatchaman* series found safe haven in the United States and would become *Battle of the Planets;* also, *Space Cruiser Yamato,* rechristened *Star Blazers,* docked Stateside.
- 1985. *Robotech,* a reedited version of three separate series from Tatsunoko, went into syndicated television in the United States.
- 1986. TMS sold its series *Galaxy High* to the CBS Television Network for Saturday morning airing — the first time a Japanese anime series appeared on American national television.
- 1988. Katsuhiro Otono's epic science-fiction feature, *Akira,* stunned Japan with its brutal vision of a neo-Tokyo; the film became the first blockbuster U.S. anime hit, reportedly selling over 100,000 copies on video and generating record grosses at theater box offices.
- 1991. AnimeCon '91 in San Jose, California, became the first major North American convention devoted exclusively to anime and manga — a significant new event in fandom.
- 1994. A major milestone year on what was quickly becoming the anime superhighway:

— Hayao Miyazaki's children's classic *My Neighbor Totoro* (1988), a hit in Japan, was released in the United States, selling a reported 500,000 video copies. Disney studio takes note of Miyazaki.

— Pioneer became the first Japanese anime company to enter the U.S. market, releasing their popular OAV series *Tenchi Muyo* practically simultaneously in Japan and the United States.

— Disney's animated feature *The Lion King* was released and immediately drew protests from fans of anime. Joining the fray, over forty Japanese cartoonists signed a letter complaining to Disney that *The Lion King* was, in fact, an uncredited derivative of Osamu Tezuka's *Jungulu Taitei Leo* (*Kimba the White Lion*). The Disney studio denied the charge. Osamu Tezuka had died in 1989; Tezuka Studio claimed that Tezuka would have been honored by Disney drawing inspiration from a Tezuka work.

• 1995. Two of Japan's greatest television hits — both from the Toei Company — *Sailor Moon* and *Dragonball* land on U.S. television. Simultaneously, U.S. singer Michael Jackson uses images from *Akira* in his music video for "Scream." *Sailor Moon* was historic in that its five teenage warrior-scouts were girls rather than boys — girls who, singly and collectively, could hold their own against any threat on Earth or in the negaverse.

• 1996. The Disney Studio buys U.S. rights to distribute all the works of fast-rising Japanese animation star Hayao Miyazaki. That same year, Manga Entertainment coproduced *Ghost in the Shell,* the most expensive Japanese anime feature (reported budget: over U.S. $10,000,000) made at that time.

• 1997. *Pokémon* (a contraction of English words *pocket* and *monster,* and animated by Shogakukan Production Company in Tokyo), arrived in the United States — big time! Fortunes were made with this series as *Pokémon* trading cards and related merchandise demonstrated beyond any doubt that an anime series could be used as a launching pad for merchandise that tied-in closely with the theme of a series. *Pokémon* thus paved the way for *Yu-Gi-Oh* and other merchandise-driven (as opposed to character-driven) series to play a prominent role in American television. That trend continued well into the twenty-first century, and showed no sign of abating, anytime soon.

• 2003. Anime, by this time no longer an underground phenomenon, had become mainstream in the Americas, with the Stanford Japan Center reporting that the anime industry is expected to grow into a global market worth more than ¥10 trillion (US$86.88 *billion*). JETRO (Japan External Trade Organization) stated that Japanese anime sales, including anime character products, surpassed US$4.51 billion in America. Wowmax Media reported that anime-related business in the United States alone grew in 2003 by another ¥60 billion (US$521.1 million).

APPENDIX 2

Ten Most Frequently Asked Questions

On the occasion of *Kimba*'s fortieth birthday in the United States — that is, the fortieth anniversary of the completion of the pilot film in which *Jungulu Taitei Leo* became *Kimba the White Lion* (November 10, 2005) — I hosted a birthday party in Glendale, California, near the Disney and Dreamworks campuses. The following week, my wife and I were in Sydney and Melbourne, Australia, helping to launch restored DVD collections of *Kimba* and *Astro Boy* series. In Australia particularly, after sitting for scores of interviews for television, radio, and print media, I was struck by the number of questions that mirrored those I had been asked a week earlier in Glendale; and those, in turn, were repeats of those I have been asked, over and over, since the fortieth birthday party for *Astro Boy* in Little Tokyo, Los Angeles (April 6, 2003).

These are the ten most frequently asked questions, foreshortened, with foreshortened answers:

1. How did you get started?

I was born Fred Laderman in Toledo, Ohio, acquired a taste for "show business" from a movie-struck cousin; graduated from Ohio State University (honored in 2004 as Distinguished Alumnus); after graduation, went to New York and was hired to write continuity for an FM radio station; then was hired by an ad agency whose owner, William "Bill" Cayton, looked to me to build a film department, where we produced commercials plus nature documentaries and adaptations of foreign cartoons. Ten years later, I went on my own to make *Pinocchio in Outer Space*, followed by *Journey Back to Oz*, for theatrical release, and *The Big World of Little Adam* for television.

2. How did you find *Astro Boy*; what made you think the show would succeed here; did you expect *Astro Boy* to become so big?

The Japanese ask me that (at least the first part), a lot. Actually, the show found *me*. An agent from Tokyo brought sample prints of *Tetsuan*

194

Celebrating Kimba's fortieth birthday at a party in Glendale, California, November 10, 2005. Left to right: Jared Cook, frequent translator for Osamu Tezuka; Sonia Owens, voice of "Kitty"; Fred Ladd, producer for NBC Enterprises; and Sadao Miyamoto, animator for Mushi Productions.

Atom to NBC Enterprises in New York, NBC thought the show had promise, their Jim Dodd knew of me as an adapter of foreign (mainly, animated) films and called me in.

As to its success in the United States, I saw *Tetsuan Atom* as a futuristic *Pinocchio,* liked the fast-paced action of the animation — even though the animation was crude — and thought that kids would be attracted to the *stories* and become loyal viewers.

Its success, so big and so swiftly, exceeded all our expectations. NBC thought it was my adaptation that did it; I thought the adaptations were okay, but "the *play's* the thing": stories of a little robot trying to find his way through the world, like a child's toy come to life, is sure-fire with kids!

3. Why the name Astro Boy — where'd that come from?

A common misconception among fans is that I made up the name *Astro Boy.* At best, that is half-true. The name of the whale in *Pinocchio in Outer Space* is Astro. NBC's Bill Breen said "Astro Boy"; that was the first time I heard those two words put together. (Recently, I've heard it said that the young son of NBC's Bill Schmidt first uttered the name.) I coined the names for all the other lead characters — Astro Girl, Doctor Elefun, Mister Pompous, Inspector Gumshoe, Police Chief McLaw.

For *Jungle Emperor Leo,* I proposed the name Simba; Bill Breen's replacement at the time was Jacques Liebenguth. Jacques (to my disappointment) changed Simba (a generic word) to Kimba, a name that I felt lacked the strength of the word Simba. Over the years, though, I have come to appreciate the name Kimba.

4. Disney's *The Lion King,* to this day, is said to have been "inspired" by *Kimba*; why didn't the Tezuka people sue?

First, I don't see the Japanese as being a litigious society. Second, Osamu Tezuka was a great admirer of Walt Disney. Tezuka's people took the position that Osamu Tezuka would have been honored to think that his creation had impressed the Disney studio enough to emulate Tezuka.

5. Of all the anime shows you've adapted —*Astro Boy, Gigantor, 8th Man, Kimba, Sailor Moon,* etc.— what's your favorite?

My number one favorite would have to be *Astro Boy.* That was the first such series ever ... there was nothing else like it anywhere ... there was no book, no precedent, to which we could refer for solutions to problems that never existed before ... we had to figure out not only how to deliver the shows on a tight schedule, but how to write and dub the shows at a $$ amount equal to what the cost would have been in Puerto Rico. We were inventing a procedure from scratch! That was challenging, that was exciting, that was fun!

After *Astro Boy,* I liked the premise for *8th Man*; I thought the concept of a cop who was half-human, half- robot was inspired (the plot possibilities were enormous!). *Kimba, Gigantor, Sailor Moon*— all those were wonderful, too — each series came with its own set of problems, no two series were alike.

6. Why do you think anime has become so popular?

Before the arrival of *Astro Boy,* animated kids' shows — even on national U.S. TV networks on Saturday morning — consisted of half-hours that were made up of three individual six-minute episodes; in other words, 18 minutes of actual new program material; the rest of the half-hour consisted of commercials, "bumpers" (those lead-ins and lead-outs from commercial breaks), standard program opening and closing, and such. But a child watching *Astro Boy* saw a 24-minute story — a single story with a beginning, a middle, and an end — an *unusual* story with strong characters and plots like nothing else on the air. There's an "edgy," often science-fiction quality in anime that is not present in domestic cartoons. Anime has captured the spirit of compelling storytelling.

7. Do you prefer the new anime series or the old?

I prefer the old series to the new — not because of nostalgia or because the original old stories were shot in artsy black and white rather than in color, but because the older shows were *character-driven.* The old shows featured strong characters and characterizations. Recall, in *G-Force* (*nee Battle of the Planets*), the heroic fellow who was second in command of the brave G-Force team was not "Mr. Nice Guy"; he had a dark underbelly and a fast trigger-finger — always ready to fire the deadly bird missile! In *Speed Racer,* the shadowy, mysterious "Racer X" turns out to be Speed's brother! Never have I seen such characters in Hollywood-made cartoons for kids. Now, the shows that I see coming from

Fred Ladd, guest speaker at AniMagic fan convention, Palmdale, California, September 2006. Subject: "The Uncensored Truth Behind *Sailor Moon*," and the rationale for cutting scenes of "over-the-top" violence. Photo: ConsPlayers.

Tokyo are driven largely by merchandise — trading cards and video games and variations thereof; *story* seems to have taken a backseat to *merchandise.* More than ever, I am convinced that Shakespeare was right: "The *play's* the thing" — not merchandise.

8. Where do you think Japanese animation is heading?

For the time being and throughout the first decade of the twenty-first century, I see anime continuing on its present course of being heavily driven by merchandise. Japanese studios have seen how revenue from a merchandise stream can exceed the income derived solely from the licensing of their product (programs). After that — who knows? One hopes that, just as anime outgrew its dependence on giant robots, it will rise above its dependence upon ancillary (subsidiary) rights, and return to the business of telling good yarns about solid — even if quirky — characters.

9. Are American animators being influenced by Japanese animators?

No doubt about it. Look, for example, at *The Powerpuff Girls*. The huge, oversized eyes on the girls are a clear throwback to the large-eye look of *Astro Boy,* introduced by Osamu Tezuka. Genndy Tartakovsky, creator of the *Dexter's Laboratory* show on Cartoon Network, makes no bones about Japanese influence on *Dexter* and his follow-up series, *Samurai Jack*. Forty years ago, Japanese animators strove to achieve an American look; now, the reverse is true. Today's young animators grew up with the likes of *Astro Boy, Gigantor,* and *Speed Racer*; how could they avoid such strong influence from the East?

10. What are you doing these days?

These days I'm doing more of what I did in *those* days — programming for young audiences. The late Mitsuteru Yokoyama, who created the giant robot that we call Gigantor (I coined the name and own the trademark), wrote, "Sometimes I think ... what kind of robot would I have created if I had been a child now?" My guess is that Yokoyama-San would have created a giant robot with AI (artificial intelligence) and — like the boy robot in the Stanley Kubrik–Steven Spielberg film *AI* — a robot with the drive, the "wish," of possessing the quality that we call "life." That robot would be *Gigantor, the Next Generation*. We're working on development of that concept now.

Question Implied, but Not Asked — Yet

Is China the Next Japan?

Of all the countries of Asia — in particular, Japan, South Korea, China — only Japan has produced anything like anime, as we in the West have come to know it. South Korea, officially ROK, the Republic of Korea, had no real animation industry until 1968, when this writer set up a boutique studio in Seoul, as has been described earlier (see Land of Morning Calm). Actually, no Korean film industry existed until around 1993, when military rule came to an end, and censorship laws were lifted in 1996. Then the rush to make features was on!

(*Note:* In 1967, Shin Dong Hun directed an animated feature, the previously mentioned *Hong Gil Dong,* that met with some success in Korea, and Century Company produced an Asian-style version of *Treasure Island.* Both features were made on admittedly primitive equipment, and animation cels had to be imported.)

Toei studios had experimented, in the late 1960s, with a Godzilla-like monster film, *Yongari,* made with a small Korean studio. No one at Toei had any enthusiasm for the feature film that resulted. But by 2006, a major South Korean–financed film called *D-War* was being prepared for global launch in 2007. Budgeted at US$70 million, a figure respectable even by U.S. standards, the special-effects driven film shows a giant dragon on a rampage through the streets of Los Angeles! The picture was even shot in English, a clear indication that the Koreans, right from the start, envisioned a major, worldwide release for the film.

South Korea now has major animation capabilities, too, nearly all housed in Seoul, but they are serving mainly as factories to produce animated works for the United States and Japan. *The Simpsons, King of the Hill,* and many other American TV series are animated in Seoul. Toei Doga-Tokyo has taken over Seoul's Dae-Won and Sei-Yong studios to animate several of Toei's TV series. Well into the twenty-first century, a few animated features had been made in Seoul (none successful in the West), but no Korean studio was churning out TV series to compare with the phenomenon of anime in Japan.

In both the United States and Japan, anyone wishing to open an animation studio is free to do so, without government subsidy.

China is different. In Communist China, the central government does subsidize animation studios and seems determined to make them competitive with others in Asia. In 2006, according to the State Administration of Radio, Film, and Television, Chinese animation studios delivered 80,000 minutes of animation, up dramatically from the previous year's 42,000 minutes. The government also announced tax breaks and grants for animation studios. Other measures to promote the industry include allowing private capital to invest, resulting in the establishment of fifteen national animation bases, plus animation schools in four art and film academies to train more skilled animators.

With that assist, the studios in China have made remarkable strides forward, especially in computerized, 3-D animation. Using that technique, no pencil-and-ink drawing is necessary — computers do it all. Chinese children's programs rendered in 3-D animation look as professional to this writer as do those similarly rendered in the Americas.

One studio, in fact — Toonring — has a series starring a little blue turtle and a man-size robot. The little turtle's role is like Kimba's (a guileless child); the robot's role is like Danl's (the child's adult mentor). The studio's 3-D technique of animation is indistinguishable from that seen in the West from studios the likes of Blue Sky Studio (*Ice Age*) or several others that have appeared since the dawn of the twenty-first century.

It is significant that major American filmmaker George Lucas, famous for his *Star Wars* sagas, has opened a studio in Asia — not in Japan, not in South Korea — but in Singapore, off the coast of China. Is Beijing to be the next Tokyo? China, the next Japan? The United States is flooded with goods made in China. Could their anime be next in line?

Index